LOST AND STRANDED

EXPERT ADVICE ON HOW TO SURVIVE BEING ALONE IN THE WILDERNESS

TIMOTHY SPRINKLE

Skyhorse Publishing

Skyhorse Publishing books may be purchased in bulk at special discounts for sales promotion, corporate gifts, fund-raising, or educational purposes. Special editions can also be created to specifications. For details, contact the Special Sales Department, Skyhorse Publishing, 307 West 36th Street, 11th Floor, New York, NY 10018 or info@skyhorsepublishing.com.

Skyhorse® and Skyhorse Publishing® are registered trademarks of Skyhorse Publishing, Inc.®, a Delaware corporation.

Visit our website at www.skyhorsepublishing.com.

10 9 8 7 6 5 4 3 2 1

Library of Congress Cataloging-in-Publication Data is available on file.

Cover design by Tom Lau
Cover photos courtesy of iStockphoto
All interior photos courtesy of iStockphoto

Print ISBN: 978-1-5107-2770-0
Ebook ISBN: 978-1-5107-2772-4

Printed in the United States of America

For anyone who has ever wanted to go exploring, but was worried that they wouldn't come back.

CONTENTS

Introduction . . . . *vii*

Chapter 1: **The Risk Is Real** **1**

Chapter 2: **Predators/Large Animals:** **7**
Bears 7
Big Cats 20
Moose 29
Wolves 39
Coyotes 50
Humans 59

Chapter 3: **Small Animals/Insects:** **68**
Snakes 68
Spiders 73
Mosquitoes/Ticks 82
Bees/Stinging Insects 92
Scorpions 102

Chapter 4: **Weather:** **110**
Flash Flood/Drowning 110
Lightning 123
Wildfire 133
Blizzard 142

Chapter 5: **Injury/Illness:** **149**
Frostbite 149
Altitude Sickness 157
Carbon Monoxide Poisoning 166
Dehydration/Heat Stroke 173

Starvation 186
Dysentery/Giardia 193
Exposure/Hypothermia 199

Chapter 6: **Hazardous Terrain:** **208**
Rockslide 208
Avalanche 213
Glacier Travel 224
Snow Blindness/Changing Weather Conditions . . 233
Getting Lost 238

Acknowledgments *248*

Interviews *250*

Bibliography *252*

Index *272*

Introduction

KNOW THIS FIRST: THIS PLACE is beautiful.

We're in a stand of 300-year-old hemlock, some of the oldest trees on the eastern seaboard, and the light mist that's gathered around us deflects the light, softening it, as if we're in a cloud forest.

The woods in this part of Virginia are heavy, thick in ways that you don't often see in the mid-Atlantic. Hemlock trees are tall, evergreens that can reach up to 200 feet, and here they're nearly that tall. High overhead, it looks as if the branches are leaning in on us. On the ground, pine needles are everywhere. It smells like Christmas.

But I don't care.

I'm focused entirely on the one fallen hemlock tree that I'm straddling, crawling spread-eagle across what can only be described as a torrent of whitewater at least twenty feet below me. A light rain falls, has been falling all night, giving everything I touch—particularly the moss that covers this log—a damp, slippery feeling that prevents my fleece gloves from getting any sort of grip.

I pull off the gloves and stuff them in a pocket, hoping that my bare hands will fare better.

No luck.

I'm able to make slow progress by scooting with my legs, pushing my body forward across the smooth parts of the log as my legs dangle on either side, my arms wrapped around it in a desperate bear hug.

In spots where branches once grew and broken shards remain, I have to shift my weight and lift myself to crawl over them. It is terrifying. The rain picks up slightly as I dismount from the log and scramble on all fours up the other bank, sticky Virginia mud on my knees and hands.

Never before have I felt so tested in the outdoors or relied so much on my gear.

And we're far from done. High water in the canyon has left the trail littered with debris and fallen trees, forcing us to crisscross the water repeatedly, often on slippery, moss-covered logs such as the hemlock above, and often over dangerously high water. Where fallen trees are not available, we cross by jumping from rock to rock in the creek itself, taking care not to slip into the water on a sprained ankle or worse.

We're backtracking, making up for a misjudgment earlier in the day that took us off course on our fifteen-mile out-and-back hike that was to take us up Ramsey's Draft creek and over its 4,000-foot peak, Big Bald Knob. We had camped the previous night some ten miles up the creek itself, on a ridge overlooking the Blue Ridge Mountains to the west of the Shenandoah Valley, with plans to follow the ridge back down to the south to complete the circuit.

Ramsey's Draft—and a rapidly approaching thunderstorm rolling in from the west—had other plans.

* * *

Ramsey's Draft is a wilderness area in central Virginia's Augusta County, near the border with West Virginia, that's part of both the George Washington and Jefferson National Forests. It is rugged, wooded open space, about as wild as you're going to get within three hours of Washington, DC.

It's also well-known as a challenging—and sometimes dangerous—place to hike.

Writing in *Backpacker* magazine in 1997, Mary Burnham said of Ramsey's Draft that "few hikes I've taken were tougher," going on to explain why—the unmarked trail, slippery stones, steep climbs, and the ever-present risk of water along the trail. "There's either too much or not enough," she wrote, describing the main trail as soggy due to the endless creek crossings and mentioning that the most-used campsites in the area are prone to flash flooding. On the flipside, once you leave the creek bed area, there is no water available at all along the trail until you reach the mountain pond at the White Oak Trail junction, more than six miles from the trailhead.

All of her points are true. The trails in this area really aren't marked, and there are miles of poison ivy and stinging nettles along the creek, along with hundreds of downed trees like the one I ended up crawling across, up along the ridge. The climbs are steep, the miles are long, and the vistas are few and far between (but more than worth it when they appear). When weather rolls in, which happens a lot here in the mountains, flash flooding and lightning strikes are both significant threats.

Ramsey's Draft is rugged, challenging, and scenic.

In the South, a "draft" is another word for a creek, and Ramsey's Draft is no exception. The waterway here, also named Ramsey's Draft, is a tributary of the Calfpasture River, which leads to the James River through Central Virginia on its way to the Chesapeake Bay. It's a fast stream, typical for the area, barreling down from deep within the mountains above, creating a wet, muddy approach to the hike that lasts for miles.

Our hike has taken us directly up the creek into a drainage that's bordered on both sides with steep ridges that top out above 3,000 feet. From the trailhead, at U.S. 250, it looks like a deep, V-shaped valley that starts out wide and comes together in a point a few miles in. From there, the trail turns up, tracing along the hillside as the ridge leads further and further into the wilderness. The climb is steep at times, though no worse than similar trails in this part of Virginia, and the forest is a welcome break from the water's edge earlier in the hike, where heavy foliage and tall stinging plants make for a tiresome few hours of work.

It is certainly worth the effort. The George Washington and Jefferson National Forests, encompassing more than 230,000 acres between them, are home to the last few remaining old growth forest stands in Virginia and some of the last in the East. This part of the country has been logged heavily dating back to the colonial days, so finding any sort of old growth—which is defined loosely as a forest that lacks any sort of human development (such as roads), has trees that are 150 years old or older, lots of decaying wood from fallen trees, and a mixed-aged canopy—locally is a treat, usually the result of either steep slopes, early protection, or a lack of commercial viability.

Ramsey's Draft has the first one covered: steep slopes.

Given the limited access—and if our hike had proven anything, it was that access to this area was and is very limited—it would be nearly impossible for loggers to get to the old-growth forest to cut it down or truck the trees out for processing once they had been felled. That often prevents it from being commercially viable as well, because timber that you can't get out, even if you can get in to cut it down, is no good to the market. The timber industry lives and dies by forest roads, access lines to remote parts of the deep woods that allow for the speedy removal of timber that's been felled by loggers, taking it out to processing plants and, eventually, the open market for sale. Steep-sloped forests are also usually dry, because they drain off quickly and can't hold much water, limiting tree growth in the first place and further limiting economic viability. Limited access like that around Ramsey's Draft not only prevents timber activity in the first place but means the stands in the area are not going to be commercially viable either.

"When the Eastern national forests were purchased around 1913, those responsible for acquiring them where looking for some of the most valuable, and therefore, least logged tracts of land," wrote journalist and trail runner Will Harlan about this Eastern old growth in 2005. "William Willard Ashe, one of the people most responsible for the surveying and acquiring of Blue Ridge National Forests, stated that 'the larger portion of the lands which have been acquired have had the timber cut off, or at least some of the best timber has been cut, but a number of fine stands have been secured within which there has never been the sound of the lumberman's axe.' But over the years, the knowledge that the national forests of the Southern Blue Ridge contain significant old-growth forests was shouted down by the myth that 'It's all been logged.' Because these forests have been essentially forgotten, the sum of old-growth present before 1940 has been reduced by Forest Service timber sales. Hopefully, as the American people become more aware of this great treasure on their public lands, the remainder can be protected in perpetuity."

Whatever the reason, the result was a well-protected piece of forest in the middle of the crowded, developed mid-Atlantic corridor. As a bonus, the rugged terrain also keeps the crowds at bay, making for a quiet, peaceful hike. Over the course of our weekend there, we only saw two other groups on the trail.

In retrospect, it maybe would have been nice to have more company out there.

* * *

But, that day, we weren't focused on the trees.

We had a bigger problem.

In fact, our problem was twofold: we had left the trail (poorly marked as it was) and were rushing to get off the mountain before a storm rolled in. The Virginia high country is home to plenty of weather year-round, but we were up there in early fall, prime season for unsettled weather, including multiday rainstorms.

In truth, we had committed one of the cardinal sins of backcountry travel, camping too far away from our destination in what we already knew were deteriorating conditions. As mentioned, the hike up from the car follows more or less along the creek until you're about halfway up the trail. From there, it climbs up the ridge and loops around several of the higher peaks in the area. As a result, good camping spots are few and far between, mostly located at the far end of the trail before it loops back around to the top of the exit ridge. Before that point, you're facing steep terrain and little open ground. You have to go all-in.

The storm rolled in late, well after the group had all gone to bed, and by the time we started to get up after dawn, the rain was falling steadily. We packed up camp in the middle of a mild downpour, ate whatever we could find in our packs for breakfast, and set out as early as possible in order to get out of the wet.

But there was a problem.

Hikes in the East are different from those in the Rocky Mountain West and elsewhere. In Virginia, climbs may not be long or high (the state's tallest peak tops out at 5,728 feet—compare that to the 14,000-plus peaks in Colorado, not to mention the 20,310-foot Mount Denali in Alaska, the tallest peak in North America), but they make up for it with their angle of attack. They're steep. The Wintergreen Ascent, an annual bicycle race that starts at Beech Grove near Skyline Drive and climbs up to Wintergreen Resort, delivers an average grade of roughly eight percent, more than twice what you'll find out West. And the hikes are no different, with stairs, roots, rocks, and other features often coming into play in order to make the hills passable.

In good weather, these make for challenging obstacles.

In the rain, those steeps go from thigh-burningly unpleasant to outright dangerous.

Soon we're on all fours, picking our way down the same climbs we charged up the previous afternoon. Mud cakes my boots, staining my knees and cuffs a deep, reddish-brown that's typical of the area. The same slopes that helped to protect those old growth hemlock trees was suddenly working against us, keeping us from a safe, on-time return trip.

Were we going the right way? The trail itself had disappeared, leaving us with little more than landmarks to work with.

Were we walking into a dead end? By crossing the stream over and over again, we didn't know where our next water crossing would be, or if there would be a safe way across when it did.

Would the weather get worse? Steady, drenching rain is unpleasant enough, but the endless threat of lightning and, worse, flash flood is enough to force poor decision-making in the backcountry.

Were we lost?

Would we make it out of this alive?

***

There is a moment in every outdoor adventure, every trip into the backcountry, when the fear of what could go wrong enters your thoughts.

It doesn't usually happen right away. And it doesn't necessarily hit you all at once. But it's always there, lurking beneath the surface.

It never starts out that way, of course. You're focused on the trip ahead, the goal that you're working toward, whether it's a waterfall, an overlook, or something similar. You're happy and optimistic. You're looking forward with excitement and anticipation to what's coming next.

But then something happens.

It doesn't have to be anything particularly big or terrible, just enough to make you notice your surroundings and think about what's going on. Maybe you step awkwardly off a loose rock and nearly turn your ankle. Maybe you hear the rustling of a bear in the nearby woods. Or maybe you notice some dark storm clouds forming off in the distance. Whatever it is, you start to notice the risks you're taking, the potential dangers you're facing just by walking through the woods.

And you get worried.

You start to think about what might go wrong. What if you stepped off that rock differently and sprained your ankle? How would you get out if you couldn't walk? Or what if you encountered that bear on the trail, instead of off in the distance? Would you know what to do to protect yourself from a potential attack? Worse, what if her cubs had been with her? What then? And what about weather? Are you prepared to manage the risk of an electrical storm in the wilderness? Do you know how to get out if you do?

It's fear.

But this is productive fear, not the bad kind.

In fact, this kind of fear is a very good, healthy thing to experience in the outdoors. It's what keeps us safe, what keeps us healthy, and what keeps us alive. By recognizing the risks we face, and acknowledging them, we're far more able to take steps to minimize those risks, stepping

xiv • LOST AND STRANDED

carefully around loose rocks when we see them, remaining alert to the potential of wildlife encounters near the trail, and formulating a plan in advance to deal with any severe weather that might crop up.

Smart adventurers take care to be smart and travel safely in the backcountry, never overlooking the little things that could get them into trouble. This kind of fear can be a powerful motivator, a force that keeps risk at bay and keeps us safe—it is situational awareness. By thinking about the perils we are facing, we're better able to prepare for them and address them in the moment.

Panic is the opposite of this.

When we panic, we take greater risks. Rather than dealing with the problem at hand (the loose rock, for instance) we focus all of our attention instead on whatever it is that's making us anxious, making us panic. We behave rashly; we rush to judgments rather than being careful, trying everything we can to simply eliminate that fear that's driving us. As a result, we often make dangerous mistakes in the process.

This fits with the textbook definition of panic, after all: "A sudden overwhelming fear, with or without cause, that produces hysterical or irrational behavior, and that often spreads quickly through a group of persons or animals."

Hysterical or irrational behavior. Sudden overwhelming fear. Nothing about panic is productive or safe in the backcountry. It causes more problems than it solves.

Psychology students will trace this back to Maslow's Hierarchy of Needs, the theory presented by Abraham Maslow in 1943 that all humans are driven by certain shared motivations, and that everything we do can be connected to one of these basic needs. His hierarchy consisted of five stages—psychological, safety, love/belonging, esteem, and self-actualization—each one reliant on the one below it. The model was based on the theory that a person had to progress from level to level in order to reach the pinnacle.

In our case, however, the fact that psychology is the most basic of human motivations tells us a lot about the damage that panic can do in the outdoors. When we're panicked about our situation, unsure about our safety, our lizard brain simply cannot focus on anything else. It cannot look to greater safety concerns like staying on course or losing track of a partner. Based on this simple fact of our biology, all we can do in that moment is address our panicked fear—fight or flight.

And that's when mistakes happen.

What's needed in the outdoors isn't panic, it isn't crippling fear, and it isn't ongoing paranoia. It's awareness. It's an understanding of what risks you're facing, what little things could get you into trouble, and what steps you can take to minimize that risk each and every minute that you're out there. It's about knowing what you're getting into and knowing how to get out of it.

Part of this, and the reason that this book exists, is the role that simple awareness has in preparing us for survival in the backcountry. Knowing not only what we're going to face but what the potential consequences are—what those potential risks can do to you—can be very empowering. Now you aren't going in blind; you're prepared for what you might face.

You don't have to be afraid that a bear might maul you, for instance, if you know that bears in the area where you're going aren't aggressive. Or maybe they're hibernating and won't be bothering you. That's one less thing to worry about, simply by knowing more about the situation you're facing.

Or let's say you're hiking through an area—like Ramsey's Draft—that is prone to flash floods. An uninformed hiker would simply bomb up the middle of the canyon, oblivious to the risk they were facing. But by knowing the flood history of the area, including when and where floodwaters usually strike, you can enjoy the area, safe in the knowledge that if weather and potential flooding does become an issue, you know where to go and how to handle the situation.

* * *

No surprise, we made it out just fine.

The weather we were worried about did eventually roll in, and we ended up walking in the rain for the better part of three hours. But there was no flash flood. No lightning strikes (at least not any near us). No one in our party got lost.

Our concerns, as they were, were overblown.

But the experience was instructive. In fact, that's why I'm writing about it today, more than twenty years after the fact.

I am by nature a very careful, cautious person in the outdoors. I plan out my route in advance, inventory and test my gear before I leave the house, and rarely go anywhere without at least notifying someone else of my plans in case of a delay.

I'm careful.

And it has served me well. Over the course of forty years exploring various backcountry locations, I have never found myself in significant danger. Never been seriously injured, never been what I would consider lost, and never had to call on others for help getting out of a tight spot.

Ramsey's Draft was a little different simply because I did not personally plan that trip. I was not in charge of our route that day, nor was I aware of the risks inherent to that hike before we left for the weekend. Granted, I should have been more careful, and I clearly violated some of my own rules on that trip.

What could we have done better or differently?

Naturally, we were never in much serious danger. Yes, weather can complicate things in the mountains, and rushed decision-making often results in less-than-clear thinking. So, we should have been more aware of our surroundings. We should have gone in with a clearer understanding not only of how challenging the hike would be but what specific and unique risks we might face out there. We were well prepared in terms of supplies and a mapped-out route, but we could have done better.

But that's the point. That's the value in making mistakes in the backcountry. They're learning experiences. Going through a scare in the woods—whether it involves getting lost, facing severe weather, dealing with an animal encounter, experiencing a health emergency, or one of the dozens of other risks that we might face—all but ensures you won't go through a similar scare again.

Think about it. The first time you come across a bear when hiking in bear country, whether there's a negative encounter or not, you will not forget the experience or make the same decisions again. Maybe you were careless in your route planning, going straight through a known feeding area. Or maybe you chose the wrong time of year, coming across a mother bear and cubs shortly before winter hibernation. Whatever the reason for the encounter, you likely made a mistake by being there in the first place.

That's an instructive, real-world lesson. Now you know how a bear might react when it sees you. You know the signs to look for in advance of another encounter. And you know that you can come across a bear in the backcountry and, handled properly, live to tell the tale.

Most importantly, by understanding what got you into the situation in the first place, you can gain a better understanding of what not to do when visiting bear country. And that can be just as powerful, or even more so, than knowing the right way to handle every situation.

CHAPTER 1

The Risk Is Real

ACCORDING TO THE CENTERS FOR DISEASE CONTROL (CDC), nearly 213,000 people are treated in emergency rooms every year for injuries sustained in the wilderness, ranging from bone fractures (27.4 percent) to sprains (23.9 percent) and traumatic brain injury (6.5 percent). The arms and legs are the most common targets, with more than 50 percent of all injuries, followed by the head and neck with nearly one-quarter.

Of these, more than half of all cases involved young people between the ages of ten and twenty-four.

"Participation in outdoor recreation is increasingly popular in the United States," said Arlene Greenspan, DrPH and coauthor of the study. "The good news is that there are ways to help stay safe while having healthy fun outdoors. For example, by wearing the appropriate helmet for snowboarding, snowmobiling, sledding and rock climbing, you can reduce your risk of having a head injury, which could become a traumatic brain injury. Helmets are one piece of equipment that can have a critical, positive impact."

According to the Outdoor Industry Association, each year more than 140 million Americans spend some $646 billion on outdoor recreation products, travel, and services, directly supporting more than six million jobs. That is a large market, and it is growing steadily every year.

As if that wasn't impressive enough, those figures are only expected to grow going forward, as increased urbanization and an interest in personal health and wellness drive more people to explore North America's wild spaces, many for the first time.

That said, 200,000 injuries out of 140 million participants seems almost insignificant. Using these figures, your chances of being injured in the wilderness—let alone dying—are a mere one-tenth of one percent. Not exactly the same risk factor as we face simply driving to and from work every day. Nearly 1.3 million people die in road crashes every year, for a daily average of more than 3,200. With the United States population of 325 million, that's four times as much.

And, according to data from the National Electronic Injury Surveillance System, which not surprisingly tracks all instances of injury across the country based on hospital emergency room reports, there are plenty of things in our everyday lives that are far more dangerous to us than outdoor recreation.

Bicycles injure nearly half a million Americans every day. So do gym equipment and bathroom fixtures. Aluminum cans injure some 300,000, with chairs and couches claiming nearly 600,000 annually. Beds? Two out of every 1,000 American has been injured—somehow—by their beds. Even our clothes are more dangerous, injuring 345,000 people every year.

Risks are everywhere; that's a fact. From slip-and-fall injuries to natural disasters and the poisons we keep under our kitchen sinks, we are surrounded by deadly risks all day every day.

But take a second and think about just what an injury in the backcountry means. Yes, we may all be at more risk walking down the stairs in the morning (2.9 million people every year hurt themselves by falling down the stairs), but when you're one of the 0.1 percent of people who gets hurt—or worse—in the outdoors, you're in a much more dire situation.

When you slip and fall down the stairs, you likely have access to a phone to call for help. You're inside, so you don't have to worry about exposure or further injury from the elements. Depending on where you live, help is nearby and can get to you fairly quickly in the form of an ambulance.

In the wilderness, none of those options exists.

When you slip on a rock, fall into a mountain stream, and break your ankle, there's no cell service available to you to call for help. If you're too injured to move or walk, you're stuck in that stream, or at best near the water's edge. Help probably can't get to you, so you have to find a way to get to it. And, most importantly, if you're alone out there, you're likely going to be alone for a long time, until another group happens along and finds you.

None of those options is particularly appealing.

And this is just a fairly basic injury, the kind of break that, near civilization, would be easily treated and fixed at your local hospital.

Outside, though, even minor injuries can spiral out of control and turn into major problems very quickly.

Consider something as simple as a spider bite. If you're allergic and pick up a bite while clearing leaves in your backyard, it's no problem. You go inside, get yourself to the hospital if needed, and get the treatment you need.

If you're miles from any hospital, though, your symptoms aren't going to wait for you to hike four hours back to your car and drive another hour to the nearest medical center. You're going to be in much worse shape than you would have otherwise, simply due to the time it will take to treat your wound and the secondary complications that may sprout up along the way.

That's what I mean when I say that injuries in the backcountry are a different ballgame.

They may not be as frequent or as common as car accidents or falling off tables (340,000 per year), but when injuries happen in the wilderness they are more serious across the board and potentially more deadly than those that happen near the home. In my view, the focus for these types of injuries isn't immediate treatment or pain relief; it's about making sure they don't get worse before you're able to get real medical attention.

It's about staying alive.

The term *first aid* is defined by Webster's dictionary as "emergency care or treatment given to an ill or injured person before regular medical aid can be obtained." Not in place of regular medical care, but before. It is intended to stabilize a situation, prevent further injury, and help the patient get to the hospital as soon as possible without doing any further damage.

In the wilderness, all medical care is first aid. Even in the case of serious injuries that call for a Flight For Life helicopter, nothing that's being done is any replacement for the true medical care that's coming later.

Stabilize and evacuate.

* * *

This book is designed to serve two purposes: to highlight the potential dangers we all face in the outdoors, and to provide real-world, actionable advice from survival experts on dealing with each scenario. My hope is that this information will help make you a smarter, better-informed backcountry traveler, more aware of the risks you face and better equipped to deal with them in the event of an emergency.

But I am no survival expert. I am not an ex-Navy SEAL or lifelong woodsman.

I am simply someone who likes to be prepared and informed and knows how to find the people who know the answers to my questions. I also know that I'm not alone. Many other people likely have the same questions that I do—for example, what do you do when you come across a mother bear and her cubs on the trail? How do you stay safe when traveling across a glacier field? How worried should you be about that spider that somehow found its way into your tent?

It is the twenty-first century and most of us, in North America at least, don't face a daily struggle for survival. We aren't facing down large predators or debilitating diseases through the normal course of our lives.

This is a good thing. This is progress as a species.

But a side effect of this progress is that many of us have lost or forgotten the skills that helped our ancestors survive and thrive in a far more dangerous world than the one we now inhabit. We have forgotten how to live, really live, off the land and our wits. We have forgotten how to live safely side by side with large predators. We have forgotten how to move through the natural world smoothly and securely, with minimal modern conveniences or gadgets.

There are literally dozens of discussions we could have around this idea that humans, as a species, have lost the ability to thrive in the wilderness, but that is simply not the purpose of this book. We're here to fill in the gaps, not explain why those gaps exist in the first place, and also reintroduce some information that used to be common knowledge in an effort to help everyday explorers better enjoy their time in the wilderness.

The approach for this is simple: story, information, expert analysis. For each of the situations we explore in this book, from wolf attacks to heatstroke, we'll start with a narrative story about someone who fell victim to that particular scenario in the backcountry. In some cases, these people died as a result. In others, they were able to get out alive. But in all cases these stories are intended to illustrate in very stark terms exactly what can go wrong in the wild and what it looks like when that happens.

From there, we will dig into the facts and the science behind each risk factor. How common, really, are blood-borne diseases that are transmitted by mosquitoes? How dangerous, really, are mountain lions? What are the real risk factors that frostbite presents? Here I share the statistics and studies around each risk, illustrating just what the reality of each situation looks like in the real world.

Then, where applicable, I loop in the experts, the real people who have been there and done that. As opposed to the science and the studies, they bring an on-the-ground focus to these discussions. In many cases they have experienced these situations in the wild. They know what it looks like to stare down a predator or fight off a disease. They know what to look for when it comes to symptoms or signs, and they know what it feels like, for example, to suffer from dehydration or snow blindness or a long list of other injuries.

Most importantly, they know how to get out alive. They've been there, they've seen it all in the field, and they are the true pros when it comes to these subjects. Selfishly, part of the reason I wrote this book in the first place is because I wanted to speak with people like this. I wanted to find out from them what these risk factors are really like in the wilderness and how they, as experts, deal with them personally. I wanted to learn more about what we really face when we spend time in the outdoors and how we can safely deal with each of these risks. Most of all, I wanted to know how to get out alive, even in the kind of worst-case scenarios I profile in this book.

And, as you'll see, it worked. Hopefully you'll get as much out of this research and reporting as I did and it makes you a happier, safer backcountry traveler in the process.

CHAPTER 2

Predators/Large Animals

Bears

Todd Orr did everything right.

He carried a canister of bear spray, he had a loaded .45 pistol in a shoulder holster, and he even shouted out "Hey, bear" every thirty seconds or so to make his presence known.

And yet he still got mauled by a grizzly bear.

Twice.

"Yeah, life sucks in bear country," the fifty-year-old said in a gruesome video he shot himself on his cell phone after the encounter, a large flap of skin hanging off his forehead and his face covered in deep cuts and scratches. Orr's story went viral when he uploaded the video to Facebook.

It happened in October 2015, when Orr hiked into Madison Valley, located about 100 miles south of Bozeman, Montana, to scout for elk. The area is well-known as grizzly country—according to a 2004 DNA study conducted by Montana Fish, Wildlife & Parks, there are roughly 900 grizzlies in the seven-million acre Northern Continental Divide Ecosystem in the western portion of the state, including Glacier National Park and the Bob Marshall Wilderness complex, making it the largest population of brown bears in the lower 48 states—and encounters with people are not uncommon. In 2015, for example, a group of tourists in the area caught a juvenile grizzly on camera from inside their car, as the bear stood up against their vehicle and sniffed at the windows. An active hunter, Orr had even encountered brown bears safely in the past, but nothing could prepare him for what would occur this time.

Despite his "Hey, bear" calls, Orr came across a sow and her cubs in a grassy, open meadow about three miles in from the trailhead. It was a sunny fall day and they were grazing an area on the upper end of the meadow. He saw them before they saw him, so he stopped and called out again, in order to alert the bears to his presence.

Typically when these situations happen, the bear hears the warning and will run off rather than confront the human.

This was not a typical day, however.

After his call, the sow looked up, saw the intruder, and immediately moved up the trail in the opposite direction. But rather than leave the area, the bear suddenly stopped, turned, and started charging at Orr.

The average grizzly can run as fast as 35 miles per hour at a dead sprint, so it can cover quite a bit of ground very quickly. Orr kept shouting, waving his arms, and trying to make himself appear big and dangerous to the bear, as it charged.

No change.

At about twenty-five feet out he unholstered his repellant and hit her with his bear spray.

No change. According to Orr, her momentum by that point was so great that it carried her right through the spray without effect.

Before he knew it, the bear was on top of him, biting at his arms, shoulders, and backpack—anything it could get to in order to inflict damage. An experienced outdoorsman, Orr lay face down in the dirt with his arms wrapped around the back of his neck in order to protect his most vulnerable areas.

"The force of each bite was like a sledge hammer with teeth," he wrote of the encounter later. "She would stop for a few seconds and then bite again. Over and over."

This went on for a few minutes before the bear, inexplicably, got up and left. Orr picked himself up, reviewed the damage, and turned back down the trail toward his truck. At this point, he had a number of puncture wounds and scratches on his arms and back, but the damage was relatively minor and he hadn't lost much blood. He expected to get back to the trailhead within the hour and drive himself to the nearest hospital.

The bear had other ideas.

"About five or ten minutes down the trail, I heard a sound and turned to find the Griz bearing down at thirty feet. She either followed me back down the trail or cut through the trees and randomly came out on the trail right behind me. Whatever the case, she was instantly on me again. I couldn't believe this was happening a second time! Why me? I was so lucky the first attack, but now I questioned if I would survive the second."

The second attack was far worse for Orr, as the bear had caught him by surprise and he wasn't able to get down into a protective position as quickly. He eventually was able to protect the back of his neck with his arms, but the bear stood on top of him, biting at his upper torso again and again.

With one bite, the bear broke his forearm, immediately numbing Orr's hand on that side and leaving nearly half his body unusable. The pain was searing and sudden, forcing Orr to gasp for breath.

As he tells the story, the sound of his reaction seemed to drive the bear crazy, triggering a "frenzy" of biting to his shoulders and upper back. Orr huddled motionless, afraid to make another sound for fear that it would set the bear off further.

A bite to his head opened up a deep cut over his ear, sending blood flooding over his face and into his eyes. He said later that the bite nearly scalped him.

"I didn't move. I thought this was the end. She would eventually hit an artery in my neck and I would bleed out in the trail. But I knew that moving would trigger more bites so a laid motionless hoping it would end."

Then, as with the first attack, the bear simply stopped. She didn't run off immediately, but instead stood on top of Orr for a moment, breathing heavily and sniffing at him.

"I could feel her breath on the back of my neck, just inches away. I could feel her front claws digging into my lower back below my backpack where she stood. I could smell the terrible pungent odor she emitted. For thirty seconds she stood there crushing me. My chest was smashed into the ground and forehead in the dirt. When would the next onslaught of biting begin? I didn't move."

But that moment never came. The bear simply walked away, leaving Orr for dead in the middle of the trail.

He lay motionless, at once terrified that with any movement the bear would come back and concerned that he might make his injuries worse. Eventually, slowly, he picked himself up off the ground, gathered whatever belongings he could, and continued down the trail back to his truck. He jogged off and on, making it back in less than forty-five minutes, losing copious amounts of blood and with large chucks of skin and flesh hanging off of him.

But he made it.

A few hours later, X-rays at the hospital revealed that the forearm bite hadn't fully broken his ulna bone but rather took a small chip out of it. Most of his injuries turned out to be arm and shoulder punctures and tears, which doctors stitched up and addressed over the course of eight hours of treatment. He'll likely have a five-inch scar on the side of his head for the rest of his life, and he was left with chilling bruises in the shape of claws and teeth across his back where the bear stood on him.

But he survived.

And that's exceedingly rare on its own. More so even than grizzly attacks, which don't happen often at all, because such encounters are generally a zero-sum game: the victim either dies as a result of their injuries, or they avoid getting attacked in the first place. Brown bears—aka grizzlies—aren't known for their gentle behavior when threatened.

When they attack, they kill. That's how it works.

But Orr's encounter, and his survival, has provided us with a deep understanding of what a bear attack is really like, offering clues to surviving one in the unfortunate instance that it happens again. Thanks to his (admittedly gruesome) video report from just minutes after the attack, bloodied and bruised, we now know exactly what a female grizzly targets when attacking, what parts of the human body are most at risk, how to protect those parts during the course of the attack, and even the bear's behavior following the attack.

Orr's wounds to the back, shoulders, and head are typical of the injuries found on corpses following bear attacks, and we have the benefit of his account of the attack to inform our own choices going forward when venturing into bear country.

Not that that is a common occurrence in most of North America.

Although the species was once widespread throughout the continent, there are now only five recognized population areas in the United States, all in the western part of the country, four in the Lower 48 plus Alaska. Montana's Northern Continental Divide area, as mentioned, is the largest grizzly habitat in the Lower 48 and it is where Orr encountered his mama bear, but there are also established populations in the Greater Yellowstone region on the Wyoming-Montana border, in Washington's North Cascades, in the Cabinet-Yaak region of northern Idaho into Canada, and in the Selkirk Mountains of southern Canada near the Idaho and Washington border.

And, since grizzlies are listed by the U.S. Fish and Wildlife Service as "threatened," we also know almost exactly how many bears live in each of these areas.

It's not many.

Although there were as many as 50,000 grizzly bears roaming North America as recently as two centuries ago, today the continental population hovers around 1,800 total living in just two percent of their former habitat. Of those, only about 900 live in the 7.6-million acre Northern Continental Divide area that, remember, is home to the greatest concentration in the Lower 48. That number has actually been growing since the early 2000s, when just 765 were being tracked in the area, and exceeds the restoration goal of 800 for the area. The Greater Yellowstone area, which has been targeted for grizzly bear restoration, is home to about 600 bears, or one per every fifteen to thirty-six square miles, while the next-densest area, the Selkirk Mountains, support a population of just thirty to fifty bears. In the Cabinet-Yaak ecosystem, there are some thirty to forty bears for a density of one grizzly per every sixty-five to eighty-six square miles, while in the North Cascades in Washington—an area of more than six million acres—there are as few as six to twenty recorded brown bears currently in the region, for a density as low as one bear per every 1,500 square miles.

For the sake of comparison, brown bears such as grizzlies can weigh anywhere between 500 and 900 pounds, though particularly large males can tip the scales at more than 1,000 pounds. Black bears, on the other hand, tend to range from 200 to 500 pounds and, despite their name, can range in color from jet black to more of a light cinnamon color, depending on where they live, that can look very brown bear–like.

Given these figures, the chances of any hiker, hunter, or other back-country visitor encountering a grizzly, let alone suffering an attack, are infinitesimally small.

For the sake of comparison, Alaska is thought to be home to about 30,000 brown bears today (plus some 100,000 of the smaller, less aggressive black bears, which are also widespread across most of the country), making it the highest-density bear habitat on the planet. And, as any Alaska resident or frequent visitor will tell you, you're more or less guaranteed to encounter a bear of some sort if you spend much time in the backcountry (and Alaska is pretty much all backcountry).

But even in the Lower 48, dangerous encounters are not unheard of, as Todd Orr's encounter proved.

In fact, according to Fish and Game records, there is roughly one fatal brown bear mauling every year in North America and one fatal encounter with one of the 750,000 black bears on the continent. Most of these attacks are defensive, when an unsuspecting victim stumbles onto the bear in its habitat and surprises the bear.

That was the case in 2014, when a Utah man was mauled to death by an unknown bear in Wyoming's Bridger-Teton National Forest. He was working for an Idaho firm that conducts environmental assessments in the backcountry for the federal government, and an autopsy revealed that he died from blunt force trauma to the head as the result of a bear bite.

"It sounds like this was a bear defending a food source—a type of attack that's quite common," John Beecham, co-chair of the Human-Bear Conflicts Expert Team of the International Union for Conservation of Nature's Bear Specialist Group, told *National Geographic* at the time.

Still, the numbers are tiny, especially considering the millions of people who go into the woods every year. Since 2000, there have been twenty-seven fatal encounters with both brown and black bears in North America—fifteen of those were in Canada, three in Alaska, two in Tennessee, and one each in New York, New Mexico, California, Pennsylvania, Colorado, Utah, and Montana. And grizzly bears aren't even at the top of this short list—they were involved in just ten of the above attacks, while black bears accounted for the other seventeen. All in, that's barely three fatalities per year.

In truth, as with most wild animal encounters, you are far more likely to scare off a bear—brown or black—than you are to antagonize it into an attack. So many things have to go wrong before a bear charges you that travel through bear country is generally safe provided you follow some basic best practices and don't go in uninformed.

Todd Orr's case, unfortunately, truly was that worst-case scenario. He surprised a mother grizzly who was grazing with her cubs, his bear spray cloud proved ineffective against her charge (even though bear spray has been found to be 98 percent effective in just such a situation), and he was unable to get to his firearm in time to serve as a final deterrent.

That wasn't even really a desirable option anyway, he said afterward.

"Had I shot and only wounded the bear, would she have been more aggressive and attacked with more ferocity or for a longer period of time, doing more damage, If she was shot and wounded, would her sounds have called the cubs in to us, now putting me in the position of her not leaving the attack scene? Had I been lucky enough to get off a shot, it certainly may not have been lethal and could have led to a wounded and irate bear."

Not to mention the reality of killing a bear that clearly had a family to support.

"I certainly wouldn't care to shoot a sow with young, defenseless cubs that would likely not survive the winter without their mother . . . I am a hunter and an outdoorsman and I do not shoot a bear just to kill it."

* * *

According to Rachel Forbes, executive director of the Grizzly Bear Foundation, a nonprofit organization based in Vancouver, British Columbia, that's dedicated to the protection and welfare of bears in Canada, the primary message she always likes so share about grizzly and black bears is that they are not, on the whole, very interested in humans.

"We don't consider them ferocious animals," she says. "The idea that a bear is going to attack you out of some sort of malicious motive is not a reality. Bears will avoid humans as much as they can, unless they are provoked, or unless you have attracted them with something that they need. Even if you've got a bag full of berries and apples and honey that you've left in your campsite, a bear may not actually care about that if he or she is already well fed and finding stuff on their own."

That being said, successful and safe travel in bear country comes down to one thing: education. Knowing not only what attracts bears but also how they behave in the wild is the most effective step that anyone can take to minimize the probability of a negative grizzly encounter. For example, Forbes explains, the prevailing myth about grizzlies in the wild is that they are constantly on the lookout for people and will charge at the slightest provocation. That couldn't be further from the truth.

"Some people think that, if you encounter a grizzly bear in the wild, if you see one, that they see you. But they may have not even noticed you. They might be totally preoccupied with their own thing, and you can just keep walking away quietly, in a nonconfrontational manner, and nothing will happen."

Large, powerful, and always to be respected, safe travel in bear country simply calls for some common sense.

The truth is, unless you're coming between them and their cubs, or unless you've done something infringing on their personal space or you're showing them that they have a reason to feel threatened by you, they won't feel threatened by you and will generally ignore you. Forbes is quick to admit that she is no expert in bear country safety and behavior, but sees her role as an educator, sharing accepted best practices and bear-related research with anyone who will listen.

Know the Country: "When you're going into the backcountry, knowing if you're going to be in bear territory or not is step one, because you may or you may not be. In the lower 48 states of the United States there's very few places that you're going to encounter grizzly bears, because they're such a threatened population. There's a lot of places in BC where now, recently, we've actually started to see grizzlies in some new areas, not because the population is increasing but because it's moving around. But there's a lot of places where you'd be out where there's no chance of seeing a grizzly, so it's not something you really need to be scared of. Or if you're out in the winter, the chances of a bear being roused from their hibernation and coming and attacking you are also very slim."

Know the Rules: "One of the obvious things you can do to not try to attract bears to where you are is keeping your smelly stuff away or packed up tightly. They have an amazing sense of smell, so making sure you're keeping your food put away and up in bear-safe containers when you're camping and out in the outdoors is obviously a really easy and helpful preventative thing to do."

Let Them Know You're There: "If you're traveling around in the back-country you want to be making noise, that kind of stuff, where if they know that you're there they'll probably avoid you and you won't have to worry about it. On the whole, traveling in groups and singing and clanking on things is good. Grizzlies are mostly solitary, but they're not necessarily asocial. They do tolerate each other. They're like humans, like generally we'll be around other people but we happen to like some people and we don't like other ones, so there will be some bears that don't like each other, and they fight or they get in arguments. Where there's reason for them to be around each other, like a plentiful food source, they're quite fine with hanging out around each other. But you won't find them in packs like you would a wolf."

Know Where to Look: The big lesson about both black and brown bears, she says, is that they can be found almost anywhere within their ranges. There are areas that they tend to frequent, but they're generally not as predictable as other wild animals in part because their diet is so diverse. They don't need to return to the same berry patch every day, for instance, because sometimes they can eat fish, or find a moose or other prey. "If they're traveling around, one thing to know is that they generally will use paths, because they will take, just like humans will, the path of least resistance between places that they want to go. If you are on a path, mountain biking or hiking, you may very well see animal tracks because animals use those paths just as much as humans do." In addition to tracks and scat, bears will also rub up against trees and claw on them, providing other clues to bear activity in the area, as well as the typical grizzly bear food sources like huckleberries, white pine trees with the pine cones that they eat, salmon spawning streams, and more.

Protect Yourself: "Bear spray is very effective if you do actually get attacked, if you're finding yourself in that situation, which is obviously going to be a bit of a last resort. But bear spray only works when it's actually sprayed on the bear, in their face. If you spray bear spray around your campsite, or on your stuff, that can actually be an attractant for them because it's smelly and interesting. Like pepper spray, bear spray works by getting in the eyes and the nose of the attacker. It doesn't work because of its smell; it needs to be in the face of the bear."

In general, she says, where you are in the world is going to influence how habituated the local bears are to people. If you are in a legitimately remote area like somewhere in the Northwest Territories of Canada, or Alaska, you're going to encounter much more wildlife than you will if you're in an area with high amounts of human traffic. In more populated areas, the animals generally know to avoid people and have learned where not to go.

"There was a couple of mother bears in an area of BC last summer, who had a lot of cubs that summer, which is great," she says. "But they were in an area of high traffic with mountain bikers and things, and they actually charged a couple of people, because they were feeling like their cubs were threatened. Conservation officers and the locals and other people let everybody know about that, to try and make people a little bit more aware and to take precautions. That's always the answer: Do your research, ask around for if the park warden or conservation officer, or even just local guiding groups, will have reports of wildlife activity in the area. Know what you're getting into and be smart."

The real issue, explains Mike McIntosh, the founder and director of the Bear With Us Sanctuary and Rehabilitation Centre for Bears in Ontario, Canada, is that many people simply perceive the risk of bear interactions incorrectly. Fear is a very emotional thing that is hard to control, leading to many misunderstandings and overreactions.

"Bears, in general, are afraid of what they don't understand," he explains. "If they see something that doesn't make sense, it just really doesn't matter what the species is [brown bear or black bear], they'll try to leave the area. A black bear, it'll run and hide or climb a tree. But if it's a surprise situation, a grizzly or brown bear may charge or attack. That's why they say to lay down and supposedly play dead if it's a brown bear attacking because it's self-defense."

Once the bear realizes that there is no real threat it will usually leave the area. Black bears, of course, are far less likely to attack, so when they do it is usually for a different reason, not fear. In those cases, McIntosh says, it's best to fight back aggressively because the bear isn't going to just run off on its own.

Still, regardless of the species of bear, it all comes down to the element of surprise. A surprised bear is a dangerous bear, and its response to that fear—its own fear of the unknown, and you—is what can sometimes injure people. That's why it's important to always be aware of your surroundings when hiking in bear country, making noise to let them know where you are. Done right, they'll run off and you'll never even know they were there. You don't want to come around a corner and catch a bear and her cubs by surprise.

And, of course, bears are also a lot smarter than we often give them credit for.

McIntosh tells of black bears that will stake out dumpsters in residential areas, waiting for people to come out with their garbage in the evening. Once they see a good mark, they'll step out of the darkness and approach the person. The person will, not surprisingly, scream and run off, dropping the bag of trash in the process. And just like that, the bear has its reward. This is a learned behavior that, just as with a dog, a bear learns quickly and is capable of repeating over and over.

Even bear bells can have this effect, he says.

"Some people feed bears because they think it's cool. They'll take food out of their backpack and toss the bear food, and sometimes they'll even do some other things like give the food out of their hand. This doesn't make the bear dangerous, this makes the bear conditioned to a reward that they expect from people. And up in Glacier Park in Montana, people would wear bells and a grizzly bear would approach and the people would panic, drop their backpacks and leave. Even though they're not intentionally feeding the bear, they're still giving the bear a reward for responding to the bells."

That's right, some grizzly bears are smart enough to, when they hear the sound of your bear bell, realize that you probably have a backpack that the bell is attached to, and there's probably food in that backpack. They know that humans tend to carry things like sandwiches, granola bars, sports drinks, and other treats in their packs, and bears like all of those every bit as much as we do.

To them, it's a dinner bell.

To combat this in the field, McIntosh always tells people to carry a simple plastic garbage bag wadded up in their pocket any time they go out into an area where bears are known to frequent. They're light, they're cheap, they're easy to carry, and, in a pinch, they can even be used to pick up trash. But on the off chance you startle a bear in the wild and the bear starts to approach you, they're one of the most effective deterrents that he's found. Just pull it out of your pocket, open it up, and whip it up and down so that it fills up with air and goes *whack, whack, whack,* while yelling, "Go away, bear!"

Remember, bears don't like uncertain situations. They don't like things they've never seen before. And chances are very good that they've never seen a person standing on a trail, whipping a garbage bag up and down over their head before. That combination of the visual bag waving and the sound is not something that the bear would be used to or have seen before. As a result, it won't be thinking that you're going to give it food because it's not going to know what to think. It never would have had that experience before.

McIntosh also says that bear spray is a good item for everyone to carry in the backcountry no matter what kinds of animals they might encounter, because it makes people feel more at ease and safe. They might react in a calmer manner to an encounter than they would if they didn't have anything to defend themselves with and just panicked.

"Even though we watch lots of nature documentaries showing bears growling, they don't growl," McIntosh says. "They don't have the capacity to growl. Those sounds are dubbed in. They're either mixed with dog or lion or both. Bears moan if they're nervous, like a very deep moan. They'll clack their teeth together. Doesn't matter what the species is. They stomp the ground with their feet. Sometimes they bluff charge. They may get a quick rush toward the perceived threat, and stop and then retreat again trying to scare the person back if the person is too close."

They're big, powerful animals, he says, but they are also very smart and predictable. By studying their behavior patterns and understanding what sets them off, traveling and camping among them can be done safely, as long as the animals are respected and the rules of traveling among them are followed.

Big Cats

Flagstaff Mountain is so close to downtown Boulder, Colorado, that you don't even need to turn your head to see the lights of the city below, and you can even hear the roar of the crowd from the University of Colorado's Folsom Field football stadium barely a mile away. Part of the Rocky Mountain foothills, Flagstaff is preserved as open space, crisscrossed by hiking trails, and is a popular destination for cyclists—drawn by Flagstaff Road's mind-numbing 12.8 percent maximum grade climb—and climbers alike. Best of all, it is so close to town that many Boulder locals can walk to the trailhead after work.

It's close.

And it is proof that you don't need to travel deep into the wilderness to encounter wild, and sometime dangerous, predators.

Case in point, a seven-year-old boy was attacked on a Flagstaff Mountain trail in 2006 within sight of the Crown Rock trailhead, a loop hike about halfway up the hill and known for its wildflowers. In what sounds like the perfect nightmare scenario for any parent, the boy was hiking with a group of eight adults when his father turned around to see his son being dragged into the woods by a mature mountain lion, or cougar. The cat had the boy's head in its mouth and had scratched him across the legs in order to disable him.

The child's screams echoed across the open space, the sun still shining at 6 p.m.

As the group told Division of Wildlife officials later, they immediately turned to face the attack, shouting and throwing rocks at the cougar in order to get it to run off. "They did everything possible to defend the boy from the lion," a state wildlife official later told reporters. "You've got to fight back with everything you have if you're attacked by a mountain lion."

In this case, it worked. The lion got scared and dropped the boy, who was by this point kicking and squirming himself in an effort to free his head from the cat's mouth, running off into the woods and leaving the victim with a series of nonlife-threatening lacerations and puncture wounds. Bleeding heavily, the boy was rushed to a nearby hospital where doctors treated his wounds and promised a full recovery.

Hiking and trail running in the Boulder foothills hasn't been quite the same since.

Sound unusual? Such encounters used to be—and in the 2006 case, an environmental services manager with the City of Boulder said that such attacks are "extremely unusual" due to the fact that mountain lions in and around Boulder are accustomed to humans and don't look at us, or our children, as potential food—but such attacks have been on the rise for years, in large part due to human encroachment into what has long been cougar habitat.

In 2005, science journalist David Baron published a book on the trend titled *The Beast in the Garden* that tracked the mountain lion population's widespread return to Colorado's Front Range through the lens of a series of attacks in the area dating back to the 1980s. As told in the book, not even the 1991 death of a jogger in nearby Idaho Springs, Colorado, was enough to convince the locals that cougars were becoming a problem, despite the warning signs—pets turning up dead, increasing instances of mountain lion sightings, cougars lying dead by the side of the road, etc. But the trend was clear: development in the region was extending into the animal's natural habit and changing the relationship between humans and the big cats.

Mountain lion encounters used to be unusual, a once-in-a-lifetime sort of thing. But, as development expanded, sightings not only became more frequent but the cats themselves grew bolder.

For example, after a large cougar chased a Denver man's dog while he and a friend were hiking near Colorado's Mount Evans in 2013, the lion laid down and stared at the man from twenty feet away, hissing and growling at the man but not remotely scared of the encounter. The hikers spent ten minutes photographing the animal with their iPhones, even climbing up into a tree at one point in order to get a better angle.

The cat never moved.

If the young victim in Boulder was lucky—he ended up with a few scars from claw marks and other injuries following his encounter—mountain biker Anne Hjelle is the poster child for how to survive a cougar attack.

She was jumped by a mountain lion in 2004 while mountain biking in Whiting Ranch Wilderness Park near Mission Viejo in Southern California. In what reads like another nightmare scenario, Hjelle's riding partner reportedly lost sight of her on the tight, twisting singletrack in the park and came around a bend in the trail to see an adult mountain lion attempting to drag her friend into the woods by her head. Evidently, the cat had jumped on her back as she rode by and tackled her off her bike.

From there, the fight began.

Her partner threw her own bike at the mountain lion as a diversion and got into a tug of war with the animal, pulling Hjelle by the legs in an attempt to get her away from the cougar, shouting at it the whole time. The cat didn't give up right away—it first let go of the rider's helmet to start attacking her face and neck—but eventually released her entirely and ran off into the brush after two other riders stopped and started throwing rocks at it.

Hjelle was airlifted to a local hospital where she—a large portion of her face hanging off by a flap of skin—eventually went through six surgeries to try and restore her badly damaged face. A week later, with some 200 stitches and staples holding together the forty bite marks the attack had left across her face and upper body, Hjelle hiked back up to the spot of the attack in an effort to move on and confront her fear head on.

"I could have curled up into a ball or gotten on with my life," she said later. "It's not easy, but I wanted to conquer my fears—just like you do in mountain biking."

And Hjelle, for all the pain and suffering she endured as a result of the attack, may have been the lucky one that day. Another mountain biker, thirty-five-year-old Mark Reynolds, was later found dead and "partially buried" near his own damaged bike in Whiting Ranch, an apparent victim of the same mountain lion earlier in the day.

The cougar itself—a 110-pound juvenile—was eventually located by wildlife officials and euthanized.

* * *

Blame the developers, right?

One thing is for sure, since the 1980s, mountain lion encounters—though still rare—have become more common in mountain communities across the Western United States, in part because more and more people are moving into the animals' natural habitat. So, as homes move into desirable foothills neighborhoods, increased encounters are simply going to happen. After all, mountain lions like to live in rocky, mountainous terrain from sea level to about 10,000 feet for many of the same reasons that people do: the environment is rich, the landscape is safe, and there are few others around to bother them.

But problems happen when humans start moving into lion country. Oftentimes, people see more of the animals than they expected, they get nervous, and often state game officials are called in to relocate or euthanize the mountain lions before they can harm any of their new neighbors. They lose their homes, and then they lose their lives.

This is how species go extinct.

But the lions themselves are apparently not taking this encroachment into their habitat lying down. They are asserting themselves, reclaiming their former homes—regardless of who lives there now—and moving into human populated areas in ways that wildlife officials have never seen before, ending up in backyards, in the suburbs, and even in downtown areas across the country.

They're even moving to do it, expanding beyond their typical ranges in the Western United States and even reappearing in parts of the East where they were considered extinct for more than a century. For example, in December 2015, wildlife officials in Tennessee confirmed the first mountain lion sighting in that state in more than 100 years, after a hunter captured photos of a cougar on his backcountry trail camera in Obion County, near the Arkansas border. That sighting followed as many as a dozen others in the state in recent years, but was the first confirmed case.

In 2008, a mountain lion from South Dakota ended up in Chicago, where police shot and killed the animal before it could cause any harm.

In 2011, one was struck and killed by a vehicle on the Wilbur Cross Parkway, near Milford, Connecticut.

For wildlife officials, this reemergence is a mixed bag. On the one hand, its good to see mountain lions, which are typically solitary animals that live and hunt within a 100-mile range, branching out and adapting in order to survive. But by increasingly moving into human-occupied terrain, whether it is in traditional mountain lion habitat or not, they're raising new threats to both the animals and the people whom they live among, potentially leading to more euthanasia, more animal control, and more bad blood between the species.

According to the U.S. Forest Service, mountain lions—which are also known regionally as cougars, panthers, or pumas—can be found anywhere there are deer, their primary food source, to eat. That means they can survive in everything from deserts to forests but they usually live in rocky canyons and mountainous terrain near low foothills. Mountainous, but not too high up where it gets cold. They prefer areas with dense undergrowth to conceal their movements, and will generally move on when confronted by a potential threat.

In the United States, they are typically found in fourteen western states, including California, Nevada, and Colorado, among others, with a small endangered population in Florida, where they are referred to as panthers. The state animal of Florida, panthers were common across the Southeast United States until European settlers arrived in the 1600s, clear cutting the local forests and destroying the animals' habitat. Today, the only Florida panthers in existence live in a small pocket down near the southern tip of the state.

This focus on the West is fairly new for the species. Not too long ago, mountain lions could be found in all lower 48 states, in a wide range of different environments and habitats. They are not considered endangered, but the Mountain Lion Foundation does consider them threatened and estimates that the United States mountain lion population does not currently exceed 30,000, saying that the species is limited in part due to habitat degradation, overhunting and accidental deaths (e.g., road kills).

"As a former New Englander who now lives among Colorado cougars, I no longer hike alone," wrote David Baron about mountain lion encounters in and around Boulder, Colorado, in a 2011 *New York Times* op-ed. "When I walk my dog in the early morning, I watch the bushes. I have educated myself on what to do if I encounter a cougar. Yell. Throw rocks. Fight back."

This fear is well-founded, as mountain lions are shockingly efficient killers. They can reach speeds of up to 50 mph in a full run, can bound as much as forty feet to pounce while running, can leap fifteen feet up into a tree, and have been known to climb over fences as tall as twelve feet. Even at a relative jog, a mountain lion can travel at 10 mph for hours, maintaining a hunting range of 100 miles. They do all that with four paws' worth of dagger-like claws that are capable of slashing through tissue, muscle, and bone at a single swipe and a mouthful of stabbing, piercing teeth that can make short work of nearly any type of prey. Adult males can grow to more than eight feet long and weigh as much as 150 pounds, with tan or gray coloring, and live up to ten years.

Mountain lions are truly apex predators.

Still, Baron admits, despite living in the middle of mountain lion habitat for more than a decade, he has never seen one in the wild and knows the animals as primarily a psychological threat.

"The cats are masters at hiding and generally leave people alone," he wrote, "which means the biggest adjustment to living with cougars is psychological. It is knowing that a creature far more powerful than you could be crouched behind the trash can, around the next tree, under the porch."

Mountain lion sightings are still rare.

Veronica Yovovich, PhD, Wildlife Conflict Specialist with the Mountain Lion Foundation in Sacramento, California, which advocates to protect North American lions, likes to tell the story of the time she met with a landowner who contacted the nonprofit after she saw a mountain lion on her property. She was in her fifties and had lived in mountain lion country her whole life, but the encounter, Yovovich says, was the first time she had actually seen one, although the homeowner was certain that she had walked past the animals hundreds of times before without seeing them.

"That to me is one of the main points I try to drive home to people," she says. "That if you spend a good amount of time in mountain lion country chances are you've walked right past one and didn't know it. Humans are very good at eradicating species that we have conflict with and mountain lions, we really just don't have that much trouble with them. They do a really good job of staying out of our way, and if they didn't we [as a species] would have gotten rid of them by now."

It doesn't hurt that mountain lions by their nature are quiet and solitary animals, preferring to stay in the shadows and avoiding conflict of any kind as they go about their lives. They come together when they're breeding and when a female is raising young, but other than that really they are quite solitary, so they don't have that tendency toward habituation that canids such as wolves, coyotes, and dogs can possess. And that's why mountain lion–human encounters, when they happen, generally last just a few seconds, and it's only when they see the tail, often as the animal is bounding away from them, that they realize what they saw.

"One of the main things with any of these [large] animals is that, we see on nature documentaries and we see on shows animals fighting with one another because it's big and it's interesting," Yovovich says. "But that's not really how the world works most of the time. These animals can't go to the emergency room, they can't take antibiotics, they can't get stitches. So any sort of physical altercations that they might have could potentially be their last."

And they know it, so mountain lions, among many other large predators, are very cautious in the wild and very slow to attack or put themselves in a position where they might get hurt. Uncertainty is the great fear of most wild animals, so any time they get into a situation where they don't entirely know what is going on—a hiker with a dog that's barking at them, someone waving their arms to look big, or any other unnatural activity—their instinct is generally to run away, not attack. They want to get out of the uncertain situation and get someplace where they can review what is going on and decide what to do.

As a result, Yovovich says, mountain lions in particular have developed what she calls a system of intimidation and posturing that they use to telegraph their intention and get themselves out of uncertain situations without having to resort to any sort of physical interaction. It's really the behavior that they use to communicate, rather than relying on brute strength, so they will perk their ears up, stare aggressively, crouch their bodies down near the ground, and do other things to make their intentions clear and buy some time so they can get out of the area.

"I've done exactly what you're not supposed to do," she says. "I've gone into the dens, I've gone into the nurseries to pull out the young to collar them or weigh them or, you know, do whatever it is that we needed to do. And in every situation I've ever been in, you're never supposed to get between mom and baby. That's a huge no-no. And I've never had a negative interaction. I've been growled at, I've been barked at but they just circled around and stayed in the area but never actually approached me."

Triggering an attack, she explains, really does require an extenuating circumstance, something that the lion feels it must address physically rather than through its more conservative means. Even if an interaction happens, it's very likely to be extremely brief and extremely fleeting. Still, it's important to know how to act and what to do in the off chance that it does happen.

According to Yovovich, "Make yourself look big. If you have a jacket, open it and try to increase your profile, how you look against the backdrop. If you have friends around you, bunch together. Talk to the animal, and if for whatever reason it doesn't run away, throw things at it, throw rocks and show the animal that you are not something it wants to mess with and that people are not nice to be around."

Because, she says, if any animal is sticking around people, it's a good lesson to teach it. Even if it's not being aggressive, even if it's being curious, it's just better for wildlife to steer clear of people. The further they stay away from people, the safer they're going to be. So throw rocks at it, back away slowly without turning your back, and extract yourself safely but expeditiously if the situation doesn't resolve itself on its own.

Again, mountain lions are skittish by nature and, unlike coyotes and other pack animals, they tend to keep to themselves. That presents a problem when it comes to interactions with people. Coyotes are moving into urban areas nationwide and they're something we're as humans seeing and interacting with them on a more regular basis. Mountain lions aren't as comfortable with people as coyotes and other animals are, so they don't have those types of "casual social interactions" with humans, Yovovich says. That means they are lesser known and less understood than animals that we see and interact with on a more regular basis, and this fact has fueled some of the fear of mountain lions among many people. We fear them because we don't know them.

"If you think about it," she says, "you can go to Yellowstone and you can drive up the road and get out of your car and get really close to the elk, the bison, the deer, the pronghorn, the wolves, the coyotes, and the bears even. There are all sorts of animals there that will allow you to get closer than animals would outside of national parks or outside of areas that are protected. There is nowhere in the world where you can go see mountain lions like that."

Moose

There's a look my dog—a pug—gives me every time he's about to get aggressive and attack. (Yes, this is something that pugs do, especially twenty-pound alpha pugs like ours.) He pulls his face wrinkles back into a wide, creepy smile, bugs out his eyes, and tucks his ears back against the side of his head.

That's the sign. That's how you know something bad is about to happen.

And it's the exact same look I once got from a moose in the Colorado mountains.

In another case of "it can happen anywhere," I was actually skiing at a Nordic ski resort in the tourist town of Breckenridge at the time, smack dab in the middle of a few dozen neighborhoods and surrounded by roads, condos, and a few hundred other skiers. The lodge was in view, and it was at the high of midday. Not an isolated, dark place.

The encounter started innocently enough. A less-than-qualified cross country skier (at the time; I've gotten better), I swung wide around a corner on a tree-lined trail through the woods. Unlike downhill terrain, most groomed cross country trails are narrow, twisting through scenic, woody terrain. In this case, the trail itself was just barely wide enough for two skiers to pass side-by-side.

It was quiet.

As I pulled out of the corner, I saw a small group, a family, stopped about fifteen yards ahead of me and all looking in the same direction. One of them, a boy of about ten, looked up at me and quietly mouthed the word, *moose*.

And there it was. Less than twenty feet off the trail, in a small snowy clearing sunk a few feet below the trail and surrounded by evergreen trees, stood a midsized female moose, probably less than 1,000 pounds. Brown and bushy, she was alone, no young or male companions to be seen, and was munching quietly on a tree branch. Moose are herbivores and have plenty to eat in the area in the summer, feasting on grasses and leafy plants, but come winter their options are far more limited, forcing some to subsist on woody plants and even bushes. The "maintained" greenery around the ski resort, then, must have been a tempting meal.

It was a stunning sight to see. Not five minutes from the parking lot in the middle of a bustling tourist village, we were face-to-face with Colorado nature. Cameras were dug out of jacket pockets, videos were shot, texts were sent to jealous relatives out of state. For five minutes, it was the highlight of the day.

Eventually the rest of the group gathered up their things, got back on their skis, and pushed off to enjoy the rest of the resort.

Suddenly, I was alone. In a surprisingly dark, tree-covered spot. On skis that I wasn't entirely qualified to operate. A hasty exit was out of the cards.

And the moose had stopped eating.

It was looking at me.

That's when I saw it. The look that my pug gives me. For some reason, this moose did not like me standing there looking at it. I, and the group before me, had disturbed its quiet lunch and it wanted me gone.

Immediately.

At first the signs were subtle. A bit of a snort, a shake of the head, and a quiet stare. But then, over the course of maybe ten seconds, the moose ratcheted up the intensity by adopting all of the "uh oh" signs that moose give, pinning back its ears, flaring its nostrils, and pulling its face tight in an expression that I can only describe as, "Move. Now!"

Moose are well-known as ungainly creatures, tall and gangly on legs that seem too long and too skinny for their burly bodies. And they're heavy too, with full-grown bull males clocking in at more than 1,800 pounds. With a full set of antlers (which this particular moose, being a female, did not have), they even seem more unlikely to be nimble movers. But an adult moose can run full out at 35 miles per hour. They can even swim at six miles per hour.

Still, I was shocked by the speed at which the moose closed the gap between itself and me. Just as I was starting to see and understand the warning signs it was sending, it was up out of the clearing and closing on me on the ski trail.

It was tall, towering over me, moving with a purposeful grace that I didn't expect.

And it was coming straight at me.

Previously, I addressed the role that fear plays in the backcountry. The fact that, when everything is stacked against you, your instincts kick in and you know on a very primal level when it is time to flee and when it is time to fight. When faced by a charging animal—be it a moose or a bear or a wolf—you really have no time to make a decision one way or the other. You just act the way you as a human are hardwired to act. You respond in the moment based on pure instinct. (OK, to a point. Instincts can be taught, as with charging grizzly bears when the best move is to stand your ground.)

Luckily for me, I was terrified. My own fear instinct kicked in with that moose running toward me and I did all I knew how to do, realizing that I had no chance of getting out of there on just my skiing ability. I threw my hands up into the air, I shouted "Hey!" at the moose repeatedly, and I waved my ski poles in its general direction.

Masculine? Not really. Intimidating? I can't imagine. But effective? Yes, it was.

Judging by its reaction, it was the poles that did the trick as the moose turned off of me almost immediately, crossed the ski trail, and disappeared into the woods on the other side. Before I even knew what happened, or felt safe, it was long gone into the dark underbrush.

And I didn't even get a good photo of it.

* * *

Moose are one of the most common animals that hikers and campers encounter in the backcountry in part because their habitat covers almost all of North America, plus parts of Scandinavia, Latvia, Estonia, and Russia. A member of the deer family, moose—called "elk" in Europe and Asia—prefer living in forested areas in temperate to subarctic climates.

Standing more than five to six feet at the shoulder—with an antler rack that can spread six feet on its own at full male maturity—a grown bull moose is a sight to behold in the wild, with a long, muzzled face

The moose is actually the most dangerous large animal in woods, and its wide range makes human–moose encounters common all over the United States.

and a large flap of skin, a "bell," hanging below its chin. As a result, moose generally prefer to graze plants at their level, eating high grasses and shrubs, plus pinecones, mosses, and lichens in the winter. In the summer, they'll wade into shallow lakes and wetlands to feed on aquatic plants.

They are generally solo animals; rather than living in herds like most deer they are usually found in small family groups. This can make them more dangerous than other similar vegetarian animals because they don't have a group to fall back on for support and safety. When threatened, or startled, moose often feel the need to attack to defend themselves.

Plus, unlike other deer, moose aren't generally afraid of humans by design. They won't run off simply because you're there, which can make it tempting to approach them to take a photo or try to pet them. As a result, they seem like easy prey—big, lumbering animals who will just stand there and look at you, blinking, while you approach. For hunters, who hunted moose nearly to extinction in the eighteenth and nineteenth centuries, before the species made a comeback in the last century, the appeal is obvious.

None of this is to say that deer themselves are not dangerous. According to the U.S. Department of Transportation, white-tailed deer actually kill about 130 Americans each year, usually by running out into the road and causing car accidents. As if that wasn't shocking enough, there are actually some 1.5 million deer-related vehicle crashes every year, injuring nearly 30,000 people and generating more than $1 billion in insurance claims. Lyme disease infections carried by deer-borne ticks account for another 13,000 injuries in the United States every year, as humans are infected by the animals.

But moose are not as dumb as they may look. Far from it. In fact, the species has developed sophisticated techniques to protect itself in the wild, and is far from helpless when approached.

This becomes more of a problem for hikers and hunters in the fall mating season, when male moose are already in a heightened state of agitation, often fighting with other males for attention from the females.

And, while moose-related fatalities are rare, more people than you might think are injured by moose every year, particularly when the animals make their way into populated areas in search of food. This has become a persistent problem in places such as Anchorage, Alaska, for instance, where moose attacks have spiked in the last several years, both during the September and October mating season as well as in the spring when calves are being birthed and cared for. The problem has become so severe—including several attacks on mountain bikers and trail runners at the city's borderline urban 1,400-acre Kincaid Park, near Ted Stevens International Airport—that "moose stompings" have become a searchable terms in the *Alaska Dispatch News*. A runner at Joint Base Elmendorf Richardson, an Air Force-Army installation, was even attacked on the base in the summer of 2014.

"Heads up fellow trail users," wrote a representative for Singletrack Advocates, a local mountain bike advocacy organization, on its Facebook page at the time. "Reports are coming in of a momma Moose with a calf on L Train. She is not shy and will defend her calf against perceived danger with force. Please avoid L Train and the top of C $. It is not advised to ride Kincaid single track during the calving season. Please be safe."

Of course, this is not just a problem in Anchorage. Rangers at Denali National Park and Preserve in the interior of Alaska consider moose to be more dangerous to visitors than grizzly bears are, due in part to the vastly increased chance of a "negative encounter" with one in and around the park.

In June 2015, a cow moose and two calves were found to be frequenting the Riley Creek Campground in the park, attracting significant attention from visitors. Not surprisingly, the cow—or female moose—was being very defensive around her calves, even though they were in a known human-occupied area, charging at those who approached her and injuring three people, one severely.

"Cow moose are good moms but not always the best neighbors if you get too close," wildlife biologist Pat Owen said on behalf of the Parks Service at the time. "Be alert and if charged by a moose run away. Duck around trees, cars, or buildings. If you are out in the open run in a zigzag since moose don't corner well."

In one case that May, a woman was charged by a moose and knocked down as she tried to run away. The cow then reared up and hit the woman's head and shoulder with its front hooves, tearing at her head and ears and causing serious lacerations that required a trip to the hospital for treatment.

Not surprisingly, then, the park requires that all visitors stay at least twenty-five yards away from any moose. This is a difficult rule to enforce; when I was there in 2016, I saw several large groups approaching moose on foot for photos in the park, and all were less than twenty-five yards away but even that is not a guarantee of safety. As with any animal encounter in a national park, the best practice is simply to stay in your car and view the moose from a safe distance. That way, even if the animal becomes agitated and turns to attack, you at least have the safety of your vehicle between his antlers and your head.

Still, moose injure far more people in the park every year than bears do.

The good news, however, is that my moose encounter in Breckenridge was fairly typical of an attack, and reading a moose's mood based on its behavior is an easy skill to develop. Yes, avoiding a moose encounter in the first place is the best plan of action. But when faced with a situation you cannot avoid, as happened to me on the ski trail, the signs are pretty standard.

* * *

Moose are big, powerful animals that can be dangerous when people get too close. But according to Jeff Yost, a biologist with Colorado Parks and Wildlife, the idea that moose "charge" or "attack" humans is, in his view, a misperception.

"More often than not when a moose runs at you in your direction, I think people will perceive that as being aggressive and they were attacked somehow," he says. "But maybe not necessarily, because people really aren't hurt that often. I mean, there are dozens and dozens of people that have told me over the years how they've been charged by a moose or chased through the woods by a moose, but rarely actually does the moose physically hurt them in any way or knock them down or anything. There's been several times when people have been nearly hurt because they've been on a trail and a moose comes running down a trail and they got to bail off the trail because it's going to go through whatever is in its way. If you're in its way, it's going to knock you down."

Moose like to follow trails just like we do since they're easier to walk on, he says, and in the winter when the snow gets packed down on ski and snowmobile trails they tend to gravitate to them. That's why moose show up so often in and around ski areas in the West, and in those cases they sometimes chase people and appear aggressive. Eventually, officials will remove troublesome animals, but still, even in the worst-case scenario, thousands of people are skiing past them every day and there have only been a handful of incidents over many years.

"When I think of something that's aggressive, it's somebody's aggressive dog and it's trying to bite your heels while you're running away from it and it's chasing you down the street," Yost says. "To me, that seems aggressive. Moose, generally, they do something for a short burst and they want to neutralize whatever it is that they feel is threatening them, and then they stop."

Having said that, occasionally someone will get knocked down and get stomped on by a moose. If that does happen, then you want to curl up in a ball and protect yourself, Yost says. Usually when the animal realizes that you're no longer a threat it will walk away and leave you alone. All it wants to do is neutralize whatever threat it sees and get away from you. Moose aren't generally scared of people, as deer and other animals are, so one usually won't go far, just far enough to put some distance between the two of you where it can keep an eye on the situation and go back to whatever it was doing before you bothered it.

"The two people that have been hurt here in town that I know of, both of them had dogs," Yost explains. "One person, their dogs were barking at the moose. The gal turned around and was going to head the other way, and next thing you know she wakes up. She got knocked down by the moose, apparently, and hit the back of her head and needed to get stitches in her head."

In the other case, he says, the victim was walking down a paved residential street with her dogs when a moose in the road was startled by a passing car and ran in her direction. "I think it saw the dogs and veered towards the lady and knocked her down. It just kept running. It literally never stopped. It ran. We had our personnel go out and try to investigate it and follow on the tracks, and it ran for several miles and out of sight. We never could find it."

The big lesson, he says, is that dogs and moose don't mix. It's generally a good idea to avoid having a dog with you, particularly off-leash, whenever you're traveling through known moose country.

The other thing that will set moose off is simply getting too close to them. And the animals don't do themselves any favors in this regard. Since they aren't scared of people, they'll just stand there, won't immediately run away, and will let humans approach them closer than they probably should without giving any sort of warning sign. But once you get too close, beyond their comfort zone, then they will lay their ears back, the hair goes up on their back, and they will let you know when they're irritated. At that point, the best move is to back off, go the other way, and leave them alone. They'll generally leave you alone and not do anything further.

Other situations where moose can become agitated are when there is a mother cow with her calves or when a moose is startled in the woods, often when a hiker comes up on them suddenly around a corner or in thick brush and the animal charges because it is frightened. Across the board, the rule is simply to keep your distance and not corner the animal.

"Really the biggest thing with moose is don't do anything stupid," Yost says. "Don't get close to them. Keep your distance from them. Watch their physical behavior, whether they act like they're irritated or angry and the ears are laid back and the hair's standing up, or they're vocalizing."

It's worth noting, too, that human-moose interactions are likely going to continue increasing going forward, as moose populations, like coyotes and other wild animals, continue to move into more populated areas as their range expands. Yost reports that there are on average anywhere from six to ten moose in downtown Steamboat Springs on any given day, plus another half dozen up the road at the local ski area, and those numbers are likely going to grow, he says. But having that many moose in such close proximity to people, and dogs, and just civilization in general is creating more problems for wildlife officials. It is in urban and semiurban areas like this where more moose-human conflicts are going to happen, versus out in the middle of the woods.

Still, Yost is upbeat about moose in general.

"They're a tremendous, watchable wildlife animal," he says, "because they're not going to run off. It's not like sometimes when you want to stop and get a picture of an elk, and as soon as the elk sees you it runs off. Well, nine times out of ten, a moose is not even going to react to you stopping your car or getting out and trying to take a picture of it. They're great with that aspect, as long as people respect them and just don't do anything dumb."

Wolves

The tiny town of Chignik, Alaska—population 79—is located about 250 miles southwest of Kodiak Island, about halfway down the Alaska Peninsula that leads out to the Aleutian Islands.

It's a remote place, accessible only by water or air, and surrounded by a long list of similarly isolated towns and villages including Chignik Lagoon, Chignik Lake, Perryville, and Ivanof Bay. There is a U.S. Post Office nearby that serves the whole peninsula. There are effectively no roads.

And there is a population that's well mixed between natives, white settlers, and Asian descendants from the other side of the Aleutians.

Given this fact, local residents are well used to encounters with wildlife. They're effectively living within nature, so sightings of bear, moose, wolves, and more are common. It's all just a fact of life in Chignik, so residents generally have an understanding and easy familiarity with large predators that those of us from the Lower 48, not to mention the more developed parts of Alaska, just don't have.

That's one reason that the 2010 death of Candice Berner was so shocking.

Berner, a thirty-two-year-old special education teacher from Slippery Rock, Pennsylvania, was living in the area that year as an employee of the Lake and Peninsula Borough School District, the state's education department for far-flung villages such as Chignik. As the only special education teacher on the peninsula, she traveled between communities, teaching kids at several different schools, starting five months earlier in August 2009.

On the day of her March 2010 death, she had flown into Chignik to work with a few students at the town's seventeen-head schoolhouse, and planned to go for a run after work to unwind. She was an active person—just 4 foot 10 inches tall and 115 pounds—and she liked to stay fit, even in her remote new home.

So she finished work, sent her timesheet into the school district, and headed out toward Chignik Lake for a jog.

And that's the last anyone heard from her.

Until the Alaska Department of Fish and Game released its report in late 2011, all the locals knew was that Berner's body was found by snowmobilers the next day at the side of the snow-covered gravel road, her body badly disfigured and surrounded by what looked like wolf tracks. If it were true that she had been stalked and attacked by a pack of wolves, it would mark the first such fatal attack in the state this century.

The report made it official: Berner had been stalked, attacked, and killed by a pack of wolves while out for her run. The case was particularly notable because it was the first time DNA evidence was used to confirm a fatal wolf attack in the state of Alaska.

The details from the report are as gruesome as they are chilling. According to Fish and Game's research based on testimony from local villagers, Berner's tracks appeared to make a sudden reversal as she came around a bend in the road, presumably when she first noticed the wolves.

Then, the wolf tracks picked up on either side of the road, with one or two of the animals stalking her on both sides as she tried to put distance between herself and the pack. Her footsteps, they said, grew further and further apart, indicating that she was running hard and picking up speed. Another set of wolf tracks appeared to run through the woods, above the road, and intercepted her.

The attack was sudden, the researchers found, and death came quickly. Still, the experience must have been terrifying for Berner, the only proof of her last moments a bloody depression in the road where she fell as the first of the wolves knocked her down, tearing at her flesh with its jaws.

Within seconds, the rest of the pack was there, joining in the attack before the victim even had time to scream out to the empty darkness around her. Even in March, Alaska only sees about ten hours of sunlight per day, leaving most of the state in a state of perpetual dusk.

Berner didn't give up without a fight. The report said that the tracks suggested she tried to crawl away from her attackers, struggling to get the animals off of her before they could do more damage in hopes of getting away and to the safety of town before it was too late.

But by this time, severely injured and losing a lot of blood, she didn't make it. As her struggles subsided and she succumbed to her wounds, the wolves pulled her body off the road, into a clearing some thirty feet away where they proceeded to finish the job. From there, she was dragged another eighty feet away and hidden in the underbrush.

"Tracks and markings in the snow indicated that the struggle with the wolves was brief and death occurred quickly," the report said.

Following the discovery of Berner's body and the Fish and Game report, the state culled wolves in a thirty-mile radius of the village, killing eight. Of those, DNA conclusively linked two of them to blood found at the scene of the attack, although state biologists said that as many as four wolves may have been involved in the encounter, as that is their usual pattern, though we may never know conclusively in this particular case.

One factor that scientists were able to confirm in the case through their inquiry was that there was no one clear reason for the attack. Berner wasn't carrying food, hadn't stumbled across a recent kill site that the wolves were protecting, the wolves hadn't become habituated to human contact, and there was no evidence of rabies among the culled animals, which is a factor that can often lead to aggression. Even the fact that she had headphones on and was listening to music was ruled to be a nonfactor.

This wasn't a defensive attack, it was pure happenstance. A case of her being in the wrong place at the wrong time and encountering the wrong pack of wolves.

"This appears to have been an aggressive, predatory attack that was relatively short in duration," the report read.

And that might be the most troubling part of all.

* * *

A wolf attack really is a nightmare scenario, something straight out of a horror movie or a Stephen King novel. Just the thought of it, a pack of snarling, snapping wolves bearing down on a helpless victim as they try to run, stumbling, though the woods, is enough to get the hair on the back of even the most experienced backcountry traveler's neck standing up. There is just something so primal, so raw, so inescapable about wolves that many people just don't know how to handle them in the wild.

So it's good news that wolf attacks on humans are very, very rare.

That attack in Alaska was certainly one of the more high-profile, well-publicized encounters in recent years, but I honestly couldn't find many other examples to share. There simply aren't that many wolf attacks, in the United States or elsewhere, to report. (In fact, there are some questions about the Alaska attack itself, whether wolves were involved in her death or came across her body after the fact.)

The U.S. Fish and Wildlife Service is blunt in its assessment: "There are no known gray wolf attacks on humans in modern times in North America. Gray wolves do take livestock, although the occurrences are rare."

The agency lists the gray wolf as "threatened" in the lower 48 states and "endangered" in the desert Southwest, with its decline driven in large part by habitat destruction and widespread hunting.

When Rick Lamplugh, the author of *In the Temple of Wolves*, was asked to research fatal wolf attacks in recent years he was only able to find two, the Alaska attack and the 2005 death of a man in northern Saskatchewan who had injuries that were "consistent with a wolf attack." In that case, investigators determined that local wolves in the area had lost their fear of people and that, by apparently feeding the pack near his home, the victim, a twenty-two-year-old geology student named Kenton Carnegie, may have played a role in his own demise by conditioning the animals to approach him for food.

"So wolves have killed two people, one in Alaska, one in Canada," Lamplugh wrote. "But what about in the lower 48 . . .?"

He went on to cite a 2002 report from the Alaska Department of Fish and Game, which came out years before the confirmed 2010 attack, that found no human deaths in North America that could be attributed to "wild, healthy wolves"—meaning nonrabid—since at least 1900. Further, in 2011, the Oregon Department of Fish and Wildlife determined that wolves have never attacked a human in the Rocky Mountain state, an assertion that was backed up by experts at the International Wolf Center later that same year, declaring the Lower 48 wolf attack–free.

So there's that side. The side that has effectively confirmed North America's backcountry to be safe from wolves. The side that has helped to rehabilitate the wolf's image in the public eye in an effort to protect the animals from further loss and promote their safety. There has long been debate over the efforts, both from wolf supporters and detractors, but the fact remains that, starting in the 1970s, wolves came to be thought of as less of a day-to-day threat to humans and more of a species that needs our help.

But there's the other side that includes both the 2005 Canada and 2010 Alaska attacks that were both confirmed and fatal. The side that sees wolves as a threat, even in North America.

The truth is, wolf attacks do happen. They happen in the northern wilds, and they happen in the Lower 48. They just aren't often fatal when they do, and they're so rare that there are few records available to confirm frequency, location, and severity. Wolves are wild animals like any other and, when stressed or when put in a bad situation— hunger and rabies are the most common contributing factors in wolf attacks—accidents and dangerous encounters do happen. In general, as with most wild animals, wolves avoid human contact at all cost

Wolf-human attacks are exceedingly rare in the modern era, but fear of the animals still persists.

and will go out of their way to keep from seeing a human. But when we try to approach the animals ourselves, or we habituate them to us by feeding them or approaching them in the wild, that's when the trouble starts.

In response to the 2005 fatality in Canada, *San Francisco Chronicle* reporter Jerry George determined that there had only been twenty-seven recorded wolf attacks on humans in North America to date, and all of the victims as of then had survived.

"Those of us who stand a few feet back from the impassioned wolf watchers have wondered when a person would fall victim to wolves," he wrote. "Wolves are wild animals. They have a long track record of killing people in Europe and elsewhere . . . but, before this, death by wolf was unknown in North America."

He's correct about Europe and other parts of the world, where attacks by wolves were borderline common up until the early twentieth century. It's no accident that wolves feature so prominently as villains in so many European fairy tales and children's stories. When you face the very real possibility of being taken by a wolf whenever you step outside your door, instilling a healthy sense of fear in your children of a wolf that might huff and puff and blow their house down probably isn't the worst idea in the world.

In fact, historical records show that 7,600 people were killed by wolves in France over the period of approximately 1300 to 1900, with 4,600 of those being taken by nonrabid wolves, which makes the whole thing even scarier. The story was similar in Germany, Italy, and parts of Eastern Europe, where rabid wolf attacks are still happening today. More than seventy people were attacked by rabid wolves in Latvia between 1992 and 2000, and more than twenty attacked in Lithuania during roughly the same time period.

And it's not just Europe.

More than 325 people were treated for rabid wolf bites in Iran in 1996, and some 700 people were killed by wolves in India's North West Provinces in 1876, a year after wolves killed more people in the area than tigers did. The animals were killing fifty people per year in Korea as recently as the 1920s.

North America has long been the exception to this trend, isolated enough from wolves' traditional hunting grounds and sparsely populated in the areas where they do live.

But then there's this: in August 2013, a sixteen-year-old boy was involved in what the Minnesota Department of Natural Resources called the "first confirmed attack" on a person by a gray wolf in that state's history. The attack, which occurred at a campground in north central Minnesota, left the victim with serious but not life-threatening injuries, and the wolf itself was later captured and euthanized by the U.S. Department of Agriculture, but the "freakish and unprecedented" incident illustrated the very real risk that exists with wolves.

"Impossible" is no longer a guarantee when it comes to wolf attacks in North America, and no place is off-limits.

* * *

"When this animal attacked me, the ferocity of the attack, I wasn't sure what part of me was hurt at first," remembers wolf handler Oliver

Starr of the attack he suffered from one of the wolves in his care. "What it felt like was my head had exploded. I believe it's because when he cuffed my arm, he did it with such force that my blood pressure skyrocketed into my brain. It literally felt like my head was like a balloon."

It happened in the Colorado mountains, not far from where Starr was living at the time, and involved one of the two wolves he was caring for at the time: Jenna and Jake. The female, Jenna, was a spayed "wolfdog" hybrid and had been with Starr for a long time by that point, but Jake was a full-bred wolf that he was fostering and had only been with him for about six months when the attack occurred. Their relationship, as Starr himself describes it, was still "uneasy."

A trip into the snowy hills to take some photos for a magazine assignment turned into a fight for survival when the 120-pound Jake mistook a tussle late in the afternoon between Starr and Jenna, who had literally been with him her whole life, as a provocation toward his mate and attacked, catching Starr off guard, grabbing him by the arm.

"It was really surprising," he says now, "the initial strike that broke both the bones in my forearms."

Starr described the attack itself in excruciating detail in a post on *Quora* in 2015:

"Having been around wolves for about ten years at that point I knew the last thing I wanted was to be in a tug of war with a wolf where my arm was the rope. With my free arm I grabbed his head and threw myself on top of him hoping that by rolling him to the ground I could regain control of the situation.

The next forty-five seconds seemed like an eternity. It felt like I was in three places at once. I could hear my assistant screaming, I could feel the incredible pain of the bones in my forearm being crushed by Jake's jaws and at the same time there was a part of my conscious that was completely detached observing the situation with the cool analytical mind of a scientist.

I distinctly remember this scientist's mind thinking 'he's much, much stronger than I expected. The pressure is incredible.'

Meanwhile, back inside my body I was in the fight of my life. I'd shoved my free hand into Jake's mouth to prevent him from fully cleaving my arm in two. Even with my fully gloved hand in his mouth I could feel things inside my arm crackling and popping as muscle, tendon and bone began to give way."

Fortunately, Starr was not alone that day and his assistant was able to pull Jake off of him in the midst of his attack and leash him to a nearby tree, the animal's aggression directed solely at Starr as the threat to its mate. Starr was then able to hike two snow-covered miles out to his truck and drive himself to the nearest hospital, where he told doctors that he had been injured while chopping wood.

As he remembers it, there was "surprisingly little blood externally but beneath the surface of the skin it was another story." His right forearm was broken in multiple places, as was the muscle on that side and several different tendons. His left hand was also broken, the result of his forcing it into the animal's mouth in an effort to fight off the attack, along with a tear in his left bicep.

Speaking to me more recently, Starr remember the incident as a significant turning point in his understanding of wolf behavior and one of the reasons he has since dedicated his life to their care and protection. He says, "I wouldn't trade it because I understand [them] so much better now in a way that very few people do. I really understand what it feels like, what they do, how they react. It was an amazing experience. It still stands out in my brain as the forty-five seconds of my life that is the most clear."

He has been working with wolves hands-on for thirty-five years, growing up in a ranching household in the rural Colorado Rockies where he first became interested in why the animals were so feared and hated by the locals. He took classes, visited zoos, and eventually got into raising large dogs, wolf dogs, and wolves. Today, he keeps several full wolves at his home in Marin Country, in the San Francisco Bay Area, including Aqutaq, a female white wolf who was bred in captivity and raised to be what Starr calls an "ambassador wolf," an animal that people can interact with to learn more about the wolf species.

"They're animals that shouldn't be underestimated," he says of his violent encounter all those years ago in Colorado. "I still suffer from those injuries today. I will never be without pain, because of the damage that he did in just a very little bit of time. They're formidable predators. Their strength and their speed is something that is completely surprising even to people who spend their lives working with them."

But even given his experience, and his look into the dark side of what wolf-human interaction can be, he maintains that they are not a threat to humans. His attack, in fact, was at the hands of a wolf, Jake, who knew him and was in his care. It was not a true wild wolf encounter. The animal felt that Starr was acting aggressively toward its mate and it reacted accordingly. Anyone who has ever stepped between an agitated, hungry dog and its food bowl knows what that reaction can look like. It was the same thing with Starr's attack. He misread the situation, acted in a way that upset the wolf, and the animal reacted.

"There were so many things I did wrong," he says. "I was in my twenties. I was very naïve. I'd never had a pure wolf before. I was very focused on the wrong thing, which was my loose female that I was afraid was going to get run over. We were a mile from this highway. I thought she might be down there. I got frustrated. You can never ever lose your patience when you're working with wild animals. Never. The minute you lose your patience, you've already lost every part of the battle with animals."

He was simply not nearly as respectful of the potential of the animals as he is today, and he admits that he got "exactly the lesson that [he] needed." The truth is, attacks only happen in very specific types of circumstances.

"To give an example," he says, "wolves are reticent to eat unfamiliar protein. When ranchers complain about losing livestock, they've worked real hard to end up in that situation. By that, I mean that they've been conspicuously lazy. Wolves will not attack something that they don't know what the point of it is. Right? They're not going to attack a giant animal that could potentially trample and kill them for no reason."

They need to know what they're getting into, and a cow, at first glance, isn't obvious prey for them. The same applies for humans. Wolves are incredibly unlikely to attack a person because we aren't their natural prey. We're too big, too volatile and the animals have learned over the years that we are not to be messed with.

"Wolves are actually relatively timid," Starr explains. "They're very, very cautious about unfamiliar things. Humans are largely both frightening and unfamiliar."

That's the good news, but Starr is the first to admit that, although human-wolf interactions are exceedingly rare, under the right circumstances they do happen and it's important to know how to respond in such a situation so as not to trigger the animal's attack response.

According to Starr, a human in that situation should respond much as they would during any other animal encounter:

- **Make yourself larger:** As mentioned, wolves don't like to take on adversaries that are much bigger than they are or are unknown quantities. Lifting your arms wide, spreading out your jacket if you have one, or huddling together if in a group are all ways to send the message that you are large and shouldn't be messed with.
- **Shout:** As skittish animals, wolves will run when confronted by a loud noise so that they can survey the scene from a safe distance. Shouting at them is an effective way to kick in this behavior and diffuse a potentially dangerous situation.
- **Back away slowly:** Turning to run creates two problems: first, you won't be able to see what the wolf is doing while your back is turned and, second, running can sometimes trigger an attack response in wolves. Backing away slowly can mitigate both of these risks.
- **Don't try to stare them down:** Wolves will sometimes perceive direct eye contact as a challenge or threat and will attack as a result. Don't send them any signals that can be taken as direct aggression on your part. They're curious animals and will sometimes approach to see what you're doing, but that doesn't necessarily indicate aggression and shouldn't be taken as such.

According to Starr, the science is getting increasingly clear that lethal removal of wolves, and nonspecific removal of predators of any kind, is creating situations where problematic encounters are more, not less, likely in the long run. In short, scapegoating wolves as deadly predators that need to be killed and controlled has made the problem worse, not better, by engraining a fear of wolves in many people who otherwise might never have a negative encounter with one.

"The thing that the public doesn't realize," he says, "that even in many cases the agriculturalists don't realize, is that the reason why wolves are so scapegoated today has more to do with oil and gas and timber and beef and such today than it does with wolves or anything that wolves do or are. It's because wolves are the species that has been granted the endangered species protection over the broadest lot of all extractible land."

Coyotes

Located on the far north point of Cape Breton Island, part of Nova Scotia, Cape Breton Highlands National Park is a true jewel of Canada's Atlantic coast. With rolling hills, deep river canyons, and steep cliffs falling off to the icy North Atlantic, the park is an ancient plateau that is among the most unique, scenic landscapes in North America and features heavily in the 185-mile Cabot Trail, a highway that circumnavigates most of the northern part of the island.

It's a barren, windswept place that's home to a wide range of plant and animal species, many of which are found nowhere else in Canada due to the park's unique maritime climate. This list includes old-growth forests, arctic-alpine plants left over from the last ice age, the Canadian lynx, rock vole, Gaspé shrew, pilot whale, and many more. The first national park in Canada's Atlantic provinces, Cape Breton Highlands remains a crown jewel of the country's parks system.

And it's popular with tourists, particularly the flagship Skyline Trail, which takes visitors out on a roughly five-mile loop overlooking the rugged coastal cliffs, that includes a well-developed section as well as about half a hike on raised boardwalks to protect the sensitive environment. From the parking lot, it's about a two-hour out-and-back hike that's usually crowded with tourists looking to spot a bald eagle, bear, or any of the other animals that make Cape Breton Island their home.

Crowded, well-developed, and near the main road, the Skyline Trail is precisely the kind of place where you would not expect to be attacked by a pair of aggressive coyotes.

Yet that is exactly what happened in October 2009 when Taylor Mitchell, nineteen, an up-and-coming folk singer, was killed by two coyotes near the start of the Skyline Trail, not far from the parking lot. She was, and remains, the only North American adult to die as a result of a coyote attack.

The day started out innocently enough. Mitchell and a group of friends had headed out for a short walk in the park and were in the process of returning to their car when a pair of coyotes—which the hikers had seen and photographed just minutes earlier—turned and started following the group. As the victim nearest the oncoming animals, Mitchell was the most seriously injured, with severe lacerations to her head and upper body. Nearby visitors witnessed the attack as it was ongoing and immediately called 9-1-1, and emergency workers were quickly able to airlift Mitchell to a nearby hospital for treatment.

She died as a result of her injuries roughly twelve hours later.

A well-known figure in the area—she had recently recorded her first album and was in the middle of a tour of the Atlantic provinces when the attack occurred—Mitchell was widely mourned after her death. In a statement, her mother, Emily, described her daughter as "a seasoned naturalist and well versed in wilderness camping. She loved the woods and had a deep affinity for their beauty and serenity. Tragically it was her time to be taken from us so soon."

Wildlife officials were equally troubled by the attack, eventually tracking down the second coyote involved and euthanizing it due to its apparent lack of fear of humans. (First responders had killed one of the coyotes at the time of the attack.) But still, questions lingered over why this had happened in the first place.

To be sure, coyote encounters do happen from time to time, and Cape Breton Highlands National Park itself had dealt with packs following too closely and occasionally nipping visitors. An eighteen-year-old American girl was bitten by a coyote in 2003 while hiking on the Skyline Trail with her parents, not far from where Mitchell was attacked.

But fatalities are rare.

"Public safety is our primary concern," said Chip Bird, the Parks Canada field unit superintendent for Cape Breton, in announcing the temporary closure of the trail, calling the attack "unprecedented and a totally isolated incident."

It's true. Like wolves, coyotes are generally pack animals, and they have been known to team up with other packs when attacking especially large or dangerous prey. But they are considered "socially flexible," meaning they don't always have to be in a pack. Sometimes they are solitary, sometimes they hunt in pairs. and sometimes they operate within a larger pack. Still, humans are never their primary hunting target. Primarily carnivores—meat makes up roughly 90 percent of the coyote's diet—they tend to eat a wide range of different foods, though deer, sheep, rabbits, rodents, birds, and other small mammals are most common. Depending on where they live, this diet may vary to include insects, smaller mammals, and even fish, with even the occasional leafy green plant thrown in for good measure.

Humans, particularly those traveling in groups, do not fit this pattern.

"If I had to guess what animal would be responsible for a fatal attack in eastern Canada, I would have guessed black bear, never coyote," Mike O'Brien, the Nova Scotia Department of Natural Resources' Manager of Wildlife Resources told *Field & Stream* magazine in 2009 as part of its special report on the Mitchell incident and coyote attacks in general.

As a rule, coyotes, like most wild animals, go out of their way to avoid contact with humans. Just seeing coyotes from a distance in the wild can be difficult, as they more often than not will simply turn and run as soon as they notice you in their space. They aren't usually aggressors, as they were in the Nova Scotia incident.

Rare, to be sure, but not unprecedented. Mitchell's death was only the second verified coyote fatality in North American history, following the 1981 death of a three-year-old girl in California. In that case, the child, Kelly Keen, was attacked in her own backyard and dragged off of the property before he parents could get to her and fight off the coyote. She was fatally injured, and remains the only person, young or old, to ever die as the result of a coyote attack in the United States. The incident also set off a widespread effort to cull coyote populations across the country, vilifying the animals in the eyes of many in an effort that continues to this day.

Coyotes do not attack humans, but that doesn't mean there aren't good reasons to be careful around them.

The Mitchell case was and is unique, as children make far more likely prey to predatory animals such as coyotes, given their small size and inability to get away or fight back as effectively.

* * *

Coyote habitats have been getting overrun by human development for the better part of a century, as American cities have expanded across the country into wild areas that were once the exclusive home of predatory carnivores like the coyote. Our desire to live in wild, wide-open spaces has us living in closer contact with coyotes than ever before. Increased contact was simply inevitable. Again, we can blame the developers for this one, right?

Actually, with this particular species, it isn't that simple.

Unlike just about every other large mammal species in North America, the coyote has actually been increasing its range over the course of the last few centuries, venturing into regions where, historically, it would not have been found. As of 2017, coyotes can be found pretty much all over the United States, including rural, urban, and suburban areas, anywhere they can find food to eat and a comfortable environment in which to live.

This is a new thing.

According to the Urban Coyote Research Project, sponsored by the government of Cook County, Illinois, prior to the eighteenth century, the coyote species was effectively limited to the prairies and deserts of Mexico and central North America, what is today the US Midwest and High Plains down into Central America. Since then, however, they have expanded their range across almost all of the United States and Canada, venturing further and further north and setting down roots in even the most urban of areas. Today they occupy an area that is more than four times the size of their original, prairie-focused range, being found everywhere from the Alaskan Arctic to Panama in the far southern reaches of Central America.

And they're still going. As recently as 2012, South American wildlife biologists had started receiving reports of coyote sightings as far away as Columbia, taking the species onto that continent for the first time in its history.

Coyotes truly are almost everywhere.

"Coyotes were initially present at the founding of the Chicago site in the eighteenth century but disappeared during most of the nineteenth and twentieth centuries," writes the Urban Coyote Research Project. "The recent expansion in distribution is unique as other large carnivore populations, such as wolves and bears, were extirpated from many portions of the United States, leading to the absence of large carnivores in most urban landscapes. The emergence of coyotes in urban systems can have important ecological implications, such as through their role as an apex carnivore and subsequent effects on prey."

Traditionally, coyotes prefer to make their homes in open areas such as prairies or meadows where they can have free range to hunt, live, and raise their young. But the coyote is nothing if not adaptable, making itself at home today in even the most urban and "nonprairie" of places. For example, in 2016, the *Village Voice,* a newspaper in New York City, reported on a coyote nicknamed Frankie that had been seen in a busy part of central Queens for nearly a decade, living in a small park that is "maybe four blocks at its widest. On one side are high-rise housing developments, and on the other, within a block, pizza parlors and corner stores make up a busy commercial district."

And Frankie is just one of the many coyotes that are believed to live in the greater New York metro area. According to the Gotham Coyote Project, the first confirmed sighting of a true coyote in the city was in 1995, when one of the low-slung gray animals was hit by a car on the Major Deegan Expressway in the Bronx. Four years later, one turned up in Central Park. And the sightings have only increased in recent years.

Wildlife experts at the Gotham Coyote Project estimate that as many as two dozen coyotes are currently living full-time in the city.

None of this comes as any surprise to those who study coyote behavior patterns. In urban areas, coyotes generally prefer to avoid human contact, hunkering down in wooded areas or low shrubs to avoid detection. They make their homes in parks and golf courses too, anywhere that they can find the open spaces they like while also few regular human interactions.

Part of their rapid expansion and habitat flexibility comes from the fact that the coyote is an "opportunistic feeder" that will pretty much eat whatever it finds. As scavengers, they can live off the small prey they find in the city—mice, rats, and other rodents—as well as larger prey, including dogs and deer, when they find it. Coyotes also aren't strict carnivores. According to research conducted by the Urban Coyote Project—in reality, they dug through more than 1,400 pieces of coyote scat in order to determine what each animal was eating—the most common foods in the coyote diet, at least in urban areas, are small rodents, fruit, deer, and rabbit. Garbage and other human waste is not their primary food source.

Wildlife experts predict that the coyote's rapid expansion will soon start to slow, as the species has effectively run out of new places to move into. As a result, coyotes are likely here to stay in many of the urban and suburban areas where they currently live, and their populations in those regions will likely increase going forward. This is clearly an issue for all of us, not just those who spend time in the backcountry.

But, even so, coyote attacks are very rare, fatal ones particularly so. Although coyotes and humans have long had confrontations and negative encounters, severe injury and death as a result seldom happens. In 2009, Stanley Gehrt, the head of the Cook County Coyote Project, co-authored a paper, "Coyote Attacks on Humans in the United States and Canada." In it, he studied the available data on coyote-human interactions and found just 142 reported attacks in the United States and Canada from 1960 to 2006.

"Most attacks were classified as predatory (37%) or investigative (22%) in nature," Gehrt wrote. "The number of reported attacks was nearly equal between adults and children, although child victims were more ($p < .001$) prevalent in predatory attacks. Future coyote attacks could be reduced or prevented through modification of human behavior and public education designed to prevent the habituation of coyotes. A standardized reporting system for coyote attack incidents would be beneficial for further investigating characteristics of coyote attack incidents."

* * *

Coyotes are, to not put too much of a point on it, not a threat to humans. As in, not at all.

So why have they been included in this book? In large part, it is due to the fact that so many people *believe* that coyotes are a threat, have heard for so long that they are to be feared and controlled, that this is an effort to set the record straight. As much as this book is about practical advice for safety in the outdoors, education and what is real and what is myth is a big part of what I'm trying to accomplish here.

And it's what Camilla Fox has been trying to accomplish for years as executive director of Project Coyote, a nonprofit organization in California that works to educate the public about the reality of increasing human-coyotes contact in an effort to protect the animals and encourage better interactions between the species.

"So much of this is about risk perception," she says, "and we think it's really important for people to recognize that coyotes are inherently shy but, like dogs, they're curious. If I was walking my dog and there was a very curious dog who just ran right up to me, I wouldn't be surprised at all. And sometimes coyotes do the same thing. Sometimes people misinterpret that behavior as aggression when it's not."

The truth, she says, is that many people are fearful of coyotes and specific coyote behaviors, like that natural curiosity, when they simply don't need to be. For example, sometimes a person will be walking their dog in the woods and a coyote will notice them and start following along or stalking them. For many people, this might seem like an aggressive act, something to be feared, or a sign of an imminent attack. But in fact, Fox says, 99 times out of 100 this type of behavior in coyotes is nothing more than curiosity. Particularly when there is a dog present, the animal is just interested in seeing what you're all about and what's going on. Nothing more.

"Your chances of running into a coyote that has menacing intentions or is going to attack you, it's incredibly rare," Fox says. "But that also doesn't mean that it is impossible. If you're recreating in any area where there are native carnivores, being aware and having all of your senses open and alert is important. When I go hike in grizzly bear country I am very alert and make noises and all that, not because I'm afraid that a bear will attack me but because it's the right things to do in their environment. We were once prey on the Serengeti, so we have to recognize and honor our sense of vulnerability and have it not propel us to be unnecessarily fearful, but instead propel us to be alert and in touch with all of our surroundings."

For coyotes, the "right things to do" will likely sound very familiar: leave them alone, don't feed them, appreciate them from a distance, and don't automatically assume that they need to be removed or killed.

They are generally solitary animals, so rather than traveling in packs like wolves and other species do, you're more likely to encounter them one at a time, or in small family groups, if you see them at all. They are, despite their innate curiosity, generally wary of people and have learned over time to steer clear of human encounters and leave us alone. We should return the favor, giving them plenty of space when we see them and not trying to approach or directly interact with them. As a species, they can become habituated, or lose their natural wariness of people, through either intentional or unintentional feeding, which creates risks for the people feeding them as well as the coyotes them-selves. Hazing or teasing a habituated coyote will generally break them of this behavior.

"The big message is that people need to educate themselves about animal behavior so that they can better understand what a coyote is doing when it is walking behind them when they're walking their dog," Fox says. "That coyote is probably demonstrating curiosity and interest in the dog and isn't necessarily going to attack. That does not mean that you should let your dog play with the coyote, no, that could lead to a dangerous situation, but better understanding of animal behavior can solve a lot of problems."

According to the fossil record, she explains, a "coyote-like" canid existed as far back as the late Pleistocene period, and like so many related animals, its history was and is constantly changing. Looking back to primitive wolves, dire wolves, and other early canids, all of which were direct competitors with coyotes for food and survival in antiquity. But when those other wolves were hunted to extinction, it opened up new habitats and new ranges to coyotes. And they expanded aggressively into those areas, as we are seeing now. They are very adaptable and resilient and intelligent animals, and they have developed a high tolerance to human activities in order to live so close to us for so long. We as a species have not been very good about returning the favor.

"As a society we don't have a lot of tolerance for predators," Fox says, "and pretty much since we set foot on this continent, as with Native Americans, we've considered native predators to be something to extricate, as we demonstrated in our federal government's predator eradication campaigns [in the nineteenth and early twentieth centuries]. "But coyotes are here to stay, and we should appreciate them, not fear them, because they have a valuable ecological role to play. The best thing we can do is leave them alone so they can self-regulate their population."

Humans

Skyland Lodge is one of the crown jewels of Shenandoah National Park in Virginia. Set near the high point of Skyline Drive at more than 3,600 feet, the luxury hotel delivers sweeping views of the Shenandoah Valley to the west, complete with the rolling hills, heavy fog, and dense greenery that this part of the country is known for.

The lodge property itself—which today includes everything from rustic cabins to high-end hotel rooms, complete with fireplaces and WiFi—predates the creation of the national park, when local entrepreneur George Freeman Pollock Jr. established a summer retreat on the spot in 1888. The idea proved popular with visitors from the nearby cities of Richmond, Virginia, and Washington, DC, and Pollock prospered. When the National Park Service established Shenandoah National Park in 1935, Skyland and several other nearby resorts were incorporated into the design and taken over by the government for operation.

That's the history of the facility, but the real draw of Skyland is its location, which Pollock himself is said to have described as "beauty beyond description." And he was right; it is a stunning spot overlooking the valley and nestled in a forest that's heavy with chestnut and red oak trees, along with the maples, ashes, and birches that are common in the area. Beyond the 105-mile Skyline Drive itself, which traces the Blue Ridge Mountains of Virginia from Front Royal in the north to Rockfish Gap in the south, where the road changes its name to the Blue Ridge Parkway, the George Washington National Forest, Shenandoah River, and many other natural attractions are nearby.

So is the famed Appalachian Trail, the 2,200-mile scenic hiking trail that stretches from Maine to Georgia. It meanders along the top of the Blue Ridge roughly parallel to Skyline Drive, taking hikers right up to and alongside the Skyland lodge.

As described by the *Virginia Trail Guide:* "The terrain along the Appalachian Trail is varied and diverse. Some sections are smooth dirt, others are jagged and rocky. The vegetation along the trail is beautiful— alternating between lush expanses of fern, thick stands of mountain laurel and majestic groves of trees. Occasionally, the trail passes beneath a scenic overlook on Skyline Drive. Uphill from the trail, you can see families taking in park scenery from the comfort of their cars."

It's a fairly easy hike through this part of Virginia, with minimal tough climbs and only a few stretches that are far away from civilization. As such, it is popular with both day hikers and through hikers alike, and is among the most-photographed stretches along the entire trail.

But the area also has a dark past.

In late May 1996, at a secluded campsite off the AT and within half a mile of Skyland, the bodies of two young women, twenty-four-year-old Julie Williams and twenty-six-year-old Lollie Winans, were found bound, gagged, and stripped naked. Both hikers had their throats cut.

Their golden retriever was later found wandering the park alone and turned over to park rangers.

The crime shocked the local community, in part because of the brutality of the crime in such a peaceful place, and in part because the women were a couple and the incident soon became considered a hate crime. But leads were slow to come, and the investigation dragged on through the summer with no solid suspects or theories as to the motive behind the killing.

It wasn't until a man named Darrell David Rice tried to run down and abduct a female bicyclist on Skyline Drive a year later that police had a credible lead in the case. In Rice's trunk were rope, duct tape, and other supplies that could be used to bind someone.

But the case didn't add up. Rice's DNA did not match hairs found at the scene of the murders, and a judge later dropped the charges against him. He did end up serving time for a string of other troubling offenses, and was indicted in the case again six years later, but the questions lingered.

As of 2016, a full twenty years after the incident, the local FBI office in Richmond still considered it an active case.

"This is a pending case, and I bristle at the term cold case," Special Agent Adam Lee told the NBC affiliate in Washington, DC, that year. "We will stop at nothing to find justice in the case and until we have exhausted every means, we continue to this day to exploit the existing evidence and to try to obtain new evidence. Julie and Lollie are not forgotten in the Richmond Division of the FBI, and we are going to aggressively pursue every lead in this case."

Since 1974, a total of eleven hikers, including Williams and Winans, have been murdered along the Appalachian Trail, a fact that casts a shadow over the entire AT community. Of those, only a handful were ever solved.

But does that mean that hiking is dangerous? That the AT is a particularly murder-happy place? Far from it, in fact. Although the murders that have occurred along the trail are troubling and often in the back of hikers' minds while they're out in the woods, they pale in comparison to total number of murders that occurred in the United States during that time. According to FBI statistics, about 14,200 people were murdered in this country in 2014, a figure that has been trending downward for decades and continues to do so. Overall, there are 4.5 murders in the United States for every 100,000 people.

That makes the sub-dozen number that have occurred on or near the AT seem like little more than a drop in the bucket.

And it is. Bill Bryson, the travel writer and author of *A Walk in the Woods,* about his attempted through-hike in the 1990s, has said of violence on the trail that, if you were to drawn a 2,000-mile line across the country in any direction, you are very likely to come across at least a dozen different murder victims. The AT isn't unique in that.

* * *

There are plenty of reasons that murder in the outdoors is especially terrifying. For one, there is almost literally nothing standing between you and a would-be assailant. For many of us, modern society is defined by a sense of security. When we're at home we can lock the doors and windows and feel relatively secure that no one is going to get in and harm us. It's even the same thing in our cars. In the worst-case scenario, we can always lock the doors and drive away from any potential hazards.

Not so in the backcountry.

Sure, a tent might seem like some sort of shelter—and it will generally effectively protect you from the elements—but a thin layer of canvas is far from the same thing as a heavy metal door and a deadbolt. Even a "lock" on a zipper pull is effectively worthless, when a few cuts from a knife can tear the tent walls to shreds in seconds. It simply isn't going to protect you from an attacker who wants to get in and harm you.

So, you're out there. You're exposed. If the worst happens, you find yourself being stalked or hunted by another person who is intent on doing you harm, there is nowhere immediately obvious for you to hide or seek protection. You can run but you cannot hide.

At least, that's the fear.

The reality of the situation is, as mentioned above, far less intense. The fact is, human-on-human attacks or, even, murders, are exceedingly rare in the outdoors, and that's even when compared with other exceedingly rare types of risk in the backcountry, such as bear or wolf attacks. If I've learned anything over the course of my research for this book, it is that most of what we consider risk factors in the outdoors and infinitesimally small. Yes, sometimes hikers and hunters get attacked by mountain lions. But we're talking about a few dozen cases over the course of decades, decades in which millions of people traveled through the same areas, participated in the same activities, and came out unscathed. The risk of animal attack in the woods is very, very small.

Murder in the backcountry is, if this is even possible, an even smaller percentage of a percentage of that risk. We're talking statistically insignificant here. Bryson was right in his comment about the risk of murder of the Appalachian Trail—the "real world" is far riskier in terms of human-on-human violence than any backcountry area. For the most part, we all go into the woods for the same reasons: to escape, to relax, and to spend some time away from the hustle and bustle of our daily lives. (Or, for Henry David Thoreau, to "live deliberately.") It's fun. It's a change of pace.

And it takes a unique set of circumstances for someone to enter that kind of environment with violence on their mind, and it should come as no surprise that attacks like this are extremely rare, even in the annals of stranger-on-stranger violence, which is what most outdoor attacks are. (As I was once told, driving to and from the trailhead is significantly more dangerous than anything you will encounter out in the wild.)

Still, this is a book about risk, and violence in the outdoors is, at least at some level, a risk. So, let's consider the options.

Protection: No discussion of violence and protection in the backcountry is complete without some mention of firearms. There are as many sides to this debate as there are outdoor enthusiasts, so I won't get too deep into the pros and cons here, but the general fact is, while sidearms and other weapons do have their place in the backcountry—e.g., hunting—personal protection rarely enters the picture, even among those who do carry when they go into the woods. Why? Because that is simply not their best use. In the case of an animal attack, in heavy tree cover, how many marksmen are there in the world who are good enough with their weapon to draw, aim, and fire in the less than two seconds that most of us have against a charging animal? Not many.

And that's not to mention the fact that most small arms are simply not strong enough to slow down let alone stop a large animal such as a bear. The same holds true for a human attack. While it would be nice to have something at hand for protection, chances are good that, in the moment, you wouldn't be able to get it when you really need it. Of course, this is all personal preference, but for me, when the choice is between a firearm that won't offer much utility in terms of personal protection (not to mention the fact that there is really no need for personal protection out there anyway) and saving a few extra pounds in my pack, I'll opt for the weight savings every time. Besides, bear spray works on people too.

Security: Given that a tent or other backcountry shelter is effectively worthless in terms of real, solid security against a human attacker, it is best, in my opinion, to give up on the idea of outdoor "security" altogether. The fact is, that is part of what we leave behind when we travel in the outdoors and it is, frankly, kind of the point. You're putting yourself out there a little bit, relying on your wits and intelligence for protection with the understanding that you, as a smart human being, can identify true risks wherever you encounter them and know well enough how to get out of those situations without retreating behind a heavy locked door.

Common Sense: And that brings us to the most important point of all. While it may seem exposed and dangerous to hike through the woods with little more than a pocket knife for "protection"—although you and I both know that it's really for opening food packets and sharpening tent stakes—a little common sense goes a long way. We've all encountered groups at campsites that, upon arrival, we simply don't like the look of or don't trust. So, we move on, find another place to bed down for the night. Or, when we get a strange vibe from someone deep in the backcountry, perhaps someone who is acting oddly aggressive toward us, we talk them down and get ourselves out of it.

The simple fact is that every backcountry traveler is in charge of their own safety in the woods, and we're all born with all the tools we need to stay safe out there. When the crutches of modern society like locks and doors are removed, we may feel vulnerable but we're really just being forced to fall back on our instincts, the same instincts that helped our ancestors, millennia ago, to survive in a world without our creature comforts or the sense of safety that we enjoy. It works, as long as we let it.

* * *

"I don't really consider other people in the outdoors a risk," explains Randi Minetor, the author of more than forty hiking and camping guidebooks who spends weeks on the trail ever year. "If you look at criminal activity and crime reports and things like that, there just isn't much there. I will tell you I researched writing [a book about] death on the Appalachian Trails—there have been eight murders on the Trails in seventy-five years of its existence—and my publisher felt that writing the book that was really just about murder was not in the spirit of the Death series [Minetor is the author of two titles in the Lyons Press series on deaths in US National Parks], so we're not doing it. I did have a chance to look at them all and it's not something that happens frequently enough to stop you from hiking, honestly. Thousands and thousands of people hike the AT every year and are not lost, you know, are not murdered."

It's true, of course, and the number above back up Minetor's assertions. Beyond the handful of murders that have occurred on the Appalachian Trail—in addition to those, an average of about four people per year die on the trail or near it from natural causes as the result of incidents that happen on the trail (falls, hypothermia, heart attacks, etc.)—as of 2017 a grand total of zero people have been murdered on the 2,654-mile Pacific Crest Trail that stretches along the US Sierra Nevada and Cascade Ranges from Mexico to Canada, and zero on the 3,100-mile Continental Divide Trail that traces the Continental Divide.

The backcountry can be desolate, dark, and feel exposed, but you're still far more likely to experience violence in an urban area than out in the wild.

Based on her own research, Minetor can also assert with authority that there have been no murders in Zion National Park to date and just two in the 120 years that Glacier National Park has been in existence.

Violence in the outdoors simply is not something that happens often enough to be something that people need to worry about.

The truth, in my opinion as well as Minetor's, it is actually rewarding to meet new people on the trail, in campsites, and elsewhere in the woods. If you're on a long-distance hike you'll often run into people who know things that you don't, who have recently passed through the areas where you are going and can report on weather conditions, trail conditions, and more. Or they might simply be more familiar with the trail than you are and able to point you in the right direction or flag landmarks or detours for you on the map.

Worst case, these new friends are good for swapping stories or sitting around the campfire.

"We have never had unpleasant encounter on the trail," Minetor says. "That's the thing. And if you're camping, and you're spending the night in the middle of the wilderness, it's just not generally where crim-inals go to look for victims. The pickings are really slim. A criminal could sit there for weeks waiting for somebody to show up. Generally, that's just not how it works."

In short: the upside of meeting new people in the wilderness well overshadows the potential risk of harm from strangers in the woods.

CHAPTER 3
Small Animals/Insects

Snakes

It's long been said, be careful what you love. Someday it will kill you.

That sentiment came true for Tony Felder Jr., an avid "rattlesnake hunter" from Oklahoma when, in September 2016, one of the snakes he'd spent so much time tracking down and capturing, turned the tables and killed him with its venomous bite. It happened near the town of Okeene, where rattlesnake hunting is considered a sport, more popular than high school football.

"I guess we all just think that won't ever happen, I guess. I don't know how to explain it. It's a passion that once you've got it, it don't go away," friend and fellow rattlesnake hunter, Dave Wilson, told the local NBC affiliate after the accident.

For more than seventy-five years, the town of Okeene has hosted the Okeene Rattlesnake Roundup, one of the oldest snake hunts in the world, the first weekend in May. A three-day event that's part rodeo, part competition, and part state fair, the Roundup features everything from live rattlesnake shows to food vendors and carnival rides. Registered hunters are taken to the "snake hunting grounds" as a group, and everything they catch is butchered for them back at the fair that weekend.

Snakes are meat in this part of Oklahoma, and the hunt started as an annual effort by local farmers and ranchers to protect their livestock by shooting as many rattlesnakes as possible. Competition took over, and the hunt became a full-blown sport by the middle of the twentieth century.

Felder and his family have been active participants in the hunt going back three generations, when his grandfather participated in the first one, bagging snakes with a tire iron. His son, Tony Felder Sr., went on to serve as the Roundup's "pit boss" for twenty years before handing the reins to his son following a serious bite. In addition to his duties in the pit, in recent years, the junior Felder had also helped round up the wild snakes that are used to stock the hunting grounds for the Roundup.

But rattlesnake hunting isn't without its risks. In a 2006 story on his family's history with the snake hunt, Felder said although he had been to the hospital three times over the years after suffering bites, he had no intention of giving up the sport as his father had done.

"I like taking risks," he said at the time. "I jumped out of a perfectly good airplane once, so why wouldn't I play with rattlesnakes?"

That all came to a sudden end when the younger Felder suffered a bite near his home in Okeene.

And it wasn't even a rattlesnake that he was hunting.

Rather, he was out counting cattle when he came across the snake, a fairly large specimen by northwest Oklahoma standards, crawling across the road. Given that a true rattlesnake hunter never sleeps, he picked up the snake and put it into a bucket to take home and show his family, and maybe take a few photos.

But once they got there, the snake had other ideas. When Felder reached into the bucket to pull it out—something he had done safely thousands of times over the years—the snake reared back and bit him squarely on the hand. The bite landed directly on a blood vessel, speeding the deadly venom throughout his body.

He was airlifted to a hospital in Oklahoma City where he later died.

Following the accident, Felder Sr. was reflective on the tragedy and on rattlesnake hunting in general. In Oklahoma, he said, the snakes are simply a part of life that everyone just has to understand and live with. Nothing that his son did that day was any riskier than anything else he had done in the past.

"We're all invincible, you know, when we're doing stuff," he said. "It don't matter what it is."

Felder's death made headlines because he was such a prominent member of Oklahoma's rattlesnake hunting community, but he was not the only victim of a rattlesnake bite in 2016. Wayne Grooms, a seventy-one-year-old South Carolina resident, died after he suffered a bite on the lower leg while hiking in the Santee National Wildlife Refuge, a 15,000-acres wetlands area in the eastern part of the state. He collapsed and died within fifteen minutes of the attack, which was later credited to either a timber rattlesnake or an Eastern diamondback rattlesnake, both of which are found in the refuge.

* * *

Snakebites are not a rare occurrence in the United States, with thousands of people suffering minor bites every year from a wide variety of snake species.

If you spend any time in the outdoors—working in the yard, hiking, mountain biking, boating, or otherwise venturing out into snake territory, which is effectively everywhere, you're going to eventually encounter a snake. Most of the time these experiences are completely benign and the snake simply slithers away when confronted. Sometimes, though, the snake will become agitated and strike, biting whoever is closest in an effort to defend itself.

What is far rarer, however, is dying from a venomous snakebite. In fact, according to the University of Florida's Department of Wildlife Ecology and Conservation, your chances of dying from a venomous snakebite in the United States is "nearly zero" due to our easy access to high-quality medical care. In this country, when you are bitten by a snake, you go to the hospital, receive treatment, and then head home to recover. That is not always the case in other parts of the world, where death by snake is far more common.

According to the UF research, some 7,000 to 8,000 people are bitten by venomous snakes in the United States each year, leading to only five or six fatalities. That puts the fatality rate at one in roughly 50 million, meaning you are nine times more likely to die from being struck by lightning than to die from a venomous snakebite. In comparison, car and motorcycle accidents kill about 37,000 Americans every year, while lung cancer claims another 162,000.

The United States has about twenty species of venomous snakes, including sixteen species of rattlesnakes, two species of coral snakes, one species of cottonmouth (or water moccasin), and one species of copperhead. Those types are generally the big four of venomous snakes in the United States, and they are all largely regional, except for rattlesnakes, which can be found across the country. Copperheads are typically found in the Eastern states and their range spreads as far as Texas, while both the coral snake and the water moccasin are both typically found in the Southern United States.

Of the 2,200 snake species worldwide, barely 20 percent of them are venomous and even fewer carry strong enough venom to kill an adult human.

Only about 20 percent of the snake species in the world are deadly, and even then cases are rare.

Snake venom is toxic when injected under the skin, by the snake, but is generally considered nontoxic when ingested in any other way. That said, venom is—like many other "dangerous" substances in this book—only harmful in very specific circumstances. For example, the CDC says that only people who are severely allergic to snake venom are at any real risk of dying from a snakebite. Even then, as long as they receive prompt medical care most people come out of the experience just fine.

It's no secret that many people have an illogical fear of snakes. This is something that goes back centuries, probably beginning as a survival instinct back when we didn't yet know which types of snakes were dangerous. They are unique-looking animals, sliding silently into and out of our lives, and when you don't know what kind of snake you're looking at, or don't yet realize that so few of them are actually harmful, they all look roughly the same. Not to mention the fact that the bite of even a nonvenomous snake hurts, it became good general policy to avoid snakes at all costs.

Snakes are also silent and stealthy when in their habitat. They sneak up on their prey—usually small mammals—and use the element of surprise to their advantage to survive. No surprise, then, that this behavior is not popular with humans. The idea of a snake, creeping silently by, is enough to send some people into a full-blown panic attack.

But the truth is, snakes rarely go on the offensive. They are defensive animals, preferring that element of surprise to attacking head on. Venomous snakes use their venom for one reason: to stun and capture their food. It is not an offensive "weapon."

Snakes, venomous and nonvenomous, will generally only attack a human when they feel threatened, smell food, or are simply afraid. People who own snakes as pets often report suffering bites after handling mice or other animals that their snake may construe as food, but most times it occurs when the snake is upset and feels cornered. In those cases, sometimes a snake will strike out not as a means to attack but rather as a warning sign to the human to stay back and give the snake some space.

Yes, snakes have feelings too.

This applies to venomous snakes in the wild as well. Get too close to a snake and it will feel threatened, feel afraid, and sometimes lash out to protect itself. The trouble in the backcountry is that, often, we can get too close to a venomous snake without even knowing it. Just heading down a trail, minding our own business, and an unseen snake hiding in the brush at the edge of the trail may sense a threat and lash out. In those cases, there's little to be done to avoid the confrontation, but it is important to understand what to do to treat the wound.

According to Mick Thow, Australia's "reptile man," snakes go through eight stages of agitation when getting upset. First, when you get too close they'll start flicking their tail before flattening themselves out and puffing out their lungs, showing you—their foe—how big and scary they can be. If that doesn't get you to move away, they'll lift the first part of their body off the ground and present a few mock strikes. The final warning is when they put their head back down and stare at you with both eyes. Due to the way most snakes' heads are shaped, they can see well to both sides but not very well straight ahead. By lowering their head, they are able to improve their depth of field and determine just how far away you are and where they need to strike. At this point, an attack is coming almost immediately.

Still, even an agitated snake doesn't always end in a venomous snakebite.

"If you can get to stage six or seven and stop hassling the animal and leave it be, it will go back to stage one again," Thow told Australia's ABC Tasmania TV in 2010.

Spiders

It's no accident that spiders get their own "phobia"—arachnophobia—unlike most other creatures out there.

Why? Because spiders tick off a lot of creepy, crawly boxes for many people. They're tiny and often hidden. They have a lot of legs. They sneak into deep, dark places and, when we're least expecting it, they strike.

And the fact that many different species of spiders carry dangerous venom isn't helping their case.

It's believed that arachnophobia—which afflicts millions worldwide, whether they want to admit it or not—developed as an evolutionary survival technique, hard wiring people to avoid the kinds of areas where spiders typically hang out or where their webs are visible. These days, the condition often results in panic attacks—sweating, heavy breathing, uncontrollable shaking—that don't dissipate until the sufferer is away from the spider-like area. A 2008 study showed that both adults and children can more quickly identify "dangerous" animals such as spiders and snakes when shown a series of photos than they can "safer" creatures such as frogs and caterpillars.

It isn't just us, either. Studies have also shown that crickets can be born with a fear of spiders based solely on their mother's own negative experiences with the predators.

So, the fear is real.

But the reality is far from that bad. In truth, death by verifiable spider bite is exceedingly rare. Only a handful of people die each year worldwide from such bites, and in most cases the victims have other contributing risk factors, such as a compromised immune system or other condition that exacerbate the bite. The development of antivenoms more than fifty years ago has effectively eliminated the risk of death by spider bite in the Western world, saving countless people.

Still, it happens.

In 2011, Jeff Seale, a forty-year-old man in Erie, Colorado, died after he suffered what doctors found to be nineteen different bites from a black widow spider. A horseman, it is believed he encountered the spider at the stables and possibly brought it back home with him on his clothing or in his gear.

"He was in really good health up until that point," his sister told a reporter after his death. "He worked at a horse stable in the evenings, and he very well could have brought one of the spiders home in his things, or picked up some stuff from one of the horse sheds and brought one of the things home."

Despite their reputation, black widow bites are poisonous but rarely fatal. Even Seale's case wasn't open and shut. He died a full two weeks after suffering the bites, and doctors still weren't sure what role the attack played in his untimely death.

Still, nineteen bites will do some damage.

Overseas, however, the problem is generally more severe.

For example, the jungles of Brazil are home to the deadliest species of spider in the world, the Brazilian wandering spider. Related to the North American wolf spider, the wandering variety is bigger, more toxic, and packs what is considered to be the most neurologically active venom of all spiders. Its bite can kill a grown man in less than fifteen minutes and is known to bite when it feels threatened or cornered as a means of protection. Worst of all, the species likes to crawl into dark, cozy spaces to rest, including inside homes and other places where humans might encounter them.

A woman in the UK even found a cocooned Brazilian wandering spider in a bunch of bananas that she bought at her local grocery store. (Why that story, and the fact that she took the bananas back to the store for a refund, made national news is a question for another day.)

Australia saw its first spider-related fatality in more than sixty years in 2016, when a twenty-two-year-old man was bitten by a redback spider and later died after receiving treatment at a hospital. Similar in appearance to the black widow, redbacks are common spiders in Australia and bites are not uncommon. The last time someone died from such a spider, however, was in 1955, before the introduction of antivenom. Today, about 250 people are treated for redback bites with antivenom every year.

(For the record, the redback isn't even the most feared spider down under. That distinction goes to the Sydney funnel-web spider. Native to Australia, these terrors range from one to three inches long and can be very aggressive when provoked, often attacking offensively from their tube-shaped burrows. According to government records, they were responsible for thirteen confirmed deaths in Australia between 1927 and 1980.)

Still, the fact is, the world is full of dangerous spiders. But the spider bites themselves aren't often the greatest risk.

And, in parts of the world where medical care is difficult to access or there is little available antivenom, this represents a real risk. That's because, even short of death, a poisonous spider bite can do real damage to you when you're alone in the woods.

Think about walking through some low brush and getting bit on the ankle or lower leg by a venomous spider. Chances are you aren't going to die, but you will still suffer. Spider bites hurt, and they swell up, and they can get infected. Maybe that bite on your ankle opens up and gets infected. Now you have a real problem that, without access to medical care, can turn into a life-threatening condition if not treated promptly.

What if you can't walk out under your own power. Or if you can't tie your boots securely over your swollen ankle. Will you be able to make it down off a rocky trail?

Or what if you're allergic to a specific species of spider and it leaves you tired and disoriented? How will you be able to help yourself in that situation?

As with many insect and smaller animal injuries, this is where the risk of a spider bite gets real. Even if you don't die from the venom itself, you are opening yourself up to a long list of potential add-on issues as a result of the bite.

And that's what you need to be prepared for.

* * *

The black widow tends to get a bad rap.

Yes, they can be scary looking, with strong, jet black legs and a deep red, hourglass-shaped marking on the body, but widow spiders such as the black widow are in fact considered nonaggressive. They usually stick close to their webs and rarely venture out for any significant amount of time, though they are fast runners when they do. Also, it's the females of the species that we identify as black widows. The males are browner and smaller, and are considered too small to be dangerous at all.

The trouble with widow spiders, and black widows in particular, is that they can be found all over the world and they tend to live near humans. They'll set up shop in garages, cabins, along trails and other areas where they can find their preferred prey—ants, caterpillars, grasshoppers, flies, beetles, etc.—but those also tend to be areas where humans are more likely to run into them. That means we tend to encounter widow spiders a lot more than we do other species, particularly in North America and Australia.

Overall, black widow spiders account for thousands of spider bite incidents worldwide every year, more than any other spider variety, as humans stumble into their webs while walking in the woods, find them in piles of firewood, and just generally put themselves in position for a bite in a variety of spider-friendly environments. For this reason, these are generally the type of spider encounters that most people have or hear about.

And they're no fun.

The bite of a black widow spider hurts. A lot. The spider's venom can cause painful muscle spasms near the injection site, "tetanus-like" contractions, nausea, vomiting, and severe pain throughout the body. Sometimes victims end up in the hospital to deal with the pain. Taken together, the symptoms are known as Latrodectus, or an illness that's caused by the bite of certain types of spiders, including the black widow.

It's no wonder that humans have, for generations, considered the black widow a "dangerous" and sometimes deadly spider.

But, as is often the case with spiders, reality doesn't always keep up with the popular perceptions.

Although Latrodectus makes for a very unpleasant experience for the victim, it is rarely fatal in humans. There hasn't been a black widow–related fatality in the United States in decades, and less than 1 percent of all bites involve medical complications, according to data from the US Poison Control Centers. While it is true that as many as 10 percent of black widow cases were fatal as recently as a century ago, modern medicine has largely eliminated the risk of dying as a result of a widow spider bite.

And it's not just the black widow.

Data regarding fatality rates for spider bites is maddeningly difficult to come by, even in this age of digital databases and searchable online records. Why? Because so few people die from verifiable spider bites that it barely qualifies as statistically significant.

While there are several different spider species that can cause bites that are considered "medically important"—meaning they can hurt you—only two of these types are found worldwide, Latrodectur and Loxosceles, while the only other two types, Phoneutria and Atrax, are regionally distributed. Even then, the bites of these medically significant spiders can vary widely in their impact, ranging from mild irritation to more severe symptoms. One thing they all have in common, though, is that they rarely, if ever, kill humans.

Consider the evidence.

According to a National Institutes of Health study from 2011, there have been a grand total of three verifiable human deaths caused by widow spiders, two in Africa and one in Greece. Ever. Even the spiders that are considered the "world's deadliest" don't fare much better. The Australian funnel-web spider has not been responsible for a verifiable human death since 1981, according to the Medical Journal of Australia, and the South American wandering spider only has ten recorded kills in Brazilian recorded history.

Dangerous, yes, but deadly, no.

In fact, research has recently shown that being bitten by a spider, a black widow or otherwise, is actually far less likely than many people think. Chris Buddle, an arachnologist at McGill University in Montreal, Canada, says what we think of as "spider bites" are not actually "bites" in the traditional sense. More often than not, the irritation we feel when encountering a spider is more likely to in fact be a skin reaction to chemicals on the spider, an infection or a sting from a related arthropod such as a flea.

"There are a lot of misconceptions about spiders," Buddle wrote on his blog in 2012. "The most common is the idea that spiders frequently bite people—they do not. Most so-called spider bites are caused by something else. Spiders generally have no interest in biting us, and would rather feed upon invertebrates. I have been working with spiders for over 15 years, and I have handled many, many kinds of live spiders and I have never been attacked by a spider."

He explains that common misperceptions about spiders have made this problem worse, conditioning both victims and medical professionals to believe, when faced with what appears to be a bite injury from a small, unseen source, that a spider must have been the culprit. Misdiagnosis is a common problem, he says, and the excuse of "it must have been a spider" isn't enough information to provide an accurate medical assessment without first considering the other possible explanations for symptoms, let alone have the spider itself available for verification.

Plus, even when bites do happen—usually when a spider is scared or startled by a human—they don't do much damage because their prey is primarily small invertebrates, not large humans, and their venom is designed to stun and subdue little more than insects. This venom might hurt us, and it can be more serious for very young and very old victims, but it is rare that it does any lasting damage, simply because most spiders do not have enough venom in their systems to hurt a 100-plus pound human.

"They are far more afraid of us than we are of them," according to Buddle. "They're not offensive."

* * *

"The risk from spiders really depends on where in the world you are," explains Dr. Norman Platnick, Curator Emeritus of the Division of Invertebrate Zoology at the American Museum of Natural History in New York City. "Because in the United States the answer becomes very simple: For spiders there is absolutely nothing to worry about. If you're in the woods, half the spiders on the planet are so small that they couldn't break your skin even if they tried to bite you. Your likelihood of being bitten by any spider anywhere is extremely small. You don't look like prey. The reaction of a spider, anything as loud and obnoxious as a human being is to be as far away as quickly as possible."

In fact, he says, the only time you're likely to get bitten by a spider in the United States is if it gets into your clothing, shoes, or bedding and you accidentally brush up against it and it can't escape. In those cases, a spider will bite as a last resort. Even then, though, 99.99 percent of the time the animal's venom will have no effect whatsoever because spider venom has evolved of the millennia to function on insects, which are the spider's prey, and not large mammals like humans. In those cases where the spider does have an effect on us with its venom—as is the case with black widows—it's something that Dr. Platnick calls "accidental chemistry," not part of evolutionary biology. "We were never part of their prey in any way, shape, form or manner."

"In many cases your largest danger is going to a physician who misdiagnoses the symptoms as appendicitis and gives you an emergency appendectomy you don't need," he says. "That's really about it. For a healthy adult, spider venom is certainly not deadly. Brown recluse venom has a nastier effect because it's tissue destroying, but, again, the only time you're going to find brown recluses in the wild is if you're specifically hunting for them because they're going to be under rocks, under logs. Again, you are not going to be bitten unless you go out of your way to. In fact, with a brown recluse it's very hard because they just are not aggressive spiders at all."

None of this is to say that spiders are universally harmless worldwide. In Australia, for instance, funnel-web spiders do tend to be more aggressive and have been known to bite adults and children, and their venom can be very serious. They are so common in that country that antivenom is widely available, but they are no fun to tangle with.

The same goes for the Phoneutria, the Brazilian wandering spider, which like the funnel-web goes out hunting in search of prey and mates. They are also quite venomous and, in Dr. Platnick's view, they "sort of know it," so they will be aggressive if encountered. Antivenom for these spiders is also available in the areas where they are found, but it's important to get to a hospital to get the antivenom as soon as possible.

In the United States, the only two spiders that have venom that affects humans are the black widow and the brown recluse, neither of which you're likely to come across deep in the woods. In fact, the only time you would have any likelihood of being bitten by a black widow is if there's a female in its web guarding an egg sac and you start bothering the female. She might bite you to protect her eggs, but of course you'd have to purposely do that.

We aren't just lucky, Dr. Platnick says, and the fact that North America is almost devoid of dangerous spiders is partly a reflection of the natural diversity patterns of species all over the planet.

"The largest diversity of things is in the tropics and the southern semi-tropics," he says, "and North America, Europe and Asia are basically depauperate of species compared to other parts of the world. By chance alone there's going to be fewer here. On the other hand, it doesn't explain why places like Australia have such an extremely high proportion of seriously venomous organisms compared to other places."

A spider bite is effectively just like a bee sting. You could have an allergic reaction to it, which might become serious just like bee stings do, but most of the time it will just ache and eventually go away. The real

A spider's venom can be powerful and its bite extremely painful, but they are only a real threat to those who are allergic to them.

risk, Platnick says, is in the case that you get bitten by a spider that is large enough to actually break the skin, and that can sometimes lead to a bacterial infection. Most of the problems that occur after actual spider bites are bacterial infections, not venom-related.

None of this will make any difference to arachnophobes, of course. The fear of spiders is very deep seated in humans, and the reasons behind this are not hard to identify.

"I think partly they can be quite hairy and they can move very quickly over very short distances," Dr. Platnick says. "They're sprinters. They're not long distance runners but they can run quickly, they can dart, so you can catch them out of the side of your eyes and be startled by them. They're running away from you, of course, because you're a source of vibrations they don't want to be anywhere near. But it's a cultural thing. They're taught by their parents to fear spiders and it's just totally ludicrous, especially in the northern hemisphere. Being afraid of spiders is absurd because the proportion of all the spiders around the world that could possibly harm you is so infinitesimally small. I've been handling spiders for 40 years and I've never been bitten, much less had an issue arising from it."

Mosquitoes/Ticks

It hardly makes sense to even write this, but the mosquito—the same tiny, buzzing insect that we all know from summer barbeques and itchy bites—is in fact the deadliest animal known to man.

It's true.

According to the World Health Organization, mosquitoes are responsible for more than one million human deaths worldwide every year. Granted, these aren't dramatic, chase-you-down-and-devour-you kinds of deaths; most are from the spread of malaria, one of the deadliest diseases in the developing world. The disease is transmitted by a tiny parasite that is carried by a certain type of mosquito, females from the Anophelese genus. Since malaria is a blood-borne illness, the mosquito is the ideal carrier, stabbing into the veins of all sorts of animals, including people, in its own daily search for food.

Believe it or not, this is the deadliest single animal on the planet, and the damage it can do is staggering.

Thanks to the humble mosquito, this parasite can infect 300 million to 500 million people with malaria every year, as the host mosquitoes are found all over the world. Most of these mosquito-related deaths in the world today happen in Sub-Saharan Africa, where the mosquito-rich environment and lack of accessible medical care combine to create a unique set of risk factors that hits young children, the elderly, and visitors from parts of the world with no malaria (and therefore no immunity) particularly hard.

Yikes.

But not in the United States, fortunately.

In fact, thanks to the still-controversial use of the synthetic pesticide DDT in the 1950s, public health officials with the National Malaria Eradication Program were able to effectively eliminate the disease in this country by killing off the mosquitoes that cause the infection. The program grew out of military efforts during World War II that fought the disease in malaria hot spots such as Southeast Asia and the Pacific theater, where US troops were being infected by the tropical disease in droves. After the war, the same approach—namely, gassing the bugs into oblivion in potentially afflicted areas—was applied across much of the US Southeast, where mosquito populations and, therefore, the risk of infection was highest. Over the course of five years in the late 1940s and early 1950s, DDT was applied inside homes and outside in parts of thirteen states where cases of malaria had been reported or were considered possible, an effort that eventually involved spraying at more than 4.6 million US homes. Combined with the systematic removal of mosquito breeding sites, drainage improvements to prevent standing water and other prevention measures, the effort was considered a success and shut down by the Centers for Disease control in 1952.

It worked.

As of 2016, malaria is considered to be well controlled in the United States and is no longer considered to be a public health concern. The CDC has shifted its role to one of "surveillance," watching for occasional outbreaks here at home and assisting in malaria control efforts in other parts of the world. (Controlled, but not eliminated. According to the National Malaria Society, "malaria may be assumed to be no longer endemic in any given area when no primary indigenous case has occurred there for three years." The disease is considered "eliminated" when transmission is no longer occurring in a specific geographic area, and "eradicated" when transmission is eliminated worldwide.) Infections do still sometimes occur here, though locally transmitted outbreaks of mosquito-borne malaria are extremely rare. Sometimes people will pick up the infection overseas and bring it home, and the CDC still sees occasional instances of "airport malaria," which refers to cases where infected mosquitoes are transported into this country via aircraft, eventually biting and infecting airport workers and others nearby upon arrival.

None of these scenarios makes for much of an outbreak, however.

Today, most real-world mosquito concerns have nothing to do with malaria, at least in the United States. Truth is, mosquitoes are excellent hosts and distribution mechanisms for all sorts of diseases and blood-borne infections, ranging from meningitis to the Zika virus, which moved into the southern United States in 2016, to much fanfare. Although the symptoms of Zika itself in adult victims are relatively mild—typically the experience includes fever, joint pain, a rash, and little else—the disease can cause severe birth defects in unborn children, leading to travel advisories for pregnant women in areas where Zika is known to be spreading. Plus, mosquitoes are known carriers of the West Nile virus and Dengue Fever, which attack the central nervous system and joints, respectively, and can both be very serious under the right circumstances.

Like malaria, all are spread by mosquitoes who have themselves been infected or are carrying the true diseased agents.

Above all, however, it's the threat of developing encephalitis from a mosquito bite that should really worry people, according to the Illinois Department of Public Health. A sudden onset disease that involves severe inflammation in the brain, causing headaches, fever, confusion, and more, encephalitis can cause lasting damage to victims as it progresses through its later stages, causing convulsions, hallucinations, stroke, and other more serious symptoms. According to a study conducted by the National Institutes of Health, the disease led to 77,000 deaths worldwide in 2013, with an instance rate of about 7.4 cases per 100,000 people in the Western world.

To be fair, even that number is not large, and the chances of being infected with a serious disease by a mosquito—and dying as a result—is small. Modern medicine has anti-malarial drugs available to help when traveling through known malaria zones, and can generally address and heal most blood-borne diseases—when doctors are able to treat them.

As with everything mentioned so far in this book, it isn't always the initial encounter that kills you. It's the waiting around for medical care, letting the disease strengthen and grow, that does the real damage. In remote regions, or where medical care is hard to find or inaccessible, the risk is naturally going to be greater than in the middle of Times Square in New York City. The difference between a mild case and a more severe one is often about treating the illness properly and quickly.

That's why it's critical to both understand the diseases and infections that can harm you in the specific area you're visiting, as well as how to spot the signs of trouble and treat any problems quickly, before they get out of hand.

Protecting yourself from an insect that's as tiny and ubiquitous as the mosquito is far from easy. They reproduce quickly by the billions, they are small enough to sneak through all but the tiniest of barriers and, as mentioned, even one bite from an infected insect can spell death for the person involved.

Much of what we know today about mosquitoes, the diseases they carry, and how to fight back against them is the result of work that the US Army did during World War II. Fighting in the South Pacific for years on end, malaria control caught many of the Army's leaders off guard in the 1940s, forcing them to develop new tools and strategies for living and working in parts of the world where malaria was common. As a result, US soldiers were suffering and dying from malaria at an alarming rate that put their entire war effort in the South Pacific at risk.

According to the US Army Heritage and Education Center, 24,000 of the 75,000 American and Filipino soldiers in the area in 1942 suffered from malaria. Overall in the region, the Army treated more than 47,000 cases of the disease in 1942, for a total infection rate of about 250 cases per 1,000 troops.

(It wasn't just the theater of war where this was a problem, either. Decades earlier, of the 26,000 employees working on the construction of the Panama Canal in 1906, a full 21,000 of them were hospitalized for malaria at some point over the course of their work in the area.)

The upside of this severe problem is that it focused the entire might and force of the US government and the country's scientific community on finding a solution to the malaria problem, dedicating resources to a single disease at a scale that had never before been attempted.

Scientists at the time already knew that malaria infection was related to the transmission of blood-borne parasites. (A French army surgeon named Charles Louis Alphonse Laveran had first identified that fact, resulting in his winning the Nobel Prize in Physiology in 1907.) They also knew that mosquitoes were the primary transmitter of these parasites, as discovered by Ronald Ross, a British officer working in

India, resulting in his winning the Nobel Prize in 1902. What took extra time, then, was devising strategies to best contain and control the risk of malarial infection in the parts of the world where we were now operating, including the Panama Canal Zone, Cuba, and elsewhere.

As it turned out, the US Army was well positioned to address this problem, as it had addressed so many problems in the past: with organization, strategy, and leadership.

According to a 2000 report of the official eradication program published by the National Institutes of Health:

"The Army developed a very organized approach to the malaria problem and implemented it in an effective manner. The creation of new technical solutions was also strongly emphasized and out of this effort came the development of effective antimalaria drugs to replace quinine, of new insecticides and of more effective systems for delivering these insecticides. Some of the major new tools which came out of this research were DDT and drugs such as Atabrine and chloroquine. The availability of Atabrine and DDT revolutionized malaria control throughout the world. The knowledge and experience gained through the use of these new tools by the U.S. Army and other agencies in World War II provided the basis for a new optimism regarding malaria control which then led to the development of the global malaria eradication strategy in the post-war years."

And it's true. The lessons learned about malaria transmission and control in these years, particularly the usefulness of the synthetic pesticide DDT (which would later be banned after it was discovered to cause cancer and other environmental harm), would directly apply to the domestic eradication efforts in the 1950s and beyond. Today, malaria management comes down to two major lines of focus: case management and infection prevention.

Not to go too far down the science and medicine rabbit hole here, case management, as it is described by the CDC, simply refers to the medical treatment of patients who have already contracted malaria and focuses primarily on new drugs and drug availability in remote corners of the world. Prevention in the outdoors is what we are primarily interested in, and there the CDC has specific recommendations as well.

When traveling through malarial country, or anywhere that mosquitoes are heavy, such as the tropics, keep the following close at hand:

Bed Netting: The CDC recommends sleeping under insecticide-treated bed nettings and says that their use has been shown to reduce infection rates by as much as 20 percent when used in malarial areas. These are as simple as they sound, little more than a net that fits around a bed and has been impregnated with insecticides to keep mosquitoes away. Many mosquitoes are most active after dark, so this overnight protection is critical.

Repellent: Although DTT is banned for good reason, the EPA does maintain a list of approved insect repellents that have proven to be safe and effective against mosquitoes and other small insects. This list includes, in no particular order, DEET, Picaridin, IR3535, 2-undercanone, and even lemon oil, which is natural and even smells nice.

Sleeves: As simple as it seems, few protection measures are as effective against mosquitoes as long sleeves and long pants. These insects are creatures of opportunity. When they land on skin and find it worth a meal, they will bite. By simply exposing less skin to the world, and the mosquitoes, you can effectively lower you chances of being stung dramatically. And it's not just about arms and legs either. Hats, especially when worn with a head netting, tall boots, and neck coverings are important safety measures as well and can mean the difference between safety and infection when traveling through mosquito country, whether malaria, Zika, or another disease is active in the area or not.

The same rules apply to ticks, explains Kathy Maguire, Curator of Amphibians and Bugs at Reptile Gardens, a zoo located near Rapid City, South Dakota.

"If you ever watch any of those *Naked and Afraid* shows or any of those type of things, it's always the bugs that get them," she says. "And it's usually the mosquitoes or the little no-see-ums, the little things that end up getting the people and causing problems. It's not the spiders or bigger insects too much."

In fact, she says both mosquitoes and ticks do more damage worldwide than most other insects on the planet combined, in large part because of the role they play in transmitting diseases, including Lyme disease from ticks and malaria from mosquitoes.

For such small creatures, ticks tend to get an outsized share of attention from backcountry travelers. That's because, even though they typically measure no more 5 mm long—barely larger than a pencil eraser—ticks are parasites that can cause big problems for those that encounter them, both human and animal included.

Lyme disease is usually the number-one concern when dealing with ticks. A bacterial infection that is transmitted to humans and livestock through the bite of infected "blacklegged" ticks, more commonly called deer ticks, Lyme disease brings fever, headache, fatigue, and a characteristic bulls-eye skin rash called erythema migrans. Left untreated, it can cause permanent damage to the nervous system and the heart, but diagnosing the disease is maddeningly difficult, and it can plague victims with symptoms for years.

All this from a bug you'll never see coming.

But Lyme disease isn't the only threat from contact with ticks in the backcountry.

In 2015, a farmer in Kansas became the first and, to date, only victim of the "Bourbon virus," a new tick-borne disease that killed the previously healthy fifty-year-old in less than two weeks.

Named for Bourbon Country, Kansas, where the man lived and died, it took the CDC nearly a year to identify what exactly had killed the man.

That's often the trouble with tick-borne diseases. They tend to come with a wide array of symptoms and it can be hard to identify or remember when the actual bite happened, if the victim even notices at all. That gives doctors little to go on when it comes time to identify and treat the condition.

Not for lack of trying, of course.

In the case of the Kansas farmer, he came to the hospital after suffering what he knew was a tick bite while working out on his property on the Kansas-Missouri border about 100 miles south of Kansas City. Unlike the arid, brown parts of Kansas further to the west, eastern Kansas near where the attack occurred is still fairly lush and green, typified by low tree cover and rolling hills that, not surprisingly, look more like Missouri than not. The area is, in my experience, the last gasp of what I consider to be an Eastern landscape before the land surrenders to the dry, desert ecosystem of the Great Plains.

Upon arrival at the hospital, the man's symptoms, given that he knew he had suffered a tick bite (the tick itself was still attached to his shoulder, engorged with blood, when he found it), all lined up with Lyme disease. He had a fever, was fatigued, and complained of a persistent headache. Thinking he was suffering from the fairly typical tick-borne disease, doctors prescribed a round of antibiotic treatment and sent the man home.

But it didn't help.

Within days, he began to show new symptoms, including two conditions known as "thrombocytopenia" and "leukopenia," both of which involve the blood. One points to a deficiency of blood platelets that clot blood and prevent internal bleeding, while the other indicates a reduced number of white cells in the blood, slowing the body's natural healing process.

Within eleven days, his organs had failed, and he died of cardiac arrest.

Death as a result of a tick bite is not unheard of, both in the United States and abroad, but of the fifteen tick-borne diseases tracked by the CDC, few cause more than uncomfortable symptoms and can clear up with treatment. For example, Ehrlichiosis is a type of bacterial disease that is transmitted to humans and other animals via infected ticks, primarily the Texas-native Lone Star tick in the United States. Its symptoms are similar to Lyme disease—headache, fatigue, muscle aches, etc.—and since being recognized by the CDC in 1999 its infection rate has increased, due in part to better recognition on the part of health care personnel. Infections peaked in 2008 at just less than 900 cases in the United States, but 800 cases per year is typical.

Of those cases, the fatality rate for Ehrlichiosis infections in the United States hovers around 1 percent, most of which occur in patients with other contributing risk factors.

The far more common Lyme disease has followed a similar path in recent years. Although it ranks as the most commonly reported "vector-borne" illness in the United States—meaning it is transmitted by the bite of an infected arthropod such as ticks, mosquitoes, and flies—Lyme disease is not common nationwide and remains tightly concentrated in the Northeast and Upper Midwest. And, at least in this country, the fatality rate is low. According to a 2011 study conducted by the CDC, between 1999 and 2003 there were just 114 records listing Lyme disease as the cause of a person's death. In most of those cases, the disease was listed as just one of a victim's multiple health problems, so it could not be definitively singled out as their sole cause of death.

As with so many bites and infections that one might encounter in the backcountry, ticks rarely kill on their own but they can make underlying and related problems worse. You aren't going to keel over and die within days from a tick bite, even if the tick is infected with something serious.

The fact that that's pretty much exactly what happened to that Kansas farmer had experts at the CDC scratching their heads for months, particularly after a battery of tests conducted on his blood following his death came back negative for tick-borne infections. Few clues emerged until months later when further blood tests revealed the presence of "thogotoviruses." It's a type of virus that's found all over the world but, until this case, had never before been known to cause human illness in the United States. In fact, there were previously only eight other cases of human infection in the world.

To date, this is the only known case of its kind in the world, but there is some concern that it may be related to the Heartland virus, recently discovered in Missouri and also linked to tick transmission.

As with seemingly everything with tick-borne infections, we may never know for sure.

Bees / Stinging Insects

Usery Mountain Recreation Area is a county-run open space park on the east side of Phoenix, Arizona, located in the dusty, dry foothills on the way to the Fort Apache Reservation. Like most of Southern Arizona, it is a desert landscape of Saguaro cactus and scrub bush, and its hiking trails and caves are popular with day trippers and weekend campers from the nearby metro area. In the evening, the lights of Phoenix twinkle in the distance, twenty-five miles away. It is a suburban park like many throughout America.

So imagine the community's surprise when a twenty-three-year-old hiker died in the park in May 2016 after being stung more than 1,000 times by a swarm of bees.

The day started innocently enough. The victim, Alex Bestler, and a friend had come out to Usery Mountain in the morning for a hike before the heat of the day. The trails in the park mostly head up and around Pass Mountain, part of the Tonto National Forest, though the Merkle Trail where the attack occurred is located on the flats near a small hill near the trailhead for the south side of the park. According to reports, Bestler never had a chance.

He and his hiking partner stumbled across the bees early on in their hike and, within seconds, the swarm was on him, stinging him repeatedly and forcing him to the ground. His friend was able to make it to safety in a nearby bathroom, but Bestler was immediately covered from head to toe by the swarm.

A popular trail, help was immediately on scene to try and rescue Bestler from the bees, but the swarm drove them back repeatedly. Even after rangers loaded the victim onto a park ATV for evacuation, the insects continued their pursuit, stinging the rescuers and keeping Bestler covered. He was later declared dead at a local hospital.

A park spokesman later said that it was the worst bee attack he had seen in nearly two decades working at the park.

But that's not to say that bee attacks like the one that killed Alex Bestler are unheard of in the area. In fact, Arizona has developed something of a reputation for attacks like this in recent years, as has much of the US Southwest. Bees sent another man to the hospital in Phoenix the same day that Bestler was killed, and a dog in Southern California was severely injured by a swarm the very next day. A man was killed while working in his backyard garden in Douglas, near the Mexican border in 2014, the victim of what wildlife experts later estimated was a swarm of more than 800,000 bees.

Attacks on animals and livestock in the region are common.

Part of the reason for this is the increasingly warm temperatures in the desert Southwest, Reed Booth (aka "The Killer Bee Guy"), a beekeeper and bee removal expert from Bisbee, Arizona, told *Backpacker* magazine after the attacks. Bees are generally active in temperatures between 57 and 100 degrees Fahrenheit, but the hotter it gets, the more agitated the bees get.

"They're just like humans," he told the magazine. "They get hot and bothered."

But the introduction of hybrid bees—a combination of both European and Africanized honeybees—is to blame as well, creating a species of bees that are more aggressive, more prone to alarm, and gather in larger, more dangerous, swarms. These are not bees that you want to mess with.

"In 15 seconds you can have 15,000 angry bees out," Booth said, "and they don't stop stinging after you're dead."

It's not just a Southwest problem either, though that's where the hybrid bees first started to show up. As of 2016, these hybrid Africanized honeybees have been found in all Lower 48 states, and attacks are on the rise as a result. In late summer 2016, a Texas man was killed by a swarm of bees while mowing the grass on his property outside of Waco, his body found about 100 yards from his tractor, covered in bee stings.

A family member later said that the victim, fifty-four-year-old Rogerio Zuniga, had probably jumped off of the tractor and tried to run away from the attack, with the swarm in full, nightmare-level pursuit. He succumbed to his injuries and collapsed before he could get away.

Of course, bees are not alone in the world of dangerous stinging insects. Wasps and hornets too present a real threat for injury, and kill their own fair share of humans every year too, both through allergic reactions and swarm attacks such as the Arizona incident.

In many ways, the wasp is more dangerous than the honeybee, even an Africanized one. That's because there are two types of wasps: social and solitary. The vast majority of wasps are solitary, meaning they live alone and keep to themselves, but because of their lone wolf behavior they are also far less likely to encounter a person, let alone sting them. Social wasps, on the other hand, are a different matter. When a social wasp stings an animal that it considers a threat, it emits a chemical signal that alerts other nearby wasps to the threat, often leading to a rapidly forming swarm that can inflict real damage on a victim. That's why, when you get stung once by a wasp you always seem to get stung multiple times. Killing a wasp when you see it generally just makes matters worse, for the same reason.

"It's not so much that you've killed a wasp, it's that you've threatened a wasp or their wasp home," explained the American Chemical Society in a video series it produces called *Reaction* that "uncovers the chemistry of everyday life."

Plus, based on the design of their stingers, wasps can sting a victim over and over again. Bees have barbed stingers that stay behind in the victim after an attack, killing the bee in the process.

It happened to an eighty-three-year-old man in Wales in 2015, who died as a result of "thousands" of wasp stings after accidentally disturbing a large nest while staying at a home on vacation. As in the Arizona attack, the swarm grew quickly, stinging him repeatedly. At one point, family members reported that the swarm was so thick on the man that they couldn't even see his face. He managed to escape the initial attack, but later died of anaphylactic shock.

On the flipside, experts have shown that simply remaining calm in the presence of a wasp, simply letting it sit on your skin and investigate you, can not only prevent a sting from occurring in the first place but can also limit the release of this "alarm chemical." Stinging insects generally won't make the first move. Rather, they will only attack when they have been agitated or feel threatened by a quick movement.

In that way, these insects are no different from any of the other animals mentioned in this book. Staying calm in the face of danger goes a long way when dealing with an uncertain situation.

That is not to say that there is no risk here at all, of course.

Bees, wasps, and other stinging insects are among the deadliest "nonhuman animals" in the United States, killing as many as 100 people in this country every year, according to the CDC. Granted, that's out of the thousands and thousands of people who are stung annually by these insects, but for those select few who are allergic to the venom that these stings deliver, anaphylactic shock as a severe allergic reaction is not unheard of and, absent immediate medical care, can and does prove fatal. This pales in comparison to the 600,000-plus who die every year because of mosquito-transmitted malaria, as reported by the World Health Organization, but it easily dwarfs the "real" threatening animals that we all think about when we venture out into the woods—bears, mountain lions, and wolves.

Bees, wasps, and hornets kill more humans in a single year than the big three of North America predators have since records started being kept more than a century ago. And they are not alone. According to research from the Merck pharmaceutical company, as many as four times as many people die from bee stings in the United States every year than die from snake bites, and fire ants, a particularly type of aggressive stinging ant that is common in the US Southeast, are credited with killing an average of thirty people every year and stinging as much as 40 percent of the population in their range.

Compare that to venomous snakes and lizards, which combined kill six people in the United States each year; dogs, which kill twenty-eight Americans annually; and "other mammals" (mostly deer-on-car incidents), which kill another fifty-plus each year. Even cows—yes, cows—can be deadly, credited with some twenty deaths annually. All of these figures are from CDC's database.

(For the sake of further comparison, it is also worth mentioning the animal that is far and away the deadliest thing out there in terms of annual deaths are humans themselves. According to the CDC's numbers, there are more than 16,000 homicides nationwide in the United States every year, and another 41,000 people commit suicide annually. When compared to even the "deadliest" bees, it's clear that the real risk in this world lies with ourselves.)

"Stings by bees, wasps, and hornets are common throughout the United States," Merck writes. "Some ants also sting. The average person can safely tolerate 10 stings for each pound of body weight. This means that the average adult could withstand more than 1,000 stings, whereas 500 stings could kill a child. However, in a person who is allergic to such stings, one sting can cause death due to an anaphylactic reaction (a life-threatening allergic reaction in which blood pressure falls and the airway closes)."

Anyone who has ever experienced a bee or hornet sting—which is generally 100 percent of the population—knows what they feel like and how much they hurt. It is like getting stabbed by a very tiny, very painful needle that grows and grows in intensity immediately after the fact. I remember encountering a wasp's nest one time on a group hike in Jefferson National Forest near Virginia's Shenandoah Valley. The first in our group came across several of the insects gathered on the trail, and apparently agitated them, causing them to sting him repeatedly in an attempt to chase him off. Once that was done, the rest of us in turn got to walk the gauntlet and suffer the stings of the wasps. More than twenty years later, I can still clearly remember the burning, hot pain I experienced that day after one of the insects got me in the shoulder while I ran to avoid them. And that is fairly typical when it comes to severe stings like this. My wife experienced a hornet sting while walking barefoot on the beach in Santa Barbara, California, nearly a decade ago, and to this day, any mention of going to the beach in California brings back this memory.

Stings are warnings from the insect kingdom, and we aren't supposed to make the same mistake again.

According to Merck, the typical bee, wasp, or hornet sting is a red, swollen, and "sometimes itchy" area at the sight of impact that is usually no more than about a half-inch in diameter. Pain is immediate, but does tend to subside over the next couple of days.

For most of us, fortunately, that is the end of is. Lesson learned.

But some people experience stings that grow dramatically to two inches or more, sometimes swelling even more than is normal. This type of allergic reaction to a wasp or hornet sting is not common, but the reactions can vary widely from a simple rash, "itching all over, wheezing, trouble breathing, and shock," per Merck.

And this is where things can get dangerous for those people who are allergic to stings. As the reaction progresses, without medical care the symptoms can quickly become dangerous to the patient, and location becomes an issue. In the backcountry, no matter how well-intentioned or prepared, it can be difficult to get a patient to the hospital in time, turning what is generally a benign injury into something truly life-threatening.

That said, preparation is key, and most people who suffer from severe insect allergies are taught at a very early age to be vigilant about potential stings and be prepared to treat the injury on their own if needed. This can include carrying medication to treat and clean the sting, or even packing an EpiPen to address the possibility of severe allergic reaction when far from medical care. It may be the Boy Scout in me, but the mantra I remember when it comes to stings and allergies is "prepare, prepare, prepare."

But it's never perfect.

In 2014, a Virginia woman, thirty-two-year-old Sarah Harkins, died after being stung by a wasp in her yard. She was allergic, and maybe she knew that, but her death came as a result of the combination of the sting reaction as well as a fatal aneurism that the episode triggered. It was a deadly combination of risk factors that is difficult to predict and nearly impossible to completely prevent.

* * *

"We don't deal with people's psyches too much, because if people are afraid of spiders or stinging insects or something like that, they just are. You can't just undo it automatically. But I think the information of how to deal with them all is pretty similar actually," says Dr. Eric Mussen, a retired professor of entomology at the University of California, Davis, and the author of several books on beekeeping and bee behaviors. Over the course of his career, he has focused his research on managing bees—both European honeybees and other varieties of bees—for maximum field production while minimizing the potential for pesticide damage to pollinator populations.

He has, by his own admission, been stung a lot, many thousands of times over the course of his career working with bees and as a recreational beekeeper.

But that's OK, because the human body can withstand quite a bit of bee or wasp venom. In fact, with most European honeybee colonies, which are the variety that we are most likely to encounter in North America, you have to, as he explains it, "press the issue" to suffer more than twenty stings or so from a single colony. They just aren't that aggressive, and more healthy adults who are not allergic can handle twenty stings at one time without suffering any long-term injury. It will hurt like hell, but they will survive.

Africanized bees are a different matter, but we'll come back to the unique challenges they present in a moment.

For Dr. Mussen, who has spent a lifetime around stinging insects, the message is simple: leave them alone. It doesn't matter if you are dealing with wasps, hornets, or honeybees; the general rule is that they will not give you a hard time unless you do one of two things: disturb their nest or get into their "defensive area" and do something that draws them out to defend their turf. That's it. These are not complex animals.

"If you're having a picnic, and you've been barbecuing meat and whatnot, and a wasp shows up. I used to tell my family, don't worry about it, even if they land on you, they're not going to do anything," he says, admitting however that he did once have a wasp land on him in such a situation and actually bite him as if he was the source of the meat it was smelling. "It's not quite perfect like that, but generally speaking, if a honey bee lands on you, which they hardly ever do, it wouldn't be there to sting, because if it were there to sting, it would have done it already."

Part of this comes down to simple biology. If a wasp or bee wants to sting you, it will stick its tarsi, which Mussen describes as the bee's toenails, into your skin, pull on the skin a little bit, and then drive its abdomen down to sting. That's just the way they work.

This is true of all stinging, flying insects. So anytime one lands on you and hasn't yet stung you, it means it probably won't. It's just there to investigate. You might want to encourage it to leave by moving a finger or your hand over gently in its direction, but once you actually touch

Stinging is a defense mechanism, meaning the party most to blame in the case of a sting is the victim, not the insect.

them, that's when things change. Generally, all they want is to be left alone, so as long as you "don't really bang them up or stimulate them too badly they'll just keep doing their thing," according to Dr. Mussen. If you disturb a hive and get a colony up flying around your face, as long as you have the presence of mind to stand still and not disturb them, they will buzz around for a while and then just give up and go home. (Admittedly, this is not the easiest thing to do in the moment.)

"But boy, if you start swinging, if you blow at them, the way you do if a fly is bothering you, you kind of blow at it, but boy, you do that at any of these stinging insects, and that CO_2 and that little wind just gives them a target, and they're right in your face. So, there's things that you don't want to do, but it is pretty much the same for all of them," says Dr. Mussen.

Africanized honeybees are an entirely different matter.

Mussen describes them as "a little more touchy," explaining that they are more aggressive than their European cousins and can be set off by something as minor as vibrations on the ground from a group walking past their nest. They still go through the same phases as typical bees and wasps—they get agitated when their nest is disturbed or their defensive zone is breached—but the difference with Africanized varieties is they go from annoyed to enraged a lot faster than most bees do. They're like a toddler throwing a temper tantrum; they go from zero to sixty in an instant.

And they can do serious damage. As opposed to those European bees that only sting maybe twenty times before moving on, a colony of Africanized honeybees will keep attacking over and over again, well past the point of disabling their victim. As a result, it is not uncommon to find victims, usually dogs or livestock, with hundreds if not thousands of stings. Mussen says he has lost dogs as large as German Shepherds to swarms of Africanized bees that would not back off, stinging them in their ear canals, up their nostrils, and in their throat. In one case a large dog died after suffering more than 2,000 stings to its head alone.

What's happening is that more bees are reacting to the alarm pheromone given off by the guard bees, the members of the colony that wait near the entrance to the nest and alert the rest of impending danger via the transmission of scent pheromones. It's a trait of Africanized bees and it's why their swarms can be so much bigger and more aggressive. Their biology is just slightly different than European bees.

And once the victim gets stung, it just gets worse.

It you don't stand still and start moving around in the face of the swarm, and this is something that applies to both Africanized varieties and more standard insects, that movement will attract some of them and eventually one of more of them will sting whatever it is that is moving around. When they do that, that same alarm pheromone that got the insects excited in the first place is now on your skin, so others will come over and sting in the same area, setting off more scents that the rest of the colony will react to. Once you're hit, that's when you're really targeted and even more bees or wasps will come out to investigate what they're smelling and react as well.

Knowing this, and knowing that this is how colonies of stinging insects behave, Mussen himself suggests two things for anyone who expects to be spending time in the backcountry where bees, particularly the Africanized type, which are most common in the US Southwest (outside of Africa, of course), wasps, and hornets. Buy a head net like you would use to prevent mosquito bites and keep it in your pocket at all times. That way, in the event that you do agitate a colony of insects and they start to sting en masse, you can pull it out quickly and protect your head and face.

"If you start getting stings in your nose, the tears will come out of your eyes so heavily," he says. "You're not crying, you're just tearing. The tears will come up so heavily, that you can't even see where you're going."

The netting will help prevent that and make it easier to get away from the nest area as quickly and safely as possible. When your eyes are watering heavily it can be very difficult to do that, and staying in the area at that point just leaves you vulnerable to more stings.

On top of that, he says, if you're allergic to stings and you know it, you should always carry an EpiPen with you. Granted, this used to be an easier investment to make when EpiPens were more reasonably priced, but whatever the cost, Mussen says anyone who is allergic needs to carry one with them.

"If you're way out in the back woods somewhere and you start an anaphylactic response, you're in hot water," he says. An EpiPen can save your life.

Scorpions

There is a scene early in the 2012 James Bond film *Skyfall* that pits Bond, in this installment played by Daniel Craig, against what is apparently a deadly scorpion. He's sitting amidst a large crowd at a beachside bar, the walls open to the tropical night, and he's participating in some sort of local drinking game, trying to down a shot without being stung by the tan scorpion that is perched on his drinking hand, its stinger raised high as if to strike. The challenge, then, is to raise the glass to his lips, empty it, and then return the glass to the bar without jostling the scorpion enough to anger it into an attack.

With one smooth motion, Bond drains the shot, shakes the animal off his hand, and traps it on the bar under his upturned glass.

The crowd goes wild.

But of course none of it was real. And I don't just mean the computer-generated scorpion itself—the filmmakers pulled together reference photos of a real blond desert hairy scorpion, the largest scorpion in North America and a reliably aggressive species—but also the risk of the entire situation. Like spiders, ants, and many other stinging insects, scorpion stings are largely harmless to humans. Yes, they hurt like hell, but these insects are designed to attack and subdue far smaller prey, like arthropods, and not something as large as a human. As a rule, small children and the elderly are at higher risk of injury from scorpion stings and should seek medical care if they're stung, but most healthy adults are OK with no treatment here in North America.

In the United States, there have only been four recorded scorpion-related deaths since 2005.

Things are different overseas, of course. There are scorpions in South America, Africa, and Asia that pack a stronger punch than the North American varieties and more often call for medical care. In Mexico, for example, 1,000 people are killed by scorpions every year, and worldwide there are roughly 3,000 annual deaths as a result of 1.2 million stings.

So, for Bond, the truth is roughly fifty-fifty.

We don't really know exactly where the bar is located when he has his encounter with the scorpion, but in reality the scene was shot in the seaside town of Fethiye, Turkey, on the Mediterranean Sea. Scorpions are common in Turkey's dry, desert climate, and several species in the region can be dangerous, so it's possible that such a contest would exist, and that onlookers would be scared for the participant.

Still, scorpions are generally not the killer that they are made out to be.

Of the 1,500 known species of scorpion on the planet, only about twenty-five of them can kill humans, and even then the conditions have to be just right for it to actually occur. In fact, most of those fatalities happen in infants and the elderly, and there are really only two species of scorpions in the world that can kill a healthy adult—the Israeli deathstalker (which, admit it, is a great name for a scorpion) and the Brazilian yellow scorpion (which isn't quite as fear inducing), though antivenoms exist to treat stings from both varieties. Most of the time when you get stung by a scorpion, you end up with some swelling and inflammation. Only rarely does the venom cause severe allergic, neurotic, or necrotic reactions that need to be treated by a doctor.

Scorpions remain a significant public health risk in the developing world, however, and more than 3,000 people are killed each year in parts of Africa, South India, the Middle East, Mexico, and Latin America.

Among the most recent that I could find was the 2007 case of a fifty-six-year-old British man who was stung by a scorpion in Thailand. Gareth Pike was stung on the thumb and tried to suck the venom out of the wound before being treated for fever at a local Thai hospital and released. After he returned home to the UK his symptoms returned and he was admitted to the hospital again, only to be released again a few days later. A week later he started feeling bad again and returned to the hospital, this time dying while under doctors' care of severe internal bleeding and liver damage.

The scorpion encounter, as Pike explained it before his death, sounds like the kind of thing that could happen to anyone at any time while vacationing in the tropics.

"I was living in a tin shack in the jungle and there were lots of black scorpions around," he said. "I was getting dressed one morning when I was stung on the thumb. I had a blister come out on my thumb and foot and I came out in a rash. I was in dreadful pain. I lost half my body weight and I felt very ill. I was glad to get home."

Wrong place, wrong time.

Believe it or not, one of the better-known stories of a fatal scorpion encounter comes from Greek mythology. Orion, the hunter both in legend and the night sky as a constellation, was said to have been killed by the bite of a scorpion as payback for his vanity. Apparently being the greatest hunter in the galaxy can inflate one's ego.

On the flipside, a twenty-seven-year-old woman in Malaysia broke the world record for "time spent living in a scorpion-filled box" when she spent a staggering thirty-two days alone in a glass enclosure with more than 6,000 scorpions in 2004. She was stung seven times during the attempt, but emerged relatively unharmed. Her record held until 2009, when Thailand's self-described "Scorpion Queen" spent thirty-three days in a room with 5,000 scorpions to take the "crown" for herself. She also holds the dubious record of "most time spent with a scorpion in mouth" at just over two minutes. Oddly, no one has yet decided to challenge her record as of 2017.

The lesson from all of this is simply that scorpions are not as dangerous to humans as their reputation would suggest. Like most stinging insects, their neurotoxic venom is deadly against those it was intended for—namely, insects, spiders, lizards, and small mammals such as mice—paralyzing their prey while using their claws to finish the job. But this same venom is barely enough to register more than a

Humans have feared scorpions dating back to the days of the Ancient Greeks, but that fear may never have been rooted in actual risk.

painful sting to a 100-plus pounds person. That's just the simple fact of the matter.

First, though, let's dispel another myth about scorpions: that they are insects.

While both scorpions and creatures such as spiders, ticks, and centipedes are arthropods, scorpions actually have their own branch on the arthropod family tree and are classified as Scorpiones under the category of Arachnida, which also contains spiders. The main differences from insects are technical in nature: Scorpions have eight legs instead of six. They have two body segments (the tail and the body) instead of three (the head, abdomen, and thorax) of insects. And they don't have antennae or wings.

They are simply a different type of animal.

All of that said, and with the understanding that scorpion-related fatalities are very rare, a scorpion sting is not something to mess around with. Such stings can be very painful and swell up, particularly among those people who are allergic to venomous stings, and can be problematic in their own right, even when not fatal (which most often occurs in young children and the elderly). Scorpion allergies are similar to any other sting allergy, and can lead to everything from hives and swelling to nausea, trouble breathing, and even anaphylaxis. Treatment of such cases is equally similar to honeybees and all the rest—medical care or an EpiPen. Similarly, it's when an allergic person gets stung by a scorpion deep in the backcountry and far from any type of medical attention that they can get in trouble. In these cases, preparation in the form of an EpiPen is vital.

Scorpion behavior is also fairly typical when compared to other arthropods. In short, they aren't going to go out of their way to attack you. In fact, a scorpion's sting is its last resort line of defense, and they will only use it against a human in situations where they feel cornered or threatened. They would much rather run away, hide, or feign a threat—by lifting their tail up to strike or pretending to attack—than actually go through with a sting against a foe as large and formidable as a human. They know they aren't going to really hurt you with an attack, and that it will most likely just infuriate you more, so nine times out of ten they will look to exit the situation as quickly as possible, using the possibility of a sting as a distraction mechanism.

But stings do happen, usually when the scorpion is surprised or touched inadvertently. In fact, the classic cases of scorpion stings happen when an animal hides out in the bottom of a boot or in a glove and then the owner of said boot or glove moves to put them on. Attacking is often the only thing the animal can do at that point (and is reason enough to always check your boots in the morning before putting them on).

Barring these types of situations, the rules for dealing with scorpion encounters in the wild are generally the same as with any type of stinging insects: don't sneak up on them, don't corner them, and always leave them room to leave if they want to run away. Let them control the encounter, instead of the other way around. That said, scorpions can be quite small, so it isn't always possible to avoid them on sight. They can sneak into small spaces unnoticed and are likely lurking around wherever you aren't looking whenever you're in the desert Southwest and other scorpion habitats.

That's why prevention is the key. Check your boots. Check your pack. Check your hat. Check everything you use before sticking a finger or foot into it on the off change that a scorpion has slipped inside to bed down for a while. They tend to like dark, moist, enclosed spaces, which can apply to many different things that people tend to use in the backcountry.

In truth, scorpions are actually more of a problem in the home than in the wild. Outside they are (generally) always in control of their environment. It's their turf and they can get away whenever they feel threatened or cornered (those aforementioned boots notwithstanding). But inside the home, things change. There you'll find no shortage of places for them to hide (think closets, basements, crawlspaces, etc.) and things that scorpions like (e.g., food and water), making it a constant struggle to both keep them out and manage those that do get inside. They're like mice, but, as anyone who lives in Arizona will tell you, can be much more difficult to deal with, calling for specialized mitigation professionals and prevention measures that go above and beyond most other pest control efforts.

Why? Because scorpions are resilient. Alongside cockroaches, they were found at US nuclear testing sites during World War II, surviving the test blasts more or less unscathed, so these are animals that are going to be with us for a long, long time. That's one reason that, like roaches, once they get into a home or even a neighborhood, they can be extremely difficult to completely eradicate. That can cause problems indoors from a pest control standpoint—and has led to the creation of some pretty interesting technology, such as "scorpion seal" barriers that claim to completely seal off a structure and prevent the animals from ever gaining entry—but doesn't change much about their behavior in the outdoors. They are skittish and scared of humans, that's all there is to it, and only prevent any sort of threat when cornered or provoked.

Stop me when this starts to sound familiar.

Really, scorpions are a lot like spiders, according to Kathy Maguire at Reptile Gardens in South Dakota.

"For the most part if you do get a sting it's just going to be a sting, it's not going to be a real life-threatening episode," she says. "But there are some really bad ones. It seems that the smaller ones and the lighter colored ones seem to cause more trouble. And they're generally, but not always, in warmer climates, more tropical. You know, down around Mexico they have scorpions that can cause a lot of trouble in the desert, like deathstalkers and those types."

The deathstalker is considered the most dangerous species of scorpion on the planet, despite the fact that it is usually less than three inches long and mild yellow in color. Usually found in the Middle East and Northern Africa, though some have recently turned up in North America, its venom is unusually powerful and has been known to kill small children and the elderly.

They are not to be messed with.

But still, Maguire says, the fear of scorpions is overblown. She handles them all the time, and although they can sting and they can hurt you, you aren't going to die or be seriously injured by one. You'll see them depicted in movies and on TV as these perfect killers, but once you know even a little bit about the animals you'll be able to recognize the different species and know that what you're looking at is usually harmless.

As with spiders, the rules around scorpions are straightforward. They are secretive, elusive insects by nature, and generally just want to go about their lives undetected and undisturbed, so it is good policy to afford them that right. Most of the cases of people being stung by scorpions, again as with spiders, are when the insect is hiding in their shoe or in their bedding and the victim comes along and bumps into it, scaring it into a defensive action. But, even then, the important thing to remember is that even though a scorpion will sting you and it will hurt, that's about all that's going to happen to you. Knowing the different kinds of scorpions that are out there, and which species live in the area you're visiting, can go a long way toward addressing the fear of them.

"There are a few that are really bad," Maguire says, "but the majority of them look much worse than they are. And, besides, the venom in most types of creatures is toxic enough only to kill their prey, which is a small insect also. We are not their prey."

CHAPTER 4
Weather

Flash Flood/Drowning

The desert southwest of North America is one of the most unique and beautiful places on the planet. Formed from the remains of an ancient seabed, the region is dry, rugged, and beautiful in ways that few others places can match—an explosion of reds, oranges, tans, and purples formed into rolling hills, mesas, peaks, and valleys.

The ocean is long gone, but it left behind an undulating landscape of sandstone, carved into relief by the steady erosion of the waves. In some places—such as the iconic Monument Valley on the Utah-Arizona border—this erosion has left behind stunning monoliths, the remains of long-dormant volcanoes that have been stripped down, over millions of years, to expose the dense, impermeable rock at their core. In others—and the Grand Canyon is of course the best example of this—the water has carved out vast canyons, deeper and more spectacular than anywhere else. Sandstone is a soft type of rock, susceptible to water erosion like few other types.

As a result, the Grand Canyon isn't the only canyon in the Southwest. In fact, there are thousands of slot canyons scattered all over Northern Arizona, New Mexico, California, and Utah. Southern Utah alone is the densest places on the planet in terms of slot canyons, with more than 1,000 throughout the region that includes Zion and Canyonlands National Parks, as well as Grand Staircase-Escalante National Monument and the surrounding Bureau of Land Management (BLM) land. One of the longest slot canyons in the world, named Buckskin Gulch, is located here, stretching across the southern Utah border into Arizona's Paria Canyon-Vermilion Cliffs Wilderness.

And they were all created the same way over thousands of years. A trickle of water, a crank in the rock that it can flow through, and enough time for it to carry away the bedrock a flake at a time.

In many cases, this has left behind what are known as slot canyons, narrow but deep canyons that wind their way down from the hills, driven by small streams and waterfalls. They can be a few stories deep, with sheer, near-vertical walls on either side.

And they are also often stunning to behold.

There is a well-known photo of a hiker standing deep inside one of the more popular hikes in slot canyon country looking up into a beam of light shining down and illuminating the small cavern. Surrounded by bright orange stone and standing on what appears to be a flat, dust covered floor, it makes for a striking image. And it isn't terribly unique—beautiful spots like that one can be found in any number of slot canyons across the desert Southwest.

No wonder these canyons can be tempting destinations for hikers.

That's what canyoneering guide Kaden Anderson and two friends were doing at Keyhole Canyon in Utah's Zion National Park on September 14, 2015. Located near the main road through Zion and shorter than most slot canyon hikes in the area, Keyhole has a reputation as one of the more beginner friendly locations in the park. Anderson's friends weren't experienced canyoneers like he was, so it seemed like a good, safe place to start.

But they never even got the chance that day.

As soon as they walked up to the put-in—slot canyon exploration starts at the top of the formation, requiring participants to rappel into the canyon and then work their way down to the exit at the bottom of the hill—they noticed that something was off. There was a rappel rope left in place, hanging limp against the smooth walls of the canyon. It was secured at the top but had never been removed as is usually done once a group reaches the floor of the canyon to start their hike.

Peering into the void, the group thought they saw a shoe tangled at the base of the rope. Anderson lowered himself down into the pool at the base of the rappel and confirmed what he already knew: there was a body down there, cold and dead.

Over the course of the next twenty-four hours, Zion rangers would discover the bodies of six more canyoneers, the remains of a hiking club from southern California that had ventured into Keyhole Canyon earlier that day and had been caught in a flash flood of epic proportions. It became one of the most deadly days in Zion history and a turning point for many in the canyoneering community.

How had these experienced hikers, with the latest in safety and climbing gear, fallen victim to such a basic risk? What had gone wrong?

Flash floods are far from uncommon in canyon country. After all, these are rock formations that are defined by water, created by it, and often contain pools and running streams even in the best of conditions. Runoff is a characteristic of the dry desert landscape, and since the water has nowhere else to go, it often dives down into the canyons that already exist in the landscape.

Again, this is a normal part of life in this part of the world.

Storms come and go—particularly in the fall—and can often drop a lot of water on the park in a short period of time. That was the forecast that day in September, and that's why Zion's rangers had closed off Keyhole Canyon to climbing on the day of the incident, although there were no signs to this effect at the site and groups were still able to register for permits at the ranger office.

Either way, all seven members of the Valencia Hiking Crew were deep within Keyhole Canyon when the flash flood struck, pummeling them with a wall of water that slammed the team members against the rocks of the canyon before forcing out the bottom of the canyon into Clear Creek.

The group never saw it coming, and they never stood a chance.

As horrible as the 2015 incident was, it wasn't even the worst disaster in canyoneering history. In 1997, twelve hikers were killed when a flash flood eleven feet deep swept through Antelope Canyon, another novice-friendly canyon, near Lake Powell in Arizona. One member of the party was able to survive by grabbing onto a rock ledge and hanging on for his life. The body of a woman was recovered a short time later. The bodies of the remaining victims were never found.

* * *

It is hard to argue with the appeal of slot canyon exploration. They're beautiful places, with nearly sheer sandstone walls, sandy floors, and cascading pools that look like something out of another world. And the fact that they can be so hard to access makes them all the more isolated and interesting to explore.

But that tranquil isolation comes at a price.

The typical slot canyon hike is a one-way affair. You enter near the top of the canyon, often rappelling down into the canyon a few hundred yards uphill from the canyon's exit, and work your way down the drainage, climbing over and around boulders, wading across pools and sliding down ledges. Again, these are amazing places and the appeal is clear.

But this natural, one-way arrangement can turn deadly in the case of an accident or flash flood. When the floodwaters start to rise, for example, it's not as if you can simply climb up the sheer walls of the canyon, which can be several stories high, to safety. Nor can you backtrack to a dry space near the start of the hike. The only escape is down the canyon, which is a route that generally takes some time to reach.

That's why, when canyoneers are killed in slot canyon flash floods, they are so often caught as a group. When a canyon fills suddenly with floodwaters that can be ten to twenty feet deep in minutes, there simply is no escape. Survivors of such incidents are rare, except in the unusual cases where they happen to be near the canyon's exit when the waters hit and are able to run to safety.

One way out means one way out.

The trouble with these canyons, however, is that there doesn't even need to be a storm in the area to get in trouble. Even distant rains can send floodwaters rushing down through canyon country, often trapping canyon explorers before they even realize that there is a risk.

That's what happened in the 2015 Keyhole Canyon case, which has since gone down as the worst disaster in Zion National Park's history. Although rangers had warned the group that thunderstorms were in the area and that flooding in the canyon was likely, the flash flood warning that day wasn't issued until after the group had been issued their permit and had begun their hike down the canyon. They never saw it coming.

Of course, flash flooding is about much more than just slot canyons in the desert Southwest. According to the National Weather Service, flash floods are the leading cause of weather-related deaths in the United States, killing more than 200 people every year. Over the last thirty years, an average of 127 people have died in floods annually. Doesn't seem like a ton until considering the thirty-year averages for other natural phenomenon such as lightning (seventy-three deaths), tornadoes (sixty-eight), and hurricanes (sixteen). More than 50 percent of these—and more than 70 percent in Texas alone—involve people who get trapped in their cars and swept away by floodwaters. Flash flooding deaths occur most often in Texas, and the figure there is more than double the second-place state, California.

These floods, despite their name, are often not caused by fast-moving storms or especially intense weather. In fact, the NWS says that most flash floods are actually caused by slow-moving thunderstorms that linger over an area for an especially long period of time, saturating the ground and available runoff area with heavy, sustained rains. Once the area reaches this saturation stage, the water has to go somewhere, and flash floods can form in minutes when the conditions are right, depending on the local landscape, soil conditions, and ground cover.

Once they get going, though, they can be surprisingly powerful. Anyone who has ever taken a driver's education class has likely heard the warning that as little as six inches of water can float a car, and driving through standing water of any kind is always a risk. But there's more to it than that. Yes, drivers often get caught in flash floods when they underestimate the power of the water they're passing through, but these floodwaters can also pick up 10,000-pound sandstone boulders and toss them hundreds of yards down a streambed. Or they can tear out full, healthy trees by the root, carrying them away in less than a minute. Bridges, homes, and other structures are nothing to the power of a full-blown flash flood.

All of this points to the true risk of floodwaters, particularly in the backcountry, where escape is far from certain and rescue is nonexistent. Fortunately, there is not much to remember when it comes to dealing with a flash flood in the wild, whether it's in a slot canyon, where escape is all but impossible, or in a narrow valley like the one I traveled through at Ramsey's Draft: get to higher ground.

The National Oceanic and Atmospheric Administration (NOAA) trademarked this advice with the helpful phrase, "Turn Around, Don't Drown®," that's aimed particularly at drivers, but the message is the same. When you see floodwaters get away from them.

It all comes down to preparation and education.

Know the Conditions: Check the weather forecast before heading out and know what's expected to pass through the area in the next several days. Weather reports are not always 100 percent accurate, but some information is better than none, and the off chance that heavy rains are going to be nearby is worth knowing before going out of range of cell phone or TV updates.

Know the Area: Certain areas are more subject to flash flooding than others, including low-lying areas, canyons, washes, and anywhere that the ground dips or forms a depression relative to the surrounding terrain. Know where you are going before you leave and plan accordingly. If rain is in the forecast, look at other routes.

Know the History: Floodwaters are not complicated; they go where they have always gone, and always will. Flooding strikes the same locations over and over again where the conditions are right for it. Knowing where these locations are, and either avoiding them entirely or traveling through them carefully, can go a long way toward minimizing the risk of flash flood death. When in doubt, look for signs along the road or trail.

Know the Water: Six inches of water can lift a car, so the general rule of thumb in running water is not to cross a stream that comes up over the knee. Crossing running water of any significant depth is never a good idea, and it really does take less than expected to do real damage.

Know the Way Out: Slot canyons are dangerous in the event of flash flood because their steep walls make it impossible to quickly reach higher ground. This is not always the case in the backcountry, and it is important to always be aware of not only where higher ground is relative to your position when hiking though a potential floodplain but how to get there quickly in the event of an emergency.

Sometimes you can't get to higher ground when the water starts to rise, and that's when you're in real trouble.

While we're here, let's talk about drowning itself as a risk factor.

The myth is that it's painless, just like going to sleep, allowing victims to slowly drift off into the darkness as their body's major functions start to shut down one at a time. They're suffocating, but by the time it progresses to death they are so far removed from their bodies that they feel no pain.

But that couldn't be further from the truth.

In fact, the steps that lead up to death by drowning involve plenty of pain as the body fights to survive. Need proof? Simulated drowning—aka "waterboarding"—is sometimes used as a torture technique, and is so unpleasant that the US government outlawed it in the years following the 9/11 terrorist attacks in 2001. Even "almost drowning" is terrible.

But that is unfortunate, because drowning is a fairly common way for people to die, both in the United States and worldwide. And drowning does not discriminate. Young, old, fit, fat, or otherwise, drowning victims run the gamut, succumbing in lakes, rivers, oceans, bathtubs, gutters, and anything else in between. That famous line that it is possible to drown in less than an inch of water is true, and the statistics back it up. According to the CDC, in fact, nearly 80 percent of the approximately sixty infant drowning deaths that occur every year happen in bathtubs or large buckets, and nine percent of all child drowning deaths occur in the home, where shallow water is common. Since 1984, more than 320 children have drowned in mop buckets, for a rate that averages out to roughly thirty children every year.

But this isn't just a household risk for young children. The CDC reports that about ten people, adults included, die every day in the United States as a result of nonboat-related unintentional drowning. In fact, for the decade ending 2014, there were about 3,500 fatalities of this type every year, plus another 330 who die annually in boat-related incidents. The majority, nearly 80 percent, of adult victims are male, though drowning remains a particular risk for children—it is the second leading cause of death for those aged one to four, behind only birth defects—and minorities, who face unintentional drowning rates that are "significantly higher" than those for whites across all age groups. In fact, according to the CDC, African American children between the ages of five and eighteen are 5.5 times more likely to drown in a swimming pool than white children in the same age range.

Even those who don't die can suffer greatly from drowning-related injuries. The severe brain damage caused by an extended period without oxygen can result in long-term disabilities such as memory problems and learning disabilities on up to a permanent vegetative state.

Whatever the outcome, getting there is not pleasant.

It's several minutes of panic, gasping for breath and eventually sucking water into the lungs when you try to breathe, which generally causes even more panic. And it all starts when the victim goes under, usually with two lungs full of air if they're lucky enough to take a deep breath before being submerged. In theory, that oxygen, about one liter worth, is enough to keep them alive underwater for several minutes. But drowning in practice is far removed from breath training in the protected waters of the pool, and the body's survival mode kicks in, slowing the heart rate and channeling what oxygenated blood remains directly to the blood and major organs.

This part hurts. Anyone who has ever tried to hold their breath for a minute or two knows the feeling, that strain that radiates out from the lungs to the limbs as carbon dioxide builds up in the body. Hands and feet start to tingle, and you'll start to see stars as your body's peripheral systems start to shut down. What's happening will be familiar to any runner: lactic acid caused by oxygen deprivation is building up in your extremities and causing a burning feeling throughout the body. You struggle to get oxygen into your lungs and bloodstream, but the process that has already begun is making that more and more difficult.

And this is where it gets particularly unpleasant.

As the victim struggles for air, they often start to breathe water into their lungs. When this happens, they will try to cough it back up, causing the body to involuntarily breathe more in, making the situation worse and rapidly shortening survival time. Laryngospasm is the next step, as the throat closes in an effort to seal off the air that remains in the body in order to stay alive. This is a great way to keep water out of the lungs, but causes most of the water that's being involuntarily breathed in and depositing it in the stomach. As the belly full of water builds up, it eventually weighs the victim down and they start to slip below the surface of the water, with air in their lungs and little they can do to save themselves.

From there, they lose consciousness, their brain starved for the oxygen it needs to keep functioning. Breathing stops and brain damage begins after two to three minutes underwater. It is all over in less than ten minutes.

It is worth noting that the body reacts differently whether it is drowning in freshwater or salt water. A key statistic is that a full 90 percent of all drowning deaths worldwide occur in freshwater, including lakes, pools, and other bodies of water. The ocean, which seems like an easy place to drown due to the motion of the waves and the potential riptides, is actually safer due to the fact that salt water is so

A grown adult can drown in less than an inch of water or in the open ocean.

much saltier than our blood. That means that, when we breathe it in, the body will try to dilute it by transferring the water that we all carry with us naturally into the lungs, thereby thickening the blood in the process. This slows the drowning process and can keep a victim alive for up to ten minutes, compared to a minute or two in freshwater, which is just about equal to our blood in terms of salinity and therefore quickly dilutes the blood as it's breathed in, bursting cells and leading to organ failure.

* * *

"A lot of the general backcountry principles that apply to any backcountry sport are going to apply to canyoneering," says Tom Seeley, a professional mountaineering guide with Arizona Rock & Canyon Adventures in Phoenix and Executive Director of the American Canyoneering Association. "So a lot of it is common sense."

The key to turning that common sense into action is understanding what drives the potential for flash flood in a given area. In the canyons where Seeley guides, that comes down to the watershed, or the area of water collection that's above the canyon and feeds water down into the canyon system. Some of those collection points can be very small and some can be very big and far away. Either way, if it's raining on the watershed, even if it's miles from where you are, that's building up the potential for water to rush down the canyon, even if those who are in the canyon aren't even aware that it's raining.

It's (sort of) like filling a water balloon. You can fill and fill to a point, but eventually the balloon itself is going to give out and explode from the water pressure. That's far from an ideal metaphor, but it's roughly what happens in the case of a flash flood. The watershed becomes saturated, and all that water has to go somewhere.

A lot of people will look at the weather exactly where they are and say, "Oh, it doesn't look like rain. Or maybe there's a 10 percent chance here, I feel good about that." But they may not be cognizant of the fact that, "Hey, potentially ten, twelve, fifteen miles up the road that's where we need to be looking."

A number of different factors play into watershed behavior, from ground cover, to bedrock, to even the size and location of it. For example, if water is gathering in a sandstone area, there's not going to be too much chance of dispersion. That water is just going to hit the stone surface and run off, it won't hang around and will instead travel downhill quickly. On the other hand, if there is a large watershed that is in more of a mossy, grassy area, that one is likely not going to be as big of a concern from a flood standpoint because the ground's going to suck a lot of that water in and won't flood as quickly. In those cases, saturation is going to play more of a role in how quickly and how severely the watershed floods. It all depends on the landscape.

According to Seeley, "There are some inherent problems, particularly in canyons, that people are not thinking about [when it comes to flash floods]. In general, if it's monsoon season, which is typically May to October, especially in the Southwest, it's a dangerous time to be in a canyon. The rule of thumb is if there's a chance of rain during that season you just don't go into the canyon because you're pretty much guaranteed it's going to rain, you just don't know where or when. I think the biggest challenge is it doesn't even necessarily need to be raining where you are for the canyon to flash."

Seeley's rule of thumb, he says, when he has to guide tours in canyon country during the summer months is to get into and out of the canyon as early as possible, before the afternoon storms roll in and cause problems. Most of the weather that time of year, in the desert Southwest and in most other parts of the country, happens later in the day and, as a result, that's when people are most likely to get into trouble with flash floods, the afternoon or early evening.

Maybe they plan on getting out early and they don't for some reason. Maybe now they're stuck in the canyon at midday and thunderstorms are building, and they don't really necessarily see them so they don't have a real sense of urgency. Or maybe someone gets injured during the climb and hikes down, and they get stuck in the canyon far later than they had planned. Whatever the reason, tardiness is a serious risk factor when dealing with the risk of flash floods, simply because of the natural fact that weather tends to roll in later in the day almost everywhere.

The signs of a flash flood itself are fairly clear and hard to miss. The river or stream in the canyon will change color, becoming darker as sediment and debris starts to flow down the increased water flow. And the water itself will start to rise. Sometime you'll even hear the heavier water volume coming.

The fact is, though, if you're deep in a canyon when these signs appear, it's usually too late. Getting caught in a slot canyon when a flash flood rolls through is pretty much a death sentence 100 percent of the time. Survivors are usually lucky enough to be in bigger, wider parts of the canyon when the high water strikes, and are able to scramble to higher ground. Even in the midst of a full-scale flood, it can still be possible to work your way up if the way is clear and manageable.

"The problem with some of these slot canyons is they can just be narrow enough that you can still walk through them but they're too wide that you can't really get good perches," Seeley says. "Most of the deaths that I've heard about seem to occur when someone gets caught really in a very precarious part of the canyon. Maybe just at a spot where there wasn't really a good place to scramble up and it just hit them too quick."

But even surviving a flood presents a whole new set of problems. Once the floodwaters recede, you might then be stuck high up in an area that is cut off from the trail and you can't get back down to where you started. This is a backcountry environment and you might not be prepared to spend the night alone and exposed—and likely wet from head to toe from the flood—and you soon have to deal with shelter and hypothermia and a long list of other unexpected issues.

"I can tell you from the buddies I have, anyone I know who's personally been caught in, near, or around a flash flood, those people are very, very, very, very, very gun-shy about ever even considering a canyon with even a 10 percent chance of rain in the forecast," Seeley says. "They just won't go. I think that's kind of a lesson to be learned. Really, the running joke is the canyon isn't going anywhere. It's been there typically for a couple hundred thousand years, so it'll be around next week, and next year, and the year after. The challenge comes in when you get into places like Zion with these permitting systems, and it's hard to get into some of these canyons, and now you have your permit, you won the lottery and you want to go. Now you're looking at the 20 percent chance or maybe even a 30 percent chance, it's a little more of a gray area sometimes."

As a professional guide, Seeley is always looking at exit points and safe spaces as he takes groups through canyon country, analyzing how they might get out in the event of an emergency. That's one thing he often notices in the amateurs he takes out; they aren't constantly scanning and looking for ways out. The reality sometimes is the less experienced you are, the more likely you are to be hyper-focused on the task at hand. More concerned, for example, with the rigging, your rope length, your harness and not really paying attention to the bigger picture. It makes sense—rope work at height can be dangerous and care is needed—but sometimes the minutiae distracts people from bigger issues.

At the end of the day, Seeley says, safety in flash flood comes down to knowing the terrain, understanding the flood risk, and knowing what potential hazards you are going to face when you head out. Preparation is about more than just gear and maps.

"No one would go into a canyon without enough rope," he says. "If they know the longest rappel is 100 feet, they're not going to go with twenty feet. That part people seem to really get, the nuts and bolts. But they tend to lose sight sometimes of the more abstract things. You have to really look at the big picture sometimes."

Lightning

Arizona isn't all hot and dry.

Humphrey's Peak, the state's highest point, is located near Flagstaff and rises to an elevation of 12,633 feet, placing it more in the category of Colorado's high peaks than the low hills and scrub trees that cover most of the Southwestern desert state. Capped with snow year-round, the peak rises more than 6,000 feet from the surrounding landscape, making it the twenty-sixth most prominent mountain in the lower 48 states, and a popular destination for climbers in the Kachina Peaks Wilderness Area.

Hikers, actually, because Humphrey's is also considered one of the easiest peaks to climb in the American West, calling for little more than an extended day hike to reach the summit. There is no technical climbing, no rock scrambling, and the hike itself is generally rated moderate to strenuous.

But, according to all reports, it's worth the effort. Arizona's "Little Colorado" boasts impressive views of the surrounding landscape from its summit, including the city of Flagstaff, the White Mountains, the north rim of the Grand Canyon, and even the Phoenix metro area in the distance. According to local lore, the mountain chain of which Humphrey's Peak is a part were named the "San Francisco Peaks" because it was rumored that climbers could see all the way to San Francisco, California, from the top of the range.

That rumor is certainly not true.

Still, the mountain and its evergreen forests remain an attractive backcountry destination for hikers and climbers from all over Arizona. The views are killer, the hike is pleasant—there are two main routes to the top, the low-grade Weatherford Trail, which was originally designed as a road for Model T drivers to take to the summit, and the primary Humphrey's Peak Trail, which heads up nearly five miles from the Arizona Snow Bowl—and the experience is unique in a part of the world that's better known as hot, dry, and flat.

Not to mention the fact that, in summer, when temperatures in the Phoenix area can reach well over 100 degrees Fahrenheit, the highs on the peak are far more pleasant. Snow is not uncommon.

And all this, just over two hours from Phoenix.

Certainly, that was one of the reasons that seventeen-year-old Wade Young, of Tempe near Phoenix, decided to go hiking on the peak with two friends in July 2016. The group had just graduated from high school and were celebrating some downtime when they reached the summit that hazy summer day, enjoying the break from the Arizona heat.

But cooler weather in the Southwest comes at a cost. Humphrey's Peak, given its prominence, is Arizona's most extreme weather area, a range that has seen as many as 100 lightning strikes in an hour-long period and frequently sees mid-summer squalls, despite calmer conditions down in the valley. Like most mountains, weather on the peak is bigger and more dangerous, and likely to strike at anytime, and inexperienced hikers can get caught unaware up high.

That's likely what happened to Young and his friends, who unknowingly hiked straight into one of the stronger monsoon storms to hit the region that summer. Once they reached the summit, they realized their mistake, taking advantage of the 360-degree Humphrey's Peak view to watch the storm roll in. The clouds were dark and angry, crackling with electricity and dumping heavy, cold rain. The hikers watched as lightning bolts flashed in the distance, coming closer.

Shortly before 1 p.m., they called 911 from the summit, asking authorities for help getting down in the midst of the storm. The peak is rocky and exposed, with no tree cover or other shelter, and lightning is a very real threat.

Rescuers struggled to reach them, pushed back by the bad weather, and didn't make it to the group until after 4 p.m.

They were too late.

Young was struck by lightning near the summit and later died of his injuries. His hiking companions, aged seventeen and eighteen, both survived but suffered from injuries that the Coconino County Sheriff's Office said "were likely received due to their proximity to the lightning strike." Both were able to walk off the peak, however.

It was a wild storm, but was par for the course for the peak, according to the National Weather Service. Later analysis found that there were 106 "on-the-ground" and 393 "cloud-to-cloud" lightning strikes in the area between noon and 1 p.m., when the group called 911, that day. By that point, the storm had already begun to move out.

"The onset of these storms rolls in quite rapidly," Darryl San Souci, the safety and occupational health officer at Coconino National Forest, told the *New York Daily News* after the incident. "What we tell people is be prepared before you go out and know what you need to have with you and what you need look for in case of a lightning situation."

Added spokesman Brady Smith: "You can't really predict when somebody is gonna be in a really bad situation, that's why we really harp upon knowing the conditions of where you're about to go."

Young, for his part, was remembered as an active, "happy go lucky" teen who was active in his school and was looking forward to attending college at Arizona State University in the fall. Friends commented that he was someone who was never scared to take on a new challenge, bringing a positive attitude to everything he did. He had recently been named "Tempe Top Teen" by the city's mayor in recognition for his work with local nonprofits and service organizations.

His former rugby coach said Young "got involved and . . . got off his butt and actually lived life. I think that every kid and every adult and every person out there just needs to remember that."

In this case, his death highlighted the fact that lightning simply does not discriminate—old or young, novice or experienced. As with all victims of lightning strike, and so many other backcountry accidents, Young was simply in the wrong place at the wrong time.

In a flash, it was all over.

* * *

According to the National Oceanic and Atmospheric Administration, thirty-eight people were killed by lightning in the United States in 2016, ranging from a Florida man who was struck while working in his yard to a woman in Alabama who was standing under a tree waiting out a storm. Fatal strikes happen all over the country and aren't clustered in any one region over another, which is one of the things that makes lightning dangerous.

There are no safe places. When you hear thunder, it's time to move to find shelter, because a storm is close enough to strike.

And 2016 was a fairly typical year for lightning-related fatalities. According to the National Weather Service, the United States has averaged forty-eight reported strike fatalities every year since the mid 1980s, though that number has been trending down in the last decade due to increased awareness and the simple fact that fewer people are spending significant time outside (thanks to new digital entertainment options and other distractions). Between 2006 and 2015, an average of thirty-one people were killed by lightning every year.

That's a rate of barely one fatality for every 1,000,000 people in the United States annually. And given that only 10 percent of lightning strike victims actually die from their injuries, that means about 300 people are struck each year in the United States. That's literally a one in a million chance in any given year.

Nearly 80 percent of all fatalities are men, and the peak months for lightning-related injuries and deaths coincide with the peak months for

There is no safe space outdoors in a lightning storm.

thunderstorm activity in the United States in general, July and August. This is also the time of year when people are more likely to be outside enjoying outdoor activities, so it's also when 70 percent of all lightning deaths occur. There is no age limit or minimum. In terms of demographics, fisherman have found to be more than four times more likely to be struck by lightning than golfers, who have long been considered to be at significant risk due to the fact that they can be caught out in the open area of a golf course with a bag full of metal sticks. From 2006 to 2015, thirty-three people died from lightning strike while fishing, seventeen while camping in the woods, fourteen while participating in some boating activity that was not fishing, thirteen while working in the yard, and eight while golfing. Ranch workers accounted for another sixteen deaths during that period.

(To drive these numbers to the ground, NWS data shows that the average person's odds of being struck at least once in an eighty-year life span is one in 13,000. And the odds of having someone in your life—friend, family member, or other acquaintance—are as low as one in 1,300.)

Not that lightning itself is even remotely that rare.

Worldwide, weather experts tell us that lightning strikes occur somewhere on the planet at least 100 times per second, and the average thunderstorm can produce thousands of lightning strikes per hour depending on the intensity of the storm. At any given moment, there are 1,800 active thunderstorms around the world, contributing to the 25 million cloud-to-ground lightning strikes measured in the United States alone each year.

What's more, lightning can strike as far as five to ten miles away from an active thunderstorm, delivering as much energy as a nuclear reactor and temperatures that can reach 50,000 degrees Fahrenheit.

Lightning is a massively destructive force that can literally be everywhere.

And, for those who like to explore the backcountry, that can be a good thing. There is no ambiguity here—we are all at risk. That said, lightning is a fairly predictable phenomenon and, provided we follow some basic precautions and best practices, lightning risk is fairly simple to mitigate.

To start, there are five ways that a person can be struck by lightning—directly by a bolt from cloud to body (which most often occurs in open areas like fields and parking lots), by a "side flash" when lightning strikes a tall object near where the person is located (such as when lightning strikes a tree and injures the person standing underneath it), by ground current (which is when electricity travels through the ground after a strike, potentially injuring someone far away from the strike, common in livestock), by conduction (which is when lightning travels through wires or other metal surfaces before finding a route to a victim, such as an electrical outlet in a home), and by what are known as "streamers" (which are a type of secondary lightning strike that occurs downstream of the primary strike when the main channel discharges along with other bolts).

With this information, we can infer some basic rules and precautions for instances when lightning is nearby.

- When you hear thunder or otherwise know that a thunderstorm is in the area, seek shelter immediately. Don't "wait it out," don't try to outrun it, just get inside or into a vehicle. According to the NWS, the majority of lightning-related fatalities occur to people who are in the process of seeking shelter or are nearly inside, but waited too long to act. Don't wait.
- Stay away from tall objects such as trees, flagpoles, cell phone towers, cranes, etc. during a thunderstorm, as they will likely attract lightning more than you alone will. You never want to be the tallest object in the area, but you don't want to be close to something taller either.
- Avoid open areas such as fields, instead seeking shelter among smaller trees or in low-lying areas.
- Bodies of water do not themselves attract lightning but can be excellent conductors of electricity, leading to secondary injuries. Steer clear of any water in a thunderstorm.

- Metal fencing, plumbing, and wiring can all conduct electricity over great distances, often further than you might expect, so stay far away from any metal if possible.
- Safe shelter from lightning generally means a house, garage, or other substantial structure. A tent, shed, or covered porch isn't enough as it won't provide protection from side strikes or other risk factors.

In truth, according to Dr. Joe Dwyer, a Professor of Physics and Space Sciences at Florida Institute of Technology and one of the world's leading experts on the physics of lightning strikes, lightning itself is little more than just a really, really (really, really) big spark of electricity, a very large electrical discharge.

"Most lightning starts inside thunderstorms and comes down to the ground," he says, "and when lightning strikes inside a thunderstorm most of it never leaves the storm. Maybe two thirds of it will stay up inside the thunderstorm and never come out of the cloud, so only a small fraction actually comes down to the ground."

What that means to us, he says, is that big, nasty black cloud over your head could be producing a lot of lightning well before it starts sending any to the ground. So just because you haven't seen a lightning bolt in your area yet doesn't mean there isn't any nearby lightning or no chance for it to start happening. In every thundercloud, the potential is there, even if you can't see it yet.

"You really have to pay attention to the weather," Dwyer says. "Are there thunderstorms in the area? Just stay alert. That's probably one of the most important things for lightning safety is to pay attention to your surroundings."

One myth that he is quick to dispel is that lightning never strikes the same place twice. Granted, exact strikes are uncommon, but lightning by its very nature tends to strike multiple times in the same area due to the way that electricity is conducted.

When lightning sends a bolt down to the ground, it carves a sort of conductive path between the cloud and the ground. Then, once it contacts the ground, it creates something like a short circuit between the cloud and the ground and you get a big rush of current. That is called the return stroke, and that is the bright part that we see as a lightning flash. It's a big rush of current, he explains, and it superheats the air to about 50,000 degrees Fahrenheit, which is about five times the surface temperature of the sun. This all causes the air in the immediate vicinity to rapidly expand, creating the thunder that we hear.

That's one strike.

But then, after the return stroke has reached the ground, unleashed all that force, and heated the air, the lightning will often send down another discharge in quick succession, called a "leader," down the channel it just created between the cloud and ground, recharging the channel and delivering a subsequent strike. You'll see another "short circuit," another rush of current and another return stroke, meeting the ground not far from where the first strike occurred. This process can repeat over and over again—a leader down the channel, another a return stroke; another leader down the channel, another return stroke, and on and on—and that's what causes lightning to flicker when viewed from a distance. It is a series of strikes, a flurry of them, instead of just one at a time.

"It's usually to the same location or close to the same location," Dwyer says, "though it doesn't always have to be. But often it'll be just sort of recharging the channel. You'll get a strike, the channel will start to cool and the current will die off, and then the lightning will send down another leader down the preexisting channel because it's kind of like an easy path. And that'll just repeat the process. For the subsequent strikes it doesn't have to completely re-break down the air, it can just follow the warm channel."

Whatever form the lightning's behavior takes, the discharge that it delivers is more than enough to kill you many times over. According to Dr. Dwyer, the current that rushes along the channel with each strike can easily exceed 30,000 amps of current. Considering that only a fraction of one amp is enough to kill the average healthy adult, the scale of destruction that's possible here is clear. There are very large currents and voltages involved here, and given that fact you don't even need to be directly struck by lightning to be hurt or killed by lightning. If you're standing next to a tree and it is struck there will be a lot of current flowing to the ground, and that current can find its way into your body by going up one leg and down the other. Or there might even be sparks jumping off the sides of the tree as the lightning strikes it, jumping over to hit you at the same time. There are many different ways that lightning can spread and inflict damage on the area surrounding a strike, so that's why you never want to be near anything that's likely to be struck by lightning during a thunderstorm, including trees, metal poles, and other tall, conductive objects.

The general rule for lightning safety, Dwyer explains, is that if you hear thunder, it's time to go inside. If you can actually hear thunder, then you're roughly close enough for the lightning to hurt you, so it's a good idea to go inside at that point. And in this case, "inside" would be a house or an enclosed structure, such as a car with a metal roof if you can't truly get inside. Then once you're inside, don't do anything to put yourself in electrical contact with the outside world. Avoid coming in contact with plumbing, or a phone that has a cord that plugs into the wall, anything where a wire or a metal pipe could connect to the outside world. And stay inside until thirty minutes after you hear the thunder and after the storm ends because sometimes thunderstorms will save up a real big one at the end and people go outside too early and get hurt.

Lightning isn't something you can remotely play chicken with, so whenever the conditions are right for a strike—a thunderstorm in the area is the primary risk factor—then it's time to take steps to mitigate that risk.

"There's really no safe place outside," Dr. Dwyer says. "Lightning is dangerous and there's no safe place from lightning outside. If you're inside in a closed structure, like a house or a building, then that's relatively safe, but if you're outside there's really no way to ensure your safety. There's things you can do to reduce the risk slightly, but there's no place that's really safe. Some places are more dangerous, like next to trees, but there's no place you can go, 'Okay, here I'm safe.'"

Wildfire

No one ever expected the fire to grow so fast, or get so big.

When a lightning strike started a brush fire on Bureau of Land Management land northwest of Phoenix on June 28, 2013, near the small town of Yarnell, Arizona, it was similar to the kind of fires that start all over the Western United States every year. Wildfire is a part of life in this part of the country, started by everything from lightning strikes to careless campers, and firefighters know the risks that come with working in the desert Southwest. Still, isolated, remote, and relatively small to start at less than 300 acres, what would become known as the Yarnell Hill Fire smoldered in the wilderness for a couple of days, watched by firefighters and locals but not particularly worried.

Things changed two days later, on June 30, when high winds kicked up, pushing the fire to more than 2,000 acres, turning what had been a midsized summer wildfire into a raging inferno, fed by both the persistent winds as well as acres of ready fuel thanks to the long-term drought that had been affecting the area. Temperatures that were hovering over 100 degrees Fahrenheit didn't help either.

The conditions were perfect for a monster wildfire. And that's exactly what happened.

State officials shut down twenty-five miles of Route 89 near the fire, evacuated the town of Yarnell, and issued mandatory evacuation orders for the surrounding canyon country. Hundreds of people were displaced, spending nights on the floors of high school gyms and relying on the Red Cross for aid.

And yet the fire kept coming. Days after it began, the Yarnell Hill Fire had grown to a staggering 8,300 acres and, even as late as July 2, was still largely uncontrolled. A day later, little change. It wasn't until July 10, a full twelve days after the fire started, that officials declared the fire 100 percent contained and allowed all local residents in to survey the damage.

All told, the fire destroyed 109 homes, partially damaging twenty-three others. Containment costs were later estimated at more than $4.1 million, going for aircraft support, camp support, equipment, and firefighting personnel.

But the Yarnell Hill Fire will always be remembered not for the insurance losses but for the nineteen firefighters who died in the line of duty while working to contain the blaze.

All were members of the Granite Mountain Hotshots, a highly trained group of professional backcountry firefighters who made their living fighting wildfires on the ground in places where many fear to tread. Operating in remote areas, they often have to hike their gear miles into the scene and work right in the face of the fire, cutting back brush, digging containment trenches and taking on the tough, physical work of fighting a wildfire.

That's what they were doing the morning of June 30, after the group was called in to assist with what was, at that point, a fire that was raging effectively out of control with almost no containment. According to the State of Arizona's Serious Accident Investigation Report, issued months after the incident, the Hotshots were deployed west of the town of Yarnell, fighting the fire as it moved northeast toward Model Creek and Peeples Valley, both of which had been evacuated by that point. The area is dry and rocky, typical of central Arizona, and is contoured with both hills and canyons. The firefighters eventually ended up on a ridge to the north of Route 89.

But then the winds shifted in the mid-afternoon, pushing the fire suddenly to the southeast and back toward Yarnell. Other fire teams were evacuated, leaving only the Granite Mountain team out on the fire line, stuck on the ridge in the face of a rapidly advancing fire. According to the state report, the team was in communication with fire management personnel at this point, telling them that the ridge they were standing on was "in the black"—had been burned—and assumed they were to stay there and fight.

But that didn't happen.

Officials lost contact with the crew for approximately thirty minutes following the turn of the fire, and there is still much that is not known about the team's actions in their final minutes or why they made the decisions that they did.

What we do know is that the Hotshots left the ridge, leaving "the black" and moving southeast, away from the oncoming fire through an unburned area. It is believed that they were heading toward an established safety zone at the Boulder Springs Ranch near Route 89. But rising winds kicked up the fire even more in a wide, swirling inferno, trapping the team between the ranch and the canyon rim. They had no choice but to seek the only safety they had.

Experts later estimated that the Hotshots had less than two minutes to deploy their fire shelters and dig down before the face of the fire was on top of them. They were still in the process of setting up the shelters when their position on the side of a small hill was overrun with temperatures in excess of 2,000 degrees Fahrenheit. Per the state's report: "The deployment site was not survivable."

The Granite Mountain Hotshots were approximately one mile southeast of their last known position and barely 600 yards from the relative safety of the ranch.

The Yarnell Hill Fire marked the deadliest wildland firefighter incident since the 1933 Griffith Park Fire in Los Angeles killed twenty-nine firefighters, and the deadliest day for US firefighters since September 11, 2001. It is the sixth-deadliest incident involving firefighters and the third-deadliest wildfire on record.

One member of the Hotshots, twenty-one-year-old Brendan McDonough, survived the day, serving as a lookout on the edge of the ridge site.

Two weeks later, he was on hand to read the Hot Shot's Prayer at the joint memorial service for his nineteen fallen comrades, a moment that Ray Bizal, the Southwest Regional Director of the National Fire Protection Association, who was in attendance, called particularly touching.

"As their watch, he gave them the evacuation order when the wind changed so quickly," Bizal wrote after the service. "Unfortunately, they were unable to escape. He is a brave man and a wonderful soul to have been able to say the prayer at this memorial. I cannot imagine what he is going through. His character is not being defined by the crisis he endured; his character is being defined by his tremendous reaction to that crisis. It was a moving gesture."

* * *

According to *National Geographic*, wildfires are actually far more common than many people realize. Every year, more than 100,000 wildfires on average burn some five million acres of land in the United States, with particularly bad years reaching nearly 10 million acres. The vast majority—four out of five—of these fires are started by human activities.

So it's a big problem.

But it's something of an oversimplification to say that wildfires—a term that includes forest fires, grassfires, wildland fires, and any other uncontrolled blazes fueled by weather, wind, and dry underbrush—are only the result of human carelessness. It's important to remember as well that fire, as a phenomenon, is a 100 percent natural process and is something that happens all over the world, whether humans are involved or not. Natural burns, caused by lightning strikes or other events, are part of the cycle of life, removing dead plant and animal matter and converting it back into fertile soil that the next generation of plants and animals can use to grow and thrive, before the whole cycle starts over again.

That's why the natural world is so good at catching and perpetuating wildfires.

Hot weather and drought dries out trees and plants, turning what might have been healthy, green vegetation into a literal tinderbox capable of catching fire at the slightest provocation. And as if that weren't enough, strong winds are common in the dry fire season in much of the United States, usually the late summer when the weather is driest, providing plenty of oxygen to stoke fires and energy to spread them far and wide. All of this contributes to an environment where, even if 80 percent of fires weren't being caused by humans, a full 20 percent, or 20,000 fires, would happen naturally in this country every year.

When the conditions are right, when it's hot enough, dry enough, and windy enough, all it takes is one small spark from a campfire, a carelessly tossed cigarette butt, a lightning strike, or downed power line to set off a chain reaction that turns into a deadly wildfire.

Firefighters explain that wildfires need three things to burn: fuel, oxygen, and a heat source. The fuel is easy, as any flammable material—from dry grass, to tree branches, to homes—will do, and the more fuel sources that are available in a given area, the hotter and more intensely the fire will burn there. The oxygen a fire needs comes from the air, so windy, blustery conditions can not only help to spread a fire but the ample oxygen they deliver can help stoke the fire hotter and stronger along the way. And the heat source is the spark, whatever it is that makes contact with the fuel source and starts it to burn.

That's a very high-level overview of the conditions that cause wildfires, but the proof of the destructive capabilities of these events is in the historical record itself. And, while the Yarnell Hill Fire was a tragedy of historic proportions, it was far from the largest or most destructive wildfire ever seen in North America. It turned deadly due to the landscape where it was burning and the specific conditions that trapped the Hotshots in the middle of it, but in terms of sheer scale it is difficult to top the series of wildland fires that struck Manitoba, Canada, in the summer of 1989. In total, the fires burned more than eight million acres in central and northern Manitoba, forcing the evacuation of more than 24,000 people and destroying hundreds of structures. In the United States, the Great Fire of 1910 burned more than three million across Idaho, Montana, and Washington, killing eighty-six people. More recently, the 2008 fires on California's central coast, including parts of Santa Barbara, burned more than 1.5 million acres due to extreme drought conditions in the state.

But size is not often a good judge of a wildfire's destructive capacity. Rather, fires that occur in densely populated areas—like the

Oakland "Firestorm of 1991," which burned just 1,500 acres in the hills around Oakland and Berkeley, California, but destroyed 3,500 homes and structures and killed twenty-five people, making it the deadliest and costliest wildfire in US history—are the ones that go down in the record books.

Although wildland fires are a fact of life across the state of Colorado in the summer, two recent fires near the city of Colorado Springs stand out due to the fact that they struck urban areas and did widespread damage to life and property. In 2012, the Waldo Canyon Fire, located a few miles west of the city, burned for two weeks and did more than $450 million in insured damage. It was the most destructive fire in Colorado history for barely a year, when the Black Forest Fire broke out in a heavily wooded area on the plains north of Colorado Springs, an unusual landscape for the area, destroying nearly 500 homes and doing hundreds of millions in damages.

According to the Insurance Information Institute, the 2015 fire season set a new record for the total number of recorded wildland fires in the United States, with 68,151 fires consuming more than 10 million acres of land. That was a big jump from 2014 when a similar number of total recorded fires consumed just 3.5 million acres.

The insured losses of wildfires, and the damage they can do to homes and structures, is not much of a concern in the backcountry, where wildfires do plenty of damage every year that goes completely and entirely unreported. Although it is truly horrible to lose a home to wildfire, for those who ever get caught in the path of an out of control wildland fire while in the woods themselves, the risk scenario is quite a bit different.

A full-scale wildfire can move as fast as 14 miles per hour, according to the National Interagency Fire Center, and burn hot enough to destroy almost everything in its path, including trees, roads, shelters, and more. They can be miles wide, marching steadily in one direction, or swinging wildly from one direction to the next depending on the prevailing winds.

Fire can move faster than many expect, jumping ridges and fire lines and threatening more than just the property that stands in its path.

The point is, wildland fires are fast, strong, and unpredictable. Three words that no one wants to hear when they are alone in the backcountry or on foot. Escape from a fast-moving fire is possible, but their unpredictability puts a lot of variables at play and makes the entire scenario far more dangerous than it might otherwise be.

"I have been working here for fifteen years, and there is no more 'wildfire season,'" says Michele Steinberg, manager of the National Fire Protection Association's (NFPA) Wildland Fire Operations division in Quincy, Massachusetts. "It isn't nearly as long-term predictable as it used to be, and a lot of times it's very surprising. You look at the predictions and you think, 'Really, at this time of the year, this is happening, in this location?'"

But it's true, wildfires are now happening year-round and in areas that, until recently, would have been considered fairly safe. Steinberg herself was in South Florida one recent March, beautiful weather, 75 degrees. But it was also very windy and dry; good fire weather. Sure enough, one day driving to lunch she turned a corner and saw a giant plume of smoke rising from some uninhabited utility easement land area near West Palm Beach, what turned out to be an eighty-acre brush fire.

"Fire is really, extremely situational," she says. "That's why it's very hard for us to say, blanket statement, do this because everybody's in a different situation. Under, for example, some of these western fires, you can see this thing coming for days. So people know this is coming, they're watching the behavior, they've got time to get ready. They probably have their plan ready to go stay at Grandma's house or something or at the hotel in the next town. There's behavior that lets you plan, and then there's behavior that doesn't let you plan."

That's why awareness and preplanning is critical, she says. Anyone who is living in a rural area that is prone to fire should know how to protect their home and get out in the case of an emergency. But, more than that, they should also know what fire conditions and "fire weather" look and feel like—as in Steinberg's trip to Florida, warm, dry, and windy weather can do it, and it doesn't take much to start a fire, just a spark or stray ember is enough. And that ignition can be enough to start a raging wildfire pretty easily under the right conditions.

Awareness is something that many people struggle with, Steinberg says, and part of that is due to the fact that so many of us now live in urban and suburban areas where wildfires simply aren't common so we often don't think about them, even when we're out in more fire-prone rural areas. People who are typically used to suburban living, for example, might see a plume of smoke and think it's just a smokestack or car fire, never even thinking about wildfire as a possibility.

"Just being aware," Steinberg explains, "and knowing, OK, these are the kinds of conditions where you want to behave so that you're not starting a fire. But also when you're in an area that's prone to fire, it's a real good idea to take a look at that and be aware of the risk factors."

Even the most basic precautions can be lifesaving, because wildfire is fast moving and devastating, one of the most dangerous situations to be caught on foot in the outdoors. The reason for that is that the fire itself isn't usually what kills. It's the suffocating gas that does the damage, and it can reach victims well ahead of the flames themselves. When you're outside, on foot, you're completely unprotected and unable to escape this invisible threat. Smoke is the other big threat, especially for those who are driving near a wildfire, because if you can't see where you're going you can become overwhelmed with gas and smoke even inside your car.

"The advice that we've gotten from people who are caught in that situation, and these are usually wildland firefighters or people who are out working a fire or doing a prescribed burn, is that if the wind changes and the fire's heading toward them is to basically get in a ditch if they can, to get down below the surface," Steinberg says. "As the flames pass over you, as the wind is pushing them past you, you're more likely to suffer some kind of burn to your back or something like that, but you don't want to inhale the gasses and you don't want to burn your face."

She says she's even heard stories of people saving their own lives by diving into water and staying submerged as the fire passes over them. Obviously, that's not something that you can sustain for very long, but in some cases a short period is all it takes for the danger to pass, particularly when the wind is pushing the fire through very rapidly. Since fire needs fuel and oxygen and heat to burn, once it runs out of fuel it will simply stop, so there are often situations where a wildfire will sweep through an area and not stop in one place for a long time burning.

Still, the risk of death is very real. Shortly before I spoke with Steinberg, a large grassfire had swept through parts of Texas, Oklahoma, and Kansas, killing four people who ventured out into the fields to save their livestock and were overcome before they could get out. Fire moves through grass very fast and, while it may not seem as dangerous or intense as a big "crown fire" in a forest, grassfires can be very deadly for people who get caught in them.

Her advice for dealing with wildfire is simple: don't wait.

If you see or smell smoke, don't wait around too long. Find out what's going on, contact the local law enforcement and fire authorities, and get out if advised. "Social scientists have looked at what people do in terms of an evacuation—what is their intent to evacuate, and then what do they actually do? Unfortunately, what a lot of people do is wait and see what their neighbors are going to do. When you're in a community where you may not have a whole lot of egress out of the community in a quick fashion, like you've got one road and it's up a steep hill or down a steep hill, you don't want to be waiting around because it runs into a situation where by the time you are afraid and you want to get out it's going to be too late for you to do that safely."

Also, those people that we all hear about who stay behind and defend their homes are usually very experienced firefighters or retired firefighters. They aren't amateurs. Most people really don't have the wherewithal to do what they would need to do, and it's much more dangerous for them to stay in place than to move somewhere else while the fire passes through.

"I think that, again, that wait-and-see attitude that as human beings serves us so well in other situations, doesn't serve us well in the case of wildfire," Steinberg says. "Basically, my rule of thumb is, if you're nervous about it, go. Pack your stuff and go. You're no hero for staying."

Blizzard

For me personally, the danger of whiteout winter conditions struck home not in the wilderness but in my car, sitting in I-70 traffic after a day of skiing in the Colorado High Country. It was a bright, sunny day, but somehow I had forgotten to bring my ski goggles and ended up spending the whole day in my sunglasses, which weren't polarized to protect against glare and didn't offer full coverage.

Big mistake.

After six hours on the snow, I was nearly snow-blind, with bright "lights" obscuring much of my field of vision even after I left the resort. It was as if I had spent the day staring at a light bulb—I was left with minor damage that my eye doctor later confirmed was due to excessive light exposure from the sunlight reflecting off the snow. Small comfort that also hurt my ego: it commonly happens to newbie skiers in the

Rockies, where snow and sun often coexist. For me, the problem got so bad that I eventually had to pull off and wait in a coffee shop for a few hours until my vision returned to normal.

No fun at all, but snow blindness is pretty much the best-case scenario for someone in blizzard conditions. Getting lost, falling victim to exposure, avalanche, being crushed by falling branches—the risks of backcountry travel in extreme winter weather are as numerous as they are deadly.

A group of hikers on Washington State's Mount Rainier in 2008 found out the hard way when they were trapped by a blizzard near the summit of the 14,409-foot peak.

In June.

On a mountain known for its erratic weather patterns, the three were hiking down from Camp Muir near 10,000 feet to the Paradise Glacier when they were caught in the middle of a blinding snowstorm that eventually dumped more than two feet of snow on the mountain in less than twenty-four hours.

The group was equipped for the weather—the summit of Mount Rainier is snow-covered year-round, and the hikers were experienced in glacier travel—but the ferocity of the storm caught them by surprise and quickly left them disoriented. The trail down crosses several snow-fields and can be difficult to follow even in the best of conditions, so the group decided to turn around and head back up to the relative safety of Camp Muir before they got into real trouble.

One of the three didn't make it.

Established in 1921, Camp Muir is a high-altitude camp that's most often used by climbers who are attempting to reach the summit of the peak. It consists of two structures—a public shelter and another specifically for guides—that are both small stone buildings with pit toilets and other basic services. Although the camp isn't maintained as a lodge, during the climbing season it is often crowded with climbers preparing to make their summit attempts or resting while on the way back down to the parking lot. For climbers caught in Rainier's unpredictable weather, it is often a shelter of last resort.

For the three hikers that June day, the visibility and winds got so bad that they were unable to go down or up, unsure of where the trail was or where they had come from. On top of that, the rapidly falling snow made travel difficult, preventing their eventual helicopter rescue team from reaching them for more than twelve hours.

One of the survivors later reported fighting his way through snow drifts as tall as five feet as he fought to get back to Camp Muir for help. Once he made it to safety, he led rangers back down to the other two members of his party and they were helped up to the shelter in sleds. The injured hiker—the husband of one of the survivors—was brought into camp alive, but could not be revived before rescuers could arrive to evacuate him to a nearby hospital.

According to the National Parks Services, there have been 421 fatalities on Mount Rainier as of 2016, though of course not all of them are related to severe winter weather.

Once you're lost and exposed to the elements, and can't get out, the risk factor in a blizzard goes up exponentially.

The 2008 incident highlighted the risks of climbing on Rainier, but it is far from the only blizzard-related fatality on the mountain in recent years. The climb's popularity, and its proximity to millions of potential visitors in nearby Seattle, makes for a crowded, popular destination that can easily turn deadly.

"That dayhike in good conditions can be done in shorts—it's really a great hike, but when conditions turn bad, it can turn deadly," local guide Pete Whittaker, the co-owner of Rainier Mountaineering, told *Backpacker* magazine after the incident. "There's more people who have gotten in trouble and killed between Paradise and Muir than higher up on the mountain. Because it's a great hike and so many do it, there's potential for a weather event to come in and cause trouble. Above six to seven thousand feet it can snow in any month of the year."

For example, the same thing effectively happened in March 2016 when two climbers and a snowshoer were caught in a very similar blizzard on the mountain, above Camp Muir near the Gibraltar Ledges section near the summer. A fifty-eight-year-old Norwegian climber died of hypothermia in that incident, after his group was caught out in the storm on their way to the summit and eventually had to spend a night on the mountain. Conditions proved too dangerous for a helicopter rescue the next day, and two of the three eventually made it back down to Camp Muir under their own power where they were treated and evacuated.

And they weren't the only climbers to get in trouble on Rainier during that specific snowstorm. Another snowshoer, a twenty-six-year-old man, got lost in the blizzard that night also, switching on his locator beacon so that rangers could track him as he made his way through the storm. Authorities had no way to reach him either, but were able to confirm his arrival at Camp Muir the next day, suffering from little more than frostbite.

* * *

According to the National Weather Service, a blizzard is any winter weather event that delivers sustained winds (or gusts) of 35 miles per hour combined with "considerable" falling and blowing snow for three hours or more. The general criteria that separates blizzards from more typical snowstorms is the lack of visibility, generally down to a quarter mile or less, due to the blowing, swirling snow. A "severe blizzard," per the NWS, has winds of more than 45 miles per hour, temperatures at 10 degrees Fahrenheit or lower and near zero visibility, while a "ground blizzard" is a storm that meets the wind requirement for a blizzard but doesn't have any falling snow, just snow that is being picked up off the ground and blown around, creating whiteout conditions.

None of these storms are any fun to be out in and, given the impact on visibility and travel, they are capable of crippling entire metro areas for days at a time. The Blizzard of 1888, for instance, all but shut down the Northeastern United States, killing 400 people between New York City and Boston, sinking 200 ships, and burying parts of Brooklyn under fifty-two-foot snowdrifts.

These storms have a tendency to make history when they strike major cities—in addition to the 1888 event above, who could forget the Southeast's 1993 "Storm of the Century" or "Snowmaggedon," a Nor'easter that buried most of the Washington, DC, metro area in up to three feet of snow—causing widespread power outages, inconveniences and, sometimes, deaths. But it is in the backcountry that blizzards can cause real trouble for those who get caught out in them. That's because not only do they often result in significant snowfall but whiteout conditions make travel very difficult and dangerous in the outdoors. You don't know where you are, you're not sure where you're heading and, often, many of the landmarks you might use for navigation are obscured by the weather. Getting out is, at least for the duration of the storm, effectively impossible without getting lost.

Without navigation aids, staying put is the only intelligent option, and that's where the trouble can start.

"If I go for the worst case scenario and just say I don't know exactly where I am, so I can't use my map and compass and my GPS is dying, and if I really have no way to navigate out the first thing I'm going to do is try and make sure that I'm in a safest zone as possible," says

International Mountain Guides' Robert Jantzen. "That's going to include seeing whether I need to find a way to make a shelter or dig a snow cave to get out of the wind. Get myself ready to hunker down. Once I have figured out what's the safest position I can put myself in, I'm just going to stay put."

In this scenario, the best move is to create a safe space to wait out the storm with as many resources—food, water, warm clothes, matches, gear, etc.—as you can find until the weather clears up. The trick, he says, is having the wherewithal to actually stay in your shelter until it is safe to leave and not venturing out early.

"In a whiteout it's very common to just literally walk in circles," Jantzen says, "especially if it's a flat terrain. Or you're inevitably going to slowly trend downhill into whatever valley, slough, and whatever the low point around you is. Oftentimes that's a collection zone for avalanche debris, for rock fall, and that kind of stuff. If I had no navigation, I would get myself to as good a position as possible, and stay put."

On Mount Rainier, where Jantzen works as a climbing guide, it is very common for weather to roll in and for visibility to drop to less than ten to twenty feet very quickly. In those cases, it's vitally important, for guides and everyone else, to maintain good awareness of where they are on the hill at all times and where they are going. That way, in the event of a storm, they can locate themselves on the map and use a compass to guide their descent. When conditions get too bad, the rule on the mountain is to hunker down and wait it out.

That said, Jantzen never leaves on a climb or hike without bringing along his GPS to lay a track for him to follow back in the event of an emergency. Even many of today's smartphones, including the iPhone and many Android models, come bundled with functional GPS tools that, in partnership with basic navigation apps, can provide navigation help in a pinch. The problem is many people still don't know that the technology is available in their pocket right now and, if they do, how to use it in the backcountry.

"Definitely take the tools that will help you get out of a worst-case scenario," he says. "Now, once you've got those tools, great, put them in your pack and use common sense and situational awareness to make sure you never have to dig them out."

There's no reason not to take them, he says. They don't weight much, they're pretty reliable, and even carrying extra batteries isn't going to weigh your pack down too much. And, when used in partnership with a standard map and compass, you can generally pinpoint your location anywhere on the planet within a reasonable margin of error. (As of 2017, the US government rated smartphone GPS receivers as accurate down to about a 16-foot radius. Higher-end, standalone GPS devices can cut that accuracy down to less than half that.)

And, in a whiteout or blizzard, knowing where you are is critical.

"I'd be happy if I never have to dig out my GPS again," Jantzen says, "because that meant I've been paying close enough attention to know exactly what's going on at all times. But I'm always going to take it."

CHAPTER 5

Injury/Illness

Frostbite

Topping out at a staggering 29,029 feet, the summit of Mount Everest in Nepal is the highest point on Earth and a justifiably inhospitable place where oxygen is scarce and survival is a constant struggle.

At more than five miles above sea level, the air at the summit of Everest has less than one-third as much oxygen as the rest of us enjoy down here at more sane elevations, giving the nickname for the top section of the mountain above 28,000 feet—the Death Zone—very literal implications. Above that point, the body uses oxygen up faster than it can replenish it from the atmosphere, and no amount of training or acclimatization can make up for it. Guides in the high peaks put a time limit on the Death Zone, never more than forty-eight hours. Even within that window, however, it's common for climbers in the thin air to exhibit unusual behavior, ranging from confusion to hallucinations and outright dangerous errors such as stripping off all their clothing in the subzero conditions.

The terrain at the top of the world is also harsh and unforgiving, a challenging climb even for experts at sea level. Since Edmund Hillary and Tenzing Norgay first summited Everest in 1953, about 4,000 people have climbed the mountain, and close to 300 have died in the effort.

Overall, for every ten climbers that reach the summit, one doesn't make it home.

On top of all this is the weather, with temperatures that never get above freezing and wild weather is the norm even in the best of times. In fact, temperatures on the mountain average −19 Celsius in the summer and −36 Celsius in the winter.

That's why most Everest climbers, even as far back as the Hillary and Norgay climb in 1953, attempt the mountain in May, when the weather is somewhat more predictable and the temperatures are comparatively warmer. Today, some 800 climbers take on the mountain every year, and almost all of them are there in May for the same reasons.

"Mount Everest protrudes into the stratosphere, and most of the year the summit is buffeted by winds of over 100 miles per hour that will kill a climber in minutes or even hurtle them into the void," geographer John All told *Popular Mechanics* magazine in 2012 after three climbers died on the mountain during a two-day stretch. "It is only during the onset or cession of the Asian Monsoon that these winds die down and allow climbers short seven- to ten-day windows to climb the mountain."

The winds, which can reach speeds of 175 mph, typically die down every year in May and September. Since it's usually snowing heavily on Everest in September, May is the window that makes the most sense. The conditions are marginally better, it's true, but the focus on May creates other unforeseen problems.

Less than 200 feet from the summit, on the most popular Southeast route, there is a forty-foot vertical rock wall called the Hillary step, named after the famous first person to summit the mountain. Although the climb itself up until that point is long and challenging, the step is generally considered the most difficult part of the route and the only section that calls for technical climbing skills. Unlike the long hike that is the rest of the approach, the Hillary Step requires climbers to work like they would in a climbing gym—in full alpine gear—to scale the vertical rock face.

Naturally, it takes some time to navigate this section safely. It isn't impossible, it's just a challenge.

Add in the fact that many of the 800 annual climbers on Everest these days are less experienced guide clients, rather than experienced professional climbers, and you've got the potential for waits at the bottom (and top) of the Hillary Step that can stretch for hours. So, on a typical May summit day, you've got hundreds of climbers sitting around, waiting in line for a space to open up so they can make their own push to the summit. This backlog turns what could be an eight-hour climb into a maddeningly long day that can stretch up to twenty-four hours.

That's a lot of exposure. A lot of time in the Death Zone—and a lot of time for things to go wrong.

And that's exactly what happened in 2016, when four climbers died on the summit push, during a stretch when 400 people reached the summit. One victim, a Sherpa, fell while fixing routes for the climb, while the other three, two Dutch nationals and a climber from India, succumbed to altitude sickness.

In addition to the fatalities, though, the crowding on the mountain that May revealed another of the risk factors for climbers on the rooftop of the world: frostbite. Although not typically fatal on its own, frostbite—which is technically a burn of skin and tissue caused by deep frozen temperatures—can be a debilitating injury in the backcountry that both makes other tasks far more difficult (for example, it can be all but impossible to zip up a jacket or set up a shelter with frostbitten fingers) and also opens up the victim to other injury.

Sitting around in freezing temperatures is effectively risk factor number one for frostbite.

And that's why, in addition to the four fatalities that weekend in May 2016, scores of other climbers ended up in the hospital after the fact with severe frostbite, many left scarred for life.

An official, Ang Tshering, of the Nepal Mountaineering Association, blamed the accident on poor planning on the part of the guide services, telling reporters from the Associated Press that overcrowding and bottlenecks on the mountain caused unacceptable delays that left climbers too exposed for too long.

"This was a man-made disaster that may have been minimized with better management of the teams," he said, referencing the avalanche-related fatalities that occurred on Everest during the 2015 and 2016 seasons. "The last two disasters on Everest were caused by nature, but not this one."

* * *

Frostbite is an injury caused when a person's skin or tissues literally freeze from exposure to extreme cold conditions. It most often occurs on parts of the body that are typically exposed to the elements—cheeks, ears, the nose and chin, etc.—but can also be quite destructive to extremities like fingers and toes, sometimes even forcing amputations. Any skin that is exposed to cold, windy conditions—exactly the kind of weather you'd expect to encounter high on a mountain ridge, for example—is at risk of developing frostbite, but even protected areas are at risk if the conditions are bad enough and the exposure is long enough.

The condition comes in two different flavors: frostnip and true frostbite.

Frostnip is the milder version of the two and is the first stage in the development of frostbite. It starts the same way—the skin becomes cold and red, then goes numb and hard to the touch. In the case of frostnip, it appears very mildly white and you lose all feeling in the immediate area. The good news is that frostnip can be treated with general first aid, including slowly warming the affected area, and doesn't usually result in any serious skin damage. Medical attention is normally not even required.

If the victim treats their frostbite early on in this process, between the frostnip and deep frostbite stages when the frostbite is still superficial, the skin will often end up with deep blue and purple blisters, sometimes filled with fluid.

It's when things progress to true, deep frostbite that the real trouble starts.

When skin and tissue freeze to the degree that they are classified as frostbite, you're dealing with the possibility of permanent skin damage, or damage to muscles, bones, and other systems. The complications at this point can include everything from nerve damage, to bone fractures, to severe infections, all from what is, at its core, a very simple injury. At this stage, the skin and all the tissues beneath it are frozen solid and the end result, after warming, is tissue death.

It doesn't take long to get to this stage, either. Anyone who has ever tried to watch water as it freezes into ice—which is not recommended, as it is roughly the same as watching water boil—the freezing process is slow at first, but builds upon itself over time. To use the ice cube analogy again, sometimes you can pull the tray out of the freezer after about an hour or so and you'll probably see some ice forming around the edge of each cube. Maybe there will be a thin layer of ice on top, with just the core liquid left. Whatever the case, water freezes from the outside in, and as the overall temperature of the water drops, ice begins to form faster and faster until the entire thing is a solid block.

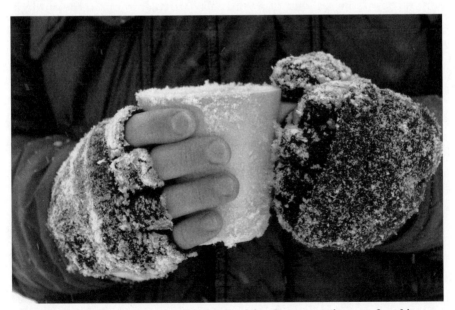

Most commonly associated with high-altitude mountaineers, frostbite can strike in the cold at any time, doing serious damage.

It's the same with our bodies. At first the skin will be cold; maybe it will go numb. From there, it turns red and warm—almost as if the cold is burning the skin, which in a way it is—before turning an unpleasant pale-white shade and taking on a hard or waxy look. At this point, the skin is frozen, and as the freeze deepens into our bodies, spreading to include the surrounding tissue, the skin will often turn black and blister. This is what causes the telltale black nose and cheeks of the injured mountaineer. If frostbite progresses into the realm of hypothermia, fever, slurred speech, drowsiness, and loss of coordination add to the mix.

The real fun part is that, since the skin goes numb fairly early in the process of developing frostbite, many people don't even realize they have it until someone else points it out to them. The numbness prevents them from feeling any of the very real pain that's associated with frozen tissue.

Given that there is effectively one treatment for frostbite, no matter how severe, and that is rewarming, either under a doctor's supervision or on your own, the real question with this particular injury in the outdoors is how to avoid it in the first place. As with most of the risk factors in this book, a little common sense goes a long way, but, particularly for mountaineers, frostbite is a particular risk in the outdoors no matter what preventative measures they take.

Stay Out of the Cold: Windy, cold conditions are what cause frostbite to form, so the near-universal advice for avoiding the injury is not to go out in that type of weather in the first place. This is where things get tricky, because you're never going to reach the summit of Mount Everest, Pike's Peak, or any other significant mountain without venturing out into cold, windy conditions. It's a simple fact of nature. That said, if you're going to be out in it, at least come armed with the knowledge of what causes frostbite and what you should avoid. The general wisdom is that the risk goes up as the temperatures go down, even with mild winds, and anything near zero Fahrenheit ticks up your risk substantially. According to the National Weather Service, a wind chill of −16.6 Fahrenheit can cause frostbite on exposed skin in less than thirty minutes. Drop that wind chill slightly to −20 Fahrenheit and frostbite appears in less than fifteen minutes.

Cover Up: Whenever venturing out into cold, windy conditions for any length of time, it is always important to wear protective clothing that's appropriate for the conditions. Jackets, pants, gloves and a hat that are rated for deep cold are required, as is protection from wet weather if that is a risk as well. For instance, a high-loft down jacket can keep the wearer warm and safe well below freezing, but as soon as it gets wet and loses its loft, it becomes effectively worthless, little more than a nylon windbreaker. Also keep in mind that tight-fitting winter clothing cannot keep the body as warm as properly fitted pieces can, because these hats, gloves, etc. need that void space between the body and the down to maintain warmth. And this should be common sense, but don't take off these items for long when you're out in the elements. As shown above, it doesn't take long for frostbite to strike.

Watch What You Touch: Up until now, we've discussed frostbite primarily as something that is caused by skin exposure to extreme cold, but direct contact with cold items—ice, frozen metal, etc.—can also cause the injury. For the most part, it's easy to avoid touching cold objects as long as you're wearing proper gloves, but this risk goes up sharply when, for instance, you're setting up a tent, working with stakes, or doing other chores around camp without your gloves on. Just like the flagpole in *A Christmas Story,* cold metal burns and skin can very easily be burned by it. The same applies to cold liquids, plastics, and anything that's left out in the extreme cold.

* * *

"It's pretty easy to avoid frostbite if you pay attention to the details," says International Mountain Guides' Robert Jantzen. "You don't want to drop a glove, it's sometimes that simple. It's not just, 'Hey, keep your gloves on.' Well yeah, but then when you're fiddling with the stove or something, and you've got to take them off. It's the little habits like, any time you take off your glove, you put it in a pocket and you zip that pocket. Those kind of little details are really the big thing for prevention."

When he sees frostbite in the field, it usually either comes from laziness or someone not paying attention to what they're doing and what the conditions are. It's not generally about losing a critical piece of gear in the middle of a blizzard and being left unprepared. It really is about preparation and paying attention to the little things: pack the right clothing for the conditions, wear it, and don't even go outside without your gear. If you start to feel yourself getting cold or your hands or feet going numb, the telltale sign of early frostnip, get back inside if you can or otherwise find a way to warm up your skin before it gets too cold.

Depending on the severity of it, frostbite can range from a mild hassle in the backcountry to a true life-threatening situation.

"If it's really severe frostbite," Jantzen says, "you can be pretty incapacitated. Especially, say you get frostbite on your feet pretty bad, your ability to then self-rescue or walk out has been compromised. If your feet ever rewarm, they'll start to swell and then wearing boots is no longer such a good option. It is a hazard in the field, as well as something to deal with when you get back home."

He doesn't worry so much about frostnip because once you rewarm yourself those symptoms tend to go away on their own. But with frostbite, and he's seen it happen in the field, when you try to rewarm yourself on the mountain, blisters and swelling start to occur in the frozen area. At that point, the only treatment is to go to the hospital, as it is very difficult to adequately treat that level of injury in the field, especially without causing additional problems. At the very least, you're looking at permanent scarring from the lost tissue, but nerve damage and other problems are likely when you aren't careful with the frostbitten area.

"There's this old tale of rubbing your frostbitten area to warm it," Jantzen says. "Or even, there's an old wives' tale of rubbing snow on the frostbitten area. Both of those are very bad ideas. That's pretty sensitive damaged tissue and you want to limit any impact or trauma to it. And then make sure, if you have to stay in the field and there's the possibility of whatever piece that got frostbitten refreezing, you don't actually want to warm it up. Warming it up and allowing fluid to return and then refreezing it actually causes a lot more damage."

Altitude Sickness

At first, the symptoms were so subtle they were easy to overlook—a little sweat on the back of the neck, a little dryness in the mouth, a slight headache.

But things progressed. Quickly.

Over the next thirty minutes, the headache turned up to pounding and I found myself losing focus, having a hard time working on any one task for long. I craved water and started to feel almost like I was drowning, wheezing in the thin air in an effort to get oxygen into my lungs.

None of this was surprising, of course. I had driven to the top of one of Colorado's tallest peaks, Mount Evans outside of Evergreen, and was experiencing the symptoms of altitude sickness as a result. Altitude sickness is extremely common and happens when someone goes quickly to high altitude, usually higher than 8,000 feet, before their body can adjust to it. For me, a Denver resident who is used to life at 5,280 feet, altitude usually isn't much of a problem, and on hikes or ski trips I'm going up slow enough to adjust along the way. But the thirty-minute trip from 5,000 to 14,000-plus feet was enough to trigger my symptoms.

It's uncomfortable, yes, and unpleasant, but altitude sickness—also called acute mountain sickness—is very common in the high country and the cure is simple: just go down to lower altitude. It doesn't matter how good of shape you're in or whether you're a man or a woman. People suffer from the condition to varying degrees based on their biology, and there is little we can do about it.

It's just a fact of life in the mountains.

The good news is that, in most situations, altitude sickness is not a major problem and doesn't usually lead to lasting damage. In situations like mine—in a parking lot in the middle of a major tourist area—I was in no real danger. I may have been feeling queasy, but I was only a few minutes' drive from feeling better, and had plenty of access to water or medical care if I needed it.

But the trouble with altitude comes when the victims are in a situation that isn't so well controlled. For example, when they're in the backcountry, when they're up on a high peak, or when they're dealing with severe weather and need to have their wits about them. That's when the symptoms of altitude sickness can put you in a bad place. It's when you're hiking in the high Rockies and start to experience headaches. Or when you're camping or trekking through a high-altitude country such as Peru or Nepal, where it's not uncommon to spend days above 15,000 feet, and have a hard time falling asleep.

That's how US astronaut Buzz Aldrin, the second man on the moon, got into trouble on a 2016 trip to Antarctica. Due to the thick layer of ice that covers the South Pole, the research station where Aldrin had been staying with his son sits at an altitude of more than 9,300 feet. Shortly after arriving, though, he started to experience some shortness of breath and other symptoms of mountain sickness.

"I had been having a great time with the group at White Desert's camp before we ventured further south," he told the *Los Angeles Times*. "I started to feel a bit short of breath so the staff decided to check my vitals. After some examination they noticed congestion in my lungs and that my oxygen levels were low, which indicated symptoms of altitude sickness."

As a result of these symptoms, the eighty-six-year-old adventurer was evacuated on a ski-equipped cargo plane to the Antarctic coast and then to New Zealand for treatment, where he spent a few days in the hospital recuperating. As a result of his altitude sickness, Aldrin had built up some congestion in his lungs that took some time to clear up.

"Once I was at sea level I began to feel much better," he said.

White Desert, the tour operator who was leading Aldrin's trip to the South Pole, said in a statement that the former astronaut was evacuated "as a precaution" following discussions with the trip doctor as well as the on-site doctor from the US Antarctic Program, the agency that manages the research station at the Pole. After landing at Christchurch, New Zealand, and transferred to the hospital for examination, doctors found that Aldrin had fluid in his lungs that was treated with antibiotics and kept overnight for observation. The company reported that his condition was stable within twenty-four hours of his evacuation and that he was in good spirits.

This experience typifies the real danger of altitude sickness. Despite his own adventure credentials—traveling to outer space and the moon, climbing Africa's Mount Kilimanjaro, jumping out of airplanes, etc.—Aldrin fell victim to the effects of the altitude like anyone else. He was not any more immune or accustomed to it than any of the rest of us would be. Worse, his age and other underlying risk factors made the condition more of a serious concern than it may have been for someone else, particularly someone of a younger age. That's the tricky part about altitude sickness and similar mountain ailments. Not only can we never be sure exactly who is going to be affected by them and to what degree but we can never be sure exactly what their symptoms are going to look like when they appear. It simply turns into a case of past experience for most sufferers, based on their symptoms on earlier trips to the mountains.

Of course, none of this is to say that Aldrin ever lost his famous can-do spirit, taking full advantage of his time on the South Pole to explore the surroundings before leaving the South Pole ahead of schedule.

And he was far from alone in his suffering.

At least one of his fellow travelers was suitably impressed, writing on Twitter before the evacuation: "I took 6 Advil this morning because of aches and pains but 86yo Buzz Aldrin is hiking around the South Pole."

* * *

Altitude sickness as a category of issues are all related to the effect of high altitude on the human body, from exposure to both low oxygen levels and low air pressure at high altitudes. In its milder forms, it is known as acute mountain sickness (AMS), but left untreated—or in the case of patients who choose not to move to lower ground when they first start noticing symptoms—it can progress to one of two related, far more serious issues: high altitude cerebral edema (HACE) or high altitude pulmonary edema (HAPE).

Both HACE and HAPE are serious injuries that are potentially fatal and can only be treated by moving to lower elevation immediately.

In the case of HAPE, the condition involves the buildup of fluid in the lungs as a result of spending too much time at elevations of usually more than 8,200 feet, according to studies, though cases have occurred as low as 4,900 feet. HACE, on the other hand, involves fluid-related swelling in the brain as a result of high-altitude travel. Of the two, HACE is less common, impacting less than one percent of the population and even then at altitudes greater than 13,000 feet.

Both conditions can be prevented through proper acclimatization, the steady process of ascending and descending a mountain over and over again over the course of several days or weeks, reaching higher each time, in order to give the body time to adjust to the change in altitude. And, although some people are more susceptible to HACE and HAPE than others, it remains a mystery as to why some suffer more than others. Health and fitness evidently have nothing to do with it, and there is effectively nothing any of us can to do improve our altitude tolerance. We are all simply born with a certain level of susceptibility to acute mountain sickness and simply need to learn to understand and function within those risks.

In truth, some mountaineers are better with altitude because they were born that way.

I happen to know that I am fairly susceptible to altitude-induced sickness, so I am very careful when I travel in the high country, making sure to drink plenty of water at all times and monitoring my symptoms along the way. As soon as I start to feel it coming on, I make my way back down to a lower elevation as soon as possible. Granted, very little of what I'm usually doing puts me at serious risk of HACE or HAPE, and I've never even come close to testing my tolerance to those conditions, but even in the 13,000 to 14,000-foot range of many of the Colorado peaks that I visit, the symptoms can be very real.

As mentioned, it starts off slowly. Starting around 8,000 feet, the early stages of AMS feel simply like you're out of breath, struggling a little bit to get enough air into your lungs. Honestly, it feels more like being out of shape than anything serious at this point, and I can generally power through it with careful, measured breaths and paying attention to my breathing.

From there, things get less specific. Your body is fighting to make do with less oxygen than it needs, so headaches, flushing, dizziness, rapid heartbeat, and other nonspecific symptoms are common. In general, if you start to feel like you have a hangover while at altitude, you're probably suffering from AMS. Going back down below 8,000 feet will usually solve the problem.

HACE and HAPE take all of these symptoms up another few notches, adding nausea, drowsiness, and disorientation to the mix, further complicating the situation for the victim because, although they

Altitude sickness feels like a hangover, it can develop quickly, and it can kill.

need to descend immediately, they may be so disoriented that they do not realize it or make bad choices. This is one of the reasons that acute AMS sufferers are sometimes found dead high on peaks, hours after they should have descended to a safer elevation. They simply became too disoriented to function and made poor choices that exacerbated their problem.

In both cases, recovery from HACE and HAPE, even with medical treatment, can take weeks and leave lasting damage.

Why all of this happens remains something of a mystery, according to the CDC, but four characteristics of the high-altitude environment—the extreme cold, low humidity, low air pressure, and high levels of ultraviolet radiation—can all work together to injure the human body.

"The biggest concern, however, is hypoxia," the agency writes. "At 10,000 ft (3,000 m), for example, the inspired PO2 is only 69% of sea-level value. The magnitude of hypoxic stress depends on altitude, rate of ascent, and duration of exposure. Sleeping at high altitude produces the most hypoxemia; day trips to high altitude with return to low altitude are much less stressful on the body."

According to the CDC, it takes at least three to five days for the body to acclimatize to high altitude, starting around 8,000 to 9,000 feet, although most of us are capable of adjusting "very well to moderate hypoxia" and can travel safely at altitude provided this process is followed.

"Acclimatization prevents altitude illness, improves sleep, and increases comfort and well-being, although exercise performance will always be reduced compared with low altitude. Increase in ventilation is the most important factor in acute acclimatization; therefore, respiratory depressants must be avoided. Increased red-cell production does not play a role in acute acclimatization."

As with everything in the backcountry, the more extreme you want to get, the more careful you need to be with your acclimatization and your efforts to avoid and address AMS. Yes, heading up to 14,000 feet and beyond in places like California, Colorado, Alaska, and Washington (Mt. Rainier and Liberty Cap, at 14,118 feet, are the state's only "fourteener") can be AMS inducing and calls for vigilance, but going big—beyond 20,000 feet in the Himalayas or in South America—requires a different level of care. Remember, altitude attacks the body in several different ways at once, sapping it of water, robbing it of oxygen, freezing it, and pummeling it with ultraviolet radiation. It makes sense, then, that higher altitudes simply mean higher levels of all these risk factors. Careful acclimatization can help minimize the overall risk, but the focus needs to be on "careful," taking extra time to go from level to level, often spending weeks on the mountain working up to those truly high altitudes.

* * *

Dr. Peter Hackett is one of the world's leading authorities on altitude-related injuries, having authored hundreds of articles on altitude issues and worked in extreme environments in the Himalayas, South America, and elsewhere as a high-altitude mountaineer and expedition doctor. And, as the head of the Institute for Altitude Medicine in Telluride, Colorado (elevation: 8,750 feet above sea level), today he sees more than his fair share of patients suffering from altitude sickness.

And they all share one thing in common: inexperience.

"Anyone can get altitude sickness," he says. "They go up too high for their own bodies. It never occurs after people are acclimatized. Really, the risk is based on your ability to acclimatize and that is based on your individual genetics, your individual physiology, how high you go and how fast you go. This process of acclimatization is time dependent and it takes a minimum of four days at any altitude over 2,500 meters or 8,000 feet. The reason there's so much individual variation in ability is because when you go into high altitude, even just going from sea level to Aspen, Colorado, which is only 8,000 feet, more than 500 genes in every cell in your body are turned on and some are turned off."

It takes a few days, he says, but once that adjustment is done you're acclimatized and you won't get altitude sickness.

Until then, however, the body is under significant stress. Even what Dr. Hackett would define as mild hypoxic stress greatly impacts your cellular biology and your gene expression. In these conditions, hundreds of different genes are activated in every cell in the body, different for each individual depending on their biology and natural genetic makeup.

"What do these genes do? They make you breathe more in response to the hypoxia of high altitude," he says. "They make you make more red blood cells. They change blood flow to your brain, into your muscles. They change enzymes that have to do with metabolism of oxygen and glucose. And they affect fluid balance. So there's all these different things going on in response to hypoxia and it's during that response time, the first couple days that people get sick."

It's not uncommon, either. According to Dr. Hackett, a full quarter of all skiers who come to the Colorado High Country from lower elevations suffer from acute mountain sickness, which generally feels like a hangover. You have a mild headache, you're irritable, maybe you'll have some nausea that gets worse when you bend over, and you probably won't feel like eating.

"The good news is that it goes away by itself in about twelve to twenty-four hours in most people," he says. "It comes on within four to eight hours after arriving at altitude, but sometimes it's delayed until after the first night at altitude. It's the altitude at which you sleep that is the most important because it's during sleep that your oxygen goes the lowest and your body is stressed the most."

That's the mild version, the type of mountain sickness that most people are familiar with and what we usually think of when we talk about AMS. It's annoying, it feels bad, but it is not life threatening. It responds to mild drugs such as Ibuprofen as well as just resting and letting your body acclimatize for twelve to twenty-four hours before going any higher.

The trouble starts when people start going very high up, very fast, without taking time to acclimatize to the altitude. In Colorado, the line for what doctors generally think of as high altitude generally starts at around 8,000 feet, though there is a threshold around 9,000 feet where people tend to get a lot sicker and symptoms tend to get worse. It makes sense, too. At Keystone, Colorado, which is at about 9,000 feet, there is about 30 percent less oxygen in the air compared to sea level. In Aspen, around 7,000 feet, there is about 20 percent less, whereas in Denver, down on the plains at 5,280 feet, there is only about 10 percent less oxygen in the air.

Dr. Hackett uses the example of climbing a 14,000-foot peak, which is well within the hypoxia zone but not uncommon in Colorado and other parts of the world. Most climbers start around 7,000 feet and get up and down the mountain in a few hours, before they get sick or start to feel the effects of the altitude. But if they were, somehow, to teleport themselves from sea level to14,000 feet and sleep overnight there, they would, in the words of Dr. Hackett, be "toast." The attack rate in that scenario would be 90 percent, impacting nearly every person no matter what their genetic predisposition is.

In this scenario, two severe forms of mountain sickness can happen. A brain edema, which effects coordination and motor skills, can develop over the course of twenty-four to forty-eight hours at extreme altitude, making the victim appear to be stumbling around and drunk. They're mentally confused, they can't walk around very well, and they cannot do simple tasks such as opening a bottle or zipping up a jacket. That's an emergency. Anyone suffering from those symptoms needs to get down to lower altitude immediate or they could die within twelve to twenty-four hours.

The other serious form of mountain sickness is the pulmonary edema, which is marked by severe trouble breathing and takes about three days to develop. It's like people can't get enough air into their lungs, which they literally can't due to the low oxygen levels. That said, the symptoms are similar to any other condition that causes fluid in the lungs: there's a rattling in the chest, they're gasping for breath and they're displaying pink, frothy sputum. It's kind of like they're drowning in their own secretions.

And it's fatal.

"If you let it go that far the odds are good the person will die," Dr. Hackett says. "To catch it early it's usually an athletic person that just doesn't put in a good day, feels a little tired, and has a cough that night. That's how you catch it early."

The number-one golden rule of all of this, he says, is never to go higher when you're sick. That's your body's way of telling you that it needs to acclimatize. Just powering through the symptoms in the hope that they will go away over time is a very bad idea and it is how people, even experienced high-altitude climbers, get in trouble with the altitude. Those that ignore this rule, he says, are the ones that die.

Certain medical conditions, such as lung disease, can make altitude sickness worse, but in general for the same rate of ascent to the same altitude, two people are going to have two different responses to hypoxia simply because of their genetics. Still, even those who are particularly susceptible to it won't have a problem if they take their time getting to altitude. A two-day trip from sea level to 7,000 feet won't cause problems, but a two-hour trip might.

"Rate of ascent plays a major, major role," Dr. Hackett says. "Even somebody who's endowed with incredible genetics would get extremely sick if we choppered them straight to Everest base camp. The rate of ascent is a stronger factor than your genetics."

Carbon Monoxide Poisoning

Tony Aspen, Colorado—playground of celebrities, socialites, and the global 1 percent—is far from what most people, myself included, would consider the backcountry.

But Aspen is a ski town, and it does sit higher than 7,000 feet, so there is at least the feeling in town that you're a little bit out there, someplace far away from the cares and worries of the real world down at sea level. After all, that's why it became a popular vacation spot in the first place. It is a world apart, six hours from the nearest major city, and set alone up in the mountains like some sort of hideaway camp, albeit one with more than its fair share of sushi restaurants and Kate Hudson sightings.

That's what drew the Lofgren family up from Denver to the mountain town in 2008. That and the vacation home rental they had won in a charity auction.

The house itself was beautiful, a luxury chateau on the mountain overlooking the town, not far from the house where actor Kevin Costner and his family live on the road into Aspen. Built just three years earlier, the 3,250-square-foot house came complete with a hot tub, chef's kitchen, private river access, and all the trimmings of a classic luxury mountain home. It sold for $8 million in 2009.

But it was one of those high-end features, the gas boiler that was used to melt snow off the patio and walkways around the house, that ended up killing the Lofgren family, including parents Caroline, forty-two; Parker, thirty-nine; and their two children: Owen, ten; and Sophie, eight, as they slept in the house on Thanksgiving night 2008. The home didn't have proper ventilation for the system, and the colorless and odorless carbon monoxide gas found its way into the bedrooms, poisoning them all before they even realized there was a risk.

Their bodies were discovered the next day, all still in bed peacefully as they had been sleeping.

The news came as a shock to the mountain town community, as well as the nation at large. How could a family be killed so quietly, so quickly, by something as simple as a construction defect? And how could officials in Pitkin County, where Aspen is located, have missed the problem in their inspections? This, remember, is the land of multimillion dollar ski mansions—aren't they held to higher standards?

In truth, carbon monoxide does not discriminate. It kills universally and equally, no matter who the victims are or how nice their house is. As long as the conditions are right—a sealed area like a house, an open-flame or gas-burning appliance and space for the gas to build up—carbon monoxide poisoning can happen. It's a maintenance issue, a construction issue, and a home engineering issue.

And, in this case, all of these factors came together in tragedy.

In the years following the Lofgren family's deaths, investigators pored over the home itself and the county's inspection standards. They discovered that, despite the fact that the house had been issued a Certificate of Occupancy following its 2005 construction, it did not have a carbon monoxide detector as required by Pitkin County, and had a long list of other construction violations. In addition to the missing CO detector, the home's HVAC system was improperly installed and the walkway boiler's exhaust vent had not been set up properly and had come disconnected from the system. The PVC exit pipe had simply come unglued from the exhaust port on the unit.

In truth, the home was a ticking time bomb. Being primarily a rental property, it was not occupied 100 percent of the time, leaving most people involved with it—the owners as well as the leasing company that managed the property—in the dark about the potential risks. What's more, the boiler was only used during snow and ice storms when there was snow to melt, so it went unnoticed until it was too late.

Lawsuits and court actions followed for years, none of which brought the Lofgren family back, but the extended family has since worked with a group of activists to both educate the public about the risks of CO as well as pass and reform carbon monoxide legislation in four states, including Colorado. They have also worked with local fire departments to ensure that every home has a functioning carbon monoxide detector in it.

"The families are dedicated to making sure that this tragedy does not happen again, and that the public is educated about the dangers of carbon monoxide and can protect themselves and their loved ones from carbon monoxide," the family said in a statement on its website.

Carbon monoxide isn't a complicated killer.

As the colorless, odorless gas builds up in a sealed structure, like a home, it slowly starts to force the oxygen out of the air, replacing it with CO. Eventually, this carbon monoxide builds up in the bloodstream of the victim breathing it in, forcing out the oxygen in their red blood cells, leading to death. The gas is created naturally whenever we burn gas, wood, charcoal, or other fuels, but only becomes a problem when it isn't vented out and allowed to build up in a contained space. That's when we start breathing it in at dangerous levels. In the home, improperly vented appliances like gas-fed furnaces are the primary cause of carbon monoxide poisoning.

It doesn't take too long for it to build up, either. Although there is often a base level of indoor carbon monoxide that we are breathing in and can safely absorb, coming from everything from cigarette smoke to cooking oils, over the course of a few hours, enough of the gas can build up in the bloodstream to cause serious damage to the heart and brain. Left unchecked, death is the next step.

That's exactly what happened in the case of the Lofgren deaths in Aspen. Following the incident, the legal system got to work, handing down indictments to a local building inspector, the area's building plan inspector, as well as the contractor who did the work. Some of those charges were later tossed out by a judge due to the fact that the statute of limitations had expired between the construction and the indictments, though a grand jury had earlier determined that, between 2004 and 2006 when the home was being approved and built, the group had contributed to the Lofgren family's deaths due to their own negligence on the job.

* * *

Unintentional carbon monoxide poisoning is one of the deadlier risks homeowners face, killing more than 5,100 people in the United States from 1999 to 2010, or an average of 430 deaths per year, according the CDC's National Vital Statistics System. It is three times more common in men (0.22 fatalities per 100,000 people) than women (0.07 per 100,000) and death rates tend to be higher among those sixty-five years and older and lower for those under twenty-five. Even for those that don't die, more than 20,000 people visit the emergency room every year suffering from carbon monoxide poisoning symptoms, and more than 4,000 of those end up staying in the hospital for treatment.

But what is it?

At the most basic level, carbon monoxide—CO—is a color-less, odorless gas that is produced anytime a fuel source is burned. So whether you're burning a log in your fireplace, a tank of propane for your grill, or a tank of gas in your car, you're creating carbon monoxide as part of the fumes. Normally this is not a problem. As long as the CO that's being created by your fireplace, gas range, truck, grill, or furnace is being properly vented off into the atmosphere—via a chimney or other vent—it can do no harm. It simply dissipates off like any other gas.

Even in cases where you might inhale some carbon monoxide in an open vented setting, around a campfire for instance, it is never able to build up into a strong-enough concentration to do much damage to humans or animals. Our bodies are able to bounce back from those trace amounts.

Carbon monoxide, a colorless, odorless gas kills about 500 people in the United States every year, sickening more than 20,000.

And the Environmental Protection Agency (EPA) monitors and regulates CO in outdoor air as part of the National Ambient Air Quality Standards of the Clean Air Act, given that the primary cause of most outdoor carbon monoxide isn't campfires and lanterns but rather emissions from cars and trucks. According to its (very dense) research, the EPA limits CO emissions at a single site to less than 35 ppm (parts per million) over the course of one hour and nine ppm over the course of eight hours. For indoor air, the current Occupational Safety and Health Administration (OSHA) limit is 50 ppm, time weighted over the course of an eight-hour work shift. That's all really pretty low, considering that medical science has yet to identify any particular health risks as the result of CO exposure at levels between one and 70 ppm, and most people don't noticing any symptoms until the levels get up over 70 ppm and stay there.

But when that venting isn't properly installed, or isn't functioning as it should, or has become disconnected, as was the case in Aspen, that's when carbon monoxide can kill. It's when it builds up and gathers together, becoming a stronger and stronger cloud—though, remember, it is colorless and odorless, so this cloud is undetectable even as it grows more and more deadly—that it becomes a real risk.

According to the EPA: "Breathing air with a high concentration of CO reduces the amount of oxygen that can be transported in the blood stream to critical organs like the heart and brain. At very high levels, which are possible indoors or in other enclosed environments, CO can cause dizziness, confusion, unconsciousness and death."

Even at lower levels, exposure to carbon monoxide is problematic for people who suffer from some types of heart disease and already have trouble getting oxygenated blood to their hearts. By introducing CO into the atmosphere that they're breathing, and thereby limiting the amount of oxygen available to them, they can be unable to get the oxygen they need to their hearts, which can at the very least produce chest pain symptoms and shortness of breath.

As the concentration of CO in the air increases, so do the symptoms, starting with those most vulnerable, including infants, the elderly, and anyone with a preexisting breathing problem. But the speed at which that happens, the time it takes carbon monoxide concentration to go from harmless, trace amounts to something that can kill can be very, very fast. Consider these cheerful examples from researchers at Iowa State University, as part of their work identifying and categorizing rick factors at specific CO concentration levels:

"400 ppm: Frontal headaches within 1-2 hours, life-threatening after 3 hours, maximum parts per million in flue gas under AGA test guidelines.

500 ppm: Often produced in garage when a cold car is started in an open garage and warmed-up for 2 minutes.

800 ppm: Dizziness, nausea and convulsions within 45 minutes. Unconsciousness within 2 hours. Death within 2-3 hours. Maximum air-free concentration from gas kitchen ranges.

1600 ppm: Headache, dizziness and nausea within 20 minutes. Death within 1 hour. Smoldering wood fires, malfunctioning furnaces, water heaters, and kitchen ranges typically produce concentrations exceeding 1,600 ppm.

3200 ppm: Concentration inside charcoal grill. Headache, dizziness and nausea within 5-20 minutes. Quickly impaired thinking. Death within 30 minutes.

6400: Headache, dizziness and nausea within 1-2 minutes. Thinking impaired before response possible. Death within 10-15 minutes."

And it pretty much goes downhill from there. The point is, CO can build up to dangerous levels a lot faster than people think, and it can kill very fast as well once it reaches these thresholds. Symptoms can vary from person to person in intensity, depending on their age and overall health, but headaches, dizziness, disorientation, nausea, and seizures are all on the list.

All that said, this is probably a good time to address why we're talking about carbon monoxide poisoning at all in a book that purports to be about health and injury risks in the outdoors, the backcountry. There is actually a very good reason that I told the story of the Lofgren family that died in Aspen to introduce the concept of CO risk, and that is because, of all the causes of accidental carbon monoxide poisoning, far and away the number-one killer is old, outdated, and faulty heating equipment. Now, to be fair, the house where the Lofgrens was killed did have a broken furnace that allowed CO to leak out into the home, but it was not old. Just poorly installed and maintained.

But carbon monoxide poisoning is covered in this book for the simple reason that, more often than not, it strikes in cabins, trailers, and other seldom used, poorly maintained structures that you're likely to encounter while traveling in the backcountry. There are many reasons that the majority of CO poisoning victims are over the age of sixty-five, but one big one is that they are staying in structures that are old and haven't been maintained over the years.

A vacation cabin off in the woods is the perfect example of this. Maybe it only gets used three or four times per year. Maybe the furnace is as old as the house is and hasn't been serviced in a decade or more. Or maybe the winters where it is located are cold and hard on systems, eventually causing leaks.

Whatever the case, backcountry travel doesn't always need to involve tents and tarps. Sometimes remote cabins are part of the experience, and often the risk of CO exposure in those structures is higher than we would like to admit.

Dehydration/Heat Stroke

The summer of 2016 was a hot one across the desert southwest.

In June, the city of Tucson, Arizona, saw its hottest day in more than twenty years when it hit 115 degrees, and Phoenix set a new daily record that same day of 118 degrees, which ranks as the fifth-hottest day in that famously hot city's history. Yuma, Arizona, to the south, reached 120 degrees that same month.

And it wasn't just a problem in Arizona. The city of Palm Springs, California, narrowly missed its all-time record on June 20 when it reached 122, while Las Vegas, Nevada, hit 115 degrees and Death Valley reached 126 degrees. Even further north, in Casper, Wyoming, and Pueblo, Colorado, records fell that summer, as 100-plus degree days became the norm for days on end.

All of this was unpleasant enough in the air-conditioned cities—I can attest that most of Denver stayed inside as much as possible that month, and all of our electric bills hit new heights as well—but was much more serious to some of those who ventured into the outdoors. In Arizona, in particular, the weather was deadly to several people who got caught in the heat unprepared.

The Ventana Canyon area northwest of Tucson is popular with day hikers and vacationers alike, and is dotted with high-end resorts and spas tucked between the foothills and scrub trees of the desert landscape. It's a beautiful area—no surprise that rooms at the resorts in the area can go for thousands of dollars per night—that's rocky, rugged, and just begging to be explored.

Evidently, that's what a group of three friends from Germany were doing on June 22 when they ventured out for a day hike on the Ventana Canyon Trail, a 9.5-mile out and back hike that Trails.com called "lightly trafficked" and rates as difficult. It takes hikers up the, no surprise, Ventana Canyon, and rewards hardy souls with both stunning rock formations and arches, as well as birds-eye views of Tucson far below. It's a pretty hike, and one that isn't impossible for fit hikers in nice weather.

The German group was prepared for the physical challenge of the hike, but not the variable that the extremely hot weather added to the mix that day. As temperatures rose, reaching 118 degrees in Phoenix by midday, the hikers ran into trouble. It is believed that the rocky canyon walls only added to these temperatures by bottling in the heat, scorching the group and draining them of their energy. Despite carrying water for the day, the extreme heat had dehydrated them quicker than expected, leaving two of the hikers strong enough to stand, let alone walk. Soon only one of them was strong enough to hike out and find help, leaving his two companions lying helpless up in the canyon to wait for rescue.

They didn't make it.

By the time help arrived from the South Arizona Rescue Organization, both of the dehydrated hikers had died as a result of their injuries.

"It really shows how critical this heat can be and how it can really sneak up on you," Phoenix Fire spokesman Capt. Larry Subervi told the *Arizona Republic* newspaper after the incident. "When we deal with temperatures like this, it can just really be unpredictable how your body is going to respond. Even backyard barbecues can be dangerous on a day like today."

The German hikers weren't the only victims of the heat that month. They weren't even the only victims that weekend. Anthony Quatela III, twenty-five, ran out of water while hiking on the Peralta Trail, a rugged hike east of Phoenix, and fell unconscious from heat exhaustion before he could make it back to the trailhead. Temperatures in the area were north of 110 degrees at the time. On top of that, a twenty-eight-year-old woman stopped breathing and died while mountain biking in the Phoenix Mountain Preserve, and a nineteen-year-old collapsed from the heat while hiking on the Finger Rock Trail near Tucson.

"It's all because they make a choice," then-Pima County Sheriff Chris Nanos told reporters at the time. "All of this is 100 percent avoidable."

Except that it isn't always that simple.

Yes, it is generally not a good idea to go hiking or biking in the middle of a heat wave, especially as severe a heat wave as the one that summer. But the body is so uniquely unsuited for extreme heat that it is easier than most people think to get in severe trouble in the outdoors and become severely dehydrated before a victim even knows what's happening.

The biology doesn't lie.

The human body loses about one liter of water per hour during strenuous activity and more when temperatures are soaring or the activity is particularly strenuous. The problem arises due to the fact that we can only effectively absorb about one-half liter of water per hour, so it is effectively impossible to replenish the water we're losing during activity that goes on for hours, such as hiking. Normally this is not a problem. We can make it through the day as long as we keep drinking water and don't overdo it, and the body can rehydrate itself when we rest in the evening.

But extreme heat speeds all of this up, dehydrating the body far faster than normal and putting us in a situation in which we cannot possibly keep up with the body's need for water. In those cases, a victim can be drinking water and doing what they think is the right thing while still becoming more and more dehydrated. And the trouble with dehydration is that is can be difficult to notice before it's too late. Once the typical symptoms of mild dehydration show up—a dry mouth, cold sweat, mild disorientation, etc.—the body is well on its way to a more serious situation and needs water immediately.

That's where the German hikers likely found themselves in Ventana Canyon that June. They made it about halfway up the trail before their symptoms caught up with them, and even drinking water at that point wasn't enough to reverse the damage that dehydration was doing to their bodies. It was simply too late, and they didn't even know they were in real trouble yet.

Their bodies lied to them, and they died as a result.

* * *

Water is life. Anyone who has ever spent time in the backcountry knows that you aren't going to get very far without a steady supply of clean, fresh water. It's a fact of life.

The reason why is simple.

The human body is made up of roughly 60 percent water. Every cell, every tissue, every hair follicle relies on water—simple, basic, clean water—in order to function properly and keep us alive. Water flushes toxins out of our vital organs, transports nutrients between cells, and helps keep tissues and mucus membranes in the throat, nose, and elsewhere moist.

But the water composition of the body is far from a steady state. We're constantly losing water throughout the day via our breath, sweat, and urine, so we need to replenish that supply on a regular basis in order to remain health and hydrated.

How much water that means exactly is up for debate, as it varies from person to person.

The general rule has long been eight glasses of water per day, every day, which translates to about half a gallon per person, but in reality there is no scientific proof to back up this claim. It's a little like the advice to change the oil in your car every 3,000 miles, even though most modern cars can go 5,000 or more between oil changes. It's a marketing message, dreamt up to both encourage drivers to get their cars serviced more often as well as making it easier to remember when to get the job done. (To be fair, years ago when the 3,000 mile idea came into vogue, drivers really did need to change their oil more often at an interval much closer to every 3,000 miles than it is today.)

In any event, the eight-cups-per-day rule has generated skepticism. Unlike oil changes, however, the truth about water intake actually leans toward more than less, with the National Academy of Medicine—a United States nonprofit that provides insights on health and medical issues—recommending thirteen cups of water (about three liters) per day for men and nine cups (a little more than two liters) per day for women after its own testing.

Either way, these recommendations are just for daily life for a healthy adult in a temperate climate. If someone is in a hot area or going through heavy exertion—say, while on a twenty-mile hike or mountain biking for three hours—their water needs go up sharply, because they're likely losing more water through sweat than they would be able to replenish with just those eight glasses per day. In fact, the Mayo Clinic recommends upping your fluid intake by two to three cups at least to make up for the water loss from any activity that makes you sweat. For activities that last longer than a short time—such as a marathon—you'll need to be replenishing fluids on a regular basis, but exactly how much you need varies from person to person.

Other hydration risk factors include the weather (hot temperatures that make you sweat), altitude (the body needs more water at altitudes higher than about 8,000 feet due to more rapid breathing), illness (when you're sick you lose water more quickly through vomiting, diarrhea, or fever-induced sweating) and pregnancy (the recommendation for pregnant women is ten cups of water every day and thirteen cups per day for women who are nursing, per the National Academy of Medicine).

Falling short of these recommendations results in dehydration, a condition that can lay low even the most fit and prepared outdoor adventurer. Technically defined as "an abnormal depletion of body fluids," dehydration occurs when water is removed from the body, leaving it without enough water to function normally. In practice, this most often occurs when water is lost through sweat, breathing, etc. and is not replenished as needed, leaving the sufferer feeling tired and dragging.

But that is just the start of the problem. Left unaddressed, dehydration can progress quickly, with excessive thirst, dark-colored urine, and general fatigue as the primary symptoms at this stage. Eventually, the victim will become dizzy and confused, having trouble understanding even simple tasks and instructions. In the backcountry, even this level of dehydration can be extremely dangerous, as victims can get lost, fall down, or otherwise hurt themselves in ways they normally would not. Over time, severe dehydration can lead to kidney damage, seizures, shock, and even death.

And dehydration does kill. The body can generally only survive a few days without any water, and every year thousands of people in the United States and elsewhere end up in the hospital as a result of dehydration and related symptoms. However, it is effectively impossible to determine how many people die specifically of dehydration every year simply because it is so global and widespread, impacting so many different types of people in different situations. Yes, hikers and hunters sometimes get lost in the woods and suffer from dehydration,

The single most common injury in the backcountry, dehydration, is also the easiest one to avoid.

but dementia patients who forget to eat and drink do too, along with inmates on hunger strikes, young children who overexert themselves, and many others. It is a condition that can affect anyone, young or old, rich or poor, anywhere in the world, and as such it likely kills far more people than we realize.

Part of the problem is the fact that, like many of the other risk factors discussed in this book, dehydration isn't always what does the ultimate killing, but it serves as a contributing factor. Aside from simply dying of thirst, repeated dehydration can lead to all sorts of internal organ damage, any one of which can quickly kill a victim. That's one reason why dehydration on its own rarely shows up on cause of death reports. It is simply one more factor that makes things worse.

But that's not to say that dehydration is not dangerous. Quite the opposite is true, particularly for the backcountry activities that we're covering in this book. Even short of death, dehydration in the woods can get a person in trouble very quickly, as the associated disorientation can lead to poor decision-making and oversights before the victim even realizes the extent of the problem. Within hours of becoming dehydrated, hikers can fall down, get lost, or otherwise get themselves into serious trouble without even realizing that they simply need to drink water.

* * *

More than a decade later, I still remember the day clearly. It was late July, hot and muggy as usual in central Virginia, and I was in the middle of training for what would be my very first half marathon.

I was living more or less alone in Charlottesville, Virginia, that summer as my wife was back in Colorado completing her legal internship as a second-year law student, so I had my days (and nights) more or less to myself. As a result, and I remember this clearly, I decided to go for a run well before work that day in order to beat the heat and get my workout out of the way early.

It turned out to be a good move.

Looking back at the weather reports now, the high temperature that day crested at north of 94 degrees Fahrenheit with nearly 50 percent relative humidity. On the ground, that felt like a heat index of 101 or higher.

My run was uneventful as usual. I'm sure I staggered my way through my usual five-mile loop, likely at a slower pace than I should have, before making my way home, cleaning up, and heading to work. I do remember the heat, though, because that was right in the middle of one of the worst hot spells of the summer, and that run on July 26, 2006, wasn't the only sauna-like one I had to endure that year.

But, most of all, I remember the heat that day because of Kelly Watt.

I knew Kelly as a high school kid, a journalism student who was working at the same weekly newspaper I was, filing local sports stories and even holding down a local column. But he was also, primarily, a gifted distance runner who was set to join the team at the College of William & Mary, my own alma mater, to compete at the Division I level in the fall of that year.

As a sportswriter, he was the real deal—I remember being surprised when I first learned that he was still in high school, his writing and editing chops were so well honed even then. But as a runner, according to those who knew him in that world, he was a rare talent, an athlete whose natural gifts were only exceeded by his personal drive and sense of purpose to be the best he could be.

"He was a risk-taker," Alex Gibby, the head track coach at William & Mary told a reporter at *The Hook*, the alt weekly where Kelly and I were both working that summer. Remembering a particular race that he watched during the recruitment process, Gibby was impressed. "He really laid it on the line," he said of Watt's late push that day. "Even though he ran into a little trouble at the end, he wasn't going to be timid."

A tough, "blue collar" type of runner, he was on track to start at William & Mary in the fall, and he was spending his summer working up his fitness to compete at the college level. That meant 5 a.m. runs before work, interval training on the rolling central Virginia roads, and even double workout days to build up his endurance. He was a young kid, eighteen years old and in the best shape of his life. He could handle the work, even in the searing Virginia heat.

"We figure we're 18, 19 years old, and we're in relatively good shape," his friend George Heeschen told *The Hook*. "We don't think anything of running alone or running in the heat."

Tragically, though, on July 26 Kelly had the day off, so he went for a run in the late afternoon, the hottest part of the hottest day in the hottest month of the year.

And he never came home from that run.

Ridge Road is an intensely scenic stretch of the Albemarle County countryside located about ten miles west of Charlottesville. It's horse country out there, so the road winds over and around rolling hills, bordered by near-endless white fencing and multimillion dollar homes, the Blue Ridge Mountains visible off in the distance. Relatively flat compared to the surrounding area, the Ridge Road run is about eight miles out and back, with intermittent shade and almost no traffic to speak of.

Under normal conditions, this makes it almost the perfect place to run. But for Kelly, when he collapsed from heat stroke at the end of his workout, the isolation of Ridge Road worked against him: it would be more than two hours before emergency workers would find him and begin treatment.

He had made it back to his car near the intersection of Ridge Road and Garth Road, but was, in his heat-related delirium, unable to get inside or get help before he collapsed into the underbrush at the side of the road. His water bottle was later found, open and empty, as if he had struggled to get a drink but was unable to get the bottle to his lips. The side of his car was covered with the desperate fingerprints of a man struggling to get inside and find shelter from the heat, even though it was unlocked.

Doctors admitted Kelly to the Intensive Care Unit at the nearby University of Virginia Medical Center and worked tirelessly to bring him back from the brink, but the damage done by the heat stroke was too severe, causing widespread organ failure and eventually fluid in his lungs that doctors could not stop.

Kelly died as a result of his injuries on Saturday, July 30, 2006. He was just eighteen years old.

The next day, his former high school teammates organized a "Take Back the Ridge" run on Ridge Road to both show support for Kelly and demonstrate their solidarity in the face of such a senseless tragedy. But Charlottesville is a running town, and in the end nearly 100 people—many of whom did not even know Kelly in life—made the trip out Garth Road to run with their peers. The event, and the story, was picked up by national media outlets, and *Runners' World* magazine even turned Kelly's story into a feature article, a cautionary tale on what can go wrong for runners, even the most fit and prepared among us, in the heat.

* * *

Dr. Edward Otten is a board certified emergency physician and professor in the University of Cincinnati Departments of Emergency Medicine and Pediatrics. A combat medic with the United States Army during the Vietnam War, he has also been involved with the Wilderness Medical Society for more than thirty years, continues to serve as a SWAT medic, and was for many years a medical advisor to NASA, helping the space agency develop programs and protocols to help its astronauts survive in the extreme climate of outer space. He is also currently part of the Department of Defense's Tactical Combat Casualty Care committee where he has helped to develop standards for combat medicine in Afghanistan and Iraq, as well as other parts of the world.

All that said, Dr. Otten is quick to point out that everything he ever learned about surviving in the outdoors that actually worked, he learned in the Boy Scouts.

"The most common problem that we're going to see with heat illness is people who are not acclimatized," he says, "and also aren't drinking and eating enough. A lot of people think it's only drinking [that matters in the heat], but if you just drink pure water without having any electrolytes you can very easily get that dilutional hyponatremia, where your sodium level goes real low."

The key, he explains, is to acclimatize yourself before you go out into a hot climate. And that is exactly what it sounds like: go out into the heat and get used to it. Just as high-altitude climbers must allow their bodies time to acclimatize to the low-oxygen environment, heat takes some getting used to as well. It isn't your imagination; people from cool weather climates really do feel the heat in a warm climate more intensely, at least for a few days, and vice versa.

"If you live in New England and you want to go down to Tucson for a two week vacation, and you just show up—and you've been living in an air conditioned house, with an air conditioned car, and an air conditioned business—you go out in the heat of day, in the heat in Sabino Canyon, you're probably going to get heat exhaustion, at least, if not possibly heatstroke."

The acclimatization process is actually physiologic. It's not just behavior and "getting used to it." Once the body is adapted to the heat, you'll start sweating at a lower temperature so you are more likely to survive in a hot climate. So, instead of waiting until your temperature is 103 for you to start sweating, for instance, you'll start sweating at 101. This way, you'll be more likely to keep cool and stay that way, and not develop a temperature of 104 or 105.

This happens, Dr. Otten explains, as the body recruits more sweat glands to produce more sweat, which is a natural response to spending time in the heat. A traveler could acclimatize by sitting in a sauna an hour or two a day, or just by spending time outside working in the yard or exercising, but the key is simply to get out where it's warm and spend some significant time out in it. People who sit around in the air conditioning their whole lives lose their ability to sweat; they don't have as many active sweat glands, so they don't sweat as much and that can be very detrimental in a hot climate.

This process also helps to actually decrease the level of electrolytes that are in people's sweat, diluting their sweat and making it less salty, so that they don't lose as much sodium or potassium as they perspire as they otherwise would. Even the blood supply to the skin ticks up in these conditions, increasing heat loss through the skin and helping to recruit even more sweat glands.

In the heat, it's all about sweating enough to keep cool. And the acclimatization process can take a week to ten days to really take hold, depending on where a person lives, according to Dr. Otten. Not taking that time, rushing the process, and overdoing it in extreme conditions, are what he sees most often in the field.

"I worked with the Desert Warfare School for the Marine Corps for several years, working on preventing heat illness in Marine reservists who show up for desert warfare training and not be acclimatized," he says. "Getting used to the heat, acclimatizing yourself. This is why Army recruits and high school football players collapse from heat exhaustion, because they're not used to being in the heat."

It doesn't take long, either. It's not uncommon to see marathon runners, people who are at least ostensibly in good shape and used to the elements, fall victim to dehydration and heatstroke on race day. And collapsing high school football players, also fit individuals, are nearly a summer tradition at schools across the hotter parts of the United States. The reason for this, Dr. Otten says, is that heat injuries are caused by a combination of factors, not just the weather. Maybe you're genetically predisposed to not being able to sweat very much, or your electrolyte levels are naturally very low so you can't lose too much in the heat before feeling weak. Certain medical conditions, drugs (including antihistamines such as Benadryl), and even plants such as gypsum weed can also interfere with the body's ability to sweat, or will boost your metabolic rate, meaning the body is generating more and more heat but isn't sweating as much to cool off.

"The most common medical problem that we see in the wilderness, no matter what you're doing, is dehydration," Dr. Otten says. "By far the most common thing. Whether you're scuba diving, you're skiing, you're kayaking, you're fishing, you're hiking, whatever, most people in the wilderness are dehydrated because you just don't drink as much fluids. When you're out there, you're out of fluids, so you don't drink as much, and you're busy doing better things. If you're rock climbing, you don't usually have a camelback or a canteen with you, so you might be out there for three to four hours in the sun, sweating, and not rehydrating yourself. Dehydration is an extremely common problem."

When it's fully hydrated, the body is simply stronger and better able to adapt to changing conditions, reducing the changes of any sort of injury. So staying hydrated is a real key to nearly every activity in the wilderness. Emergency medicine experts such as Otten talk about the "Rule of Threes" when it comes to survival: you can live three minutes without oxygen, three hours without warmth, three days without water, and three weeks without food. Naturally, oxygen is the first concern—if you end up in a car that's upside down in a river, shelter or food are not going to be your real focus—but people who don't drink any fluids for three days usually end up dying.

Much of the body's demand for water is due to the circulatory system, Dr. Otten says.

"Part of your blood pressure is due to venous return," he explains, "the blood coming back to your heart. That amount of fluid is what tells your heart how much it can pump and what your blood pressure is. If you're not keeping the tank full via sweating, or peeing a lot, or whatever you're not going to be able to produce enough blood pressure to profuse your organs. Your brain, being one of those organs, your kidneys, your liver, all those other things."

So, you need to keep an adequate amount of fluid "on board" in order for your blood pressure to be enough to serve all of your organs. If you don't, you're starving your body of the blood and oxygen it needs to function, and the results can be sudden. This is why young soldiers out on a parade ground will sometimes faint without warning.

"A lot of times, it's because they're not getting enough blood back to the heart to profuse their organs, especially their brain, so they just go to ground," Otten says. "And then they wake up once they hit the ground from fainting. That's not unusual to see."

The solution to all of these problems, he says, is hydration. Even hypothermia and frostbite, and other wilderness injuries, can be prevented simply by drinking enough water and maintaining that internal balance. In the heat, in particular, acclimatization ahead of time is critical, especially if you're planning to spend days or weeks out in it (for example, on a long hike or expedition).

"If you get heatstroke and you're by yourself, you're likely going to die, because nobody's going to save you," Dr. Otten says. "You need to recognize it and prevent heat illness before it's too late."

Starvation

Starving to death is the very definition of a worst-case scenario when it comes to being lost and stranded. Like water, the human body cannot function for long without food in some form, so death by starvation is inevitable in any situation where a victim doesn't have access to supplies or a ready food source.

Perhaps the best example, at the least the best known, of death by starvation is that of Christopher McCandless, who died in the wilds of interior Alaska in 1992 after hiking out into the bush northeast of Denali National Park alone and with no ready food supply. He was planning to challenge himself to live off the land, to become one with nature.

He starved to death in the process.

He lasted for several months, subsisting on a diet of berries and wild potatoes, but by the time his decomposing body was found by hunters in the fall of 1992, still in the abandoned old Fairbanks city bus that he was using as a shelter, he weighed less than seventy pounds and was showing clear signs of malnutrition. Though there remains some debate as to exactly what killed him—researchers considered a wide range of possibilities but in 2013 settled on lathyrism, which is caused by a toxic amino acid found in the seeds of the wild potatoes he had been eating, leading to the partial paralysis that McCandless mentioned in his journals and prevented him from going out to find food—the cause of death was determined to be starvation.

McCandless's name is well-known today thanks to Jon Krakauer's 1997 book, *Into the Wild*, which outlined the victim's travels, his philosophies, and the thought process that drove him to do what he did. (Sean Penn's 2007 film adaptation cemented his legacy in outdoor lore.)

A native of suburban Washington, DC, in Northern Virginia, McCandless graduated from Emory University in Atlanta in 1990 and immediately set off on his own version of the vagabond life, donating most of his savings to charity and crisscrossing the country in his beat-up old Datsun. He worked in a restaurant in Arizona, as a farmhand in California, and eventually ended up in Carthage, South Dakota, a tiny (population: 110 as of 2017) farming town out on the empty, windswept plains of eastern South Dakota. There, when a flash flood effectively destroyed his car, he took to the road again, hitchhiking back to the Rockies before hitching all the way up to Fairbanks, Alaska.

He wanted to live the life of a modern-day hobo, a '90s Jack Kerouac, traveling from town to town as the winds carried him, with little more than a backpack and his wits to keep him alive. He wanted to be free, and as such became extremely causal with his own health and safety.

As a native Virginian myself, I know firsthand how the woods of the east can instill a false sense of security, how spending time in the gentle, temperate arms of the Appalachian Mountains can make a person feel smarter, stronger, and overall better prepared for survival than they really are. For McCandless, who, to be fair, had spent time in the Rockies, the Sierras, and the desert of Arizona before truly heading out into the wild, it was enough to fool him into thinking he was a master survivalist. Like Thoreau, who it should always be said spent his seasons at Walden Pond within a short walk of both his own home as well as downtown Concord, Massachusetts, he wanted to live off the land and prove to himself that he was truly capable and free.

Alaska brings those realities sharply into focus—quickly.

By the time McCandless got to Fairbanks—and of all the things that he did in his short life, the simple fact that he successfully hitchhiked up from the Lower 48 to rural Alaska remains one of his most impressive accomplishments—he was set on his next challenge, the Stampede Trail. Originally built by gold miners in the early twentieth century, the trail had evolved into a semi-maintained but primitive road through the bush that heads out to the northeast from the small town of Healy, Alaska, not far from Denali.

Although the Stampede Trail is technically a rural road, it is far more dangerous than it would seem, in part because of the ever-changing conditions in the Alaskan backcountry. Bus 142, where McCandless set up camp and spent his final days, is located barely twenty miles from Healy, but the trail getting there is notoriously difficult and fraught with dangerous river crossings, taking far longer than the usual two or three days that you might expect. Depending on the weather, it can be extremely muddy, with high water and a difficult-to-follow trail. In fact, it was a high season on the Teklanika River that prevented McCandless himself from safely evacuating when he realized the gravity of his situation. That river is, of course, still there, and even modern hikers have been stranded by it when attempting to visit the bus. Beyond all that, interior Alaska is heavy with mosquitoes in the summer, with dense brush and a raw, uneven tundra landscape that can test even the hardiest of adventurers.

Given all that, it is easy to see how McCandless, who thought himself the hardiest of hardy adventurers when he got to Alaska, got into trouble. Trapped by the river, alone in the wilderness, and without supplies that he would have needed to survive a long stretch in the bush, McCandless slowly succumbed to starvation, helped along by the poisons he was also ingesting.

* * *

In the end, the story of Chris McCandless is a cautionary tale, a warning about the real risks of dying the backcountry. No, starvation is not a common way to go, in the wild or not, but it does happen, particularly in cases such as McCandless's where the victim is unprepared, unfamiliar with the terrain, and effectively doing everything in their power to starve to death.

If McCandless had studied a map he would have known that he was less than twenty miles from the town of Healy, Alaska—not to mention the sprawling tourist mecca of Denali National Park—where he could have sought shelter or found food. Or if he knew more about the local flora he would have known the risks associated with the potatoes he was eating. He was simply uninformed about what he was doing, and it caught up to him (as often happens in the unforgiving wilds of Alaska).

Of course, he is far from the only person to starve to death in the wilderness due to poor preparation.

In 2009, a forty-one-year-old man named Winston Branko Churchill disappeared in the Colorado wilderness during a hike on the 486-mile Denver-to-Durango Colorado Trail. An outsider who hated what he saw as the greed and materialism of modern society, Churchill wanted to escape into the woods and sort out all of the conflicting

It's about more than just eating to fuel your activities. It's also important to eat—and not eat—the right things.

feelings in his head. Instead, he ended up wandering off the trail and exploring the wilds of western Colorado alone, with limited supplies and limited knowledge of the area. His emaciated, mummified body was found nearly a year later, in an abandoned old mining cabin northwest of Lake City, by hikers, with no food and still wearing clothing that was inadequate for the high country. It was later determined that he slowly starved to death during his wanderings.

Outside of this discussion around starvation in the outdoors, malnutrition is a serious problem in the developing world and is an issue that the World Health Organization has flagged as the "single gravest threat to the world's public health." On the whole, starvation and hunger kill more than three million children under five worldwide every year, while a shocking 12.5 percent of the world's population, including both children and adults, or about 842 million people, are currently living with undernourishment that has yet to become severe enough to kill them.

It is a true, horrible, international health crisis.

What happened to Chris McCandless in Alaska or the "other" Winston Churchill in Colorado is not part of this crisis, but the physical reality of what happens when a person starves to death is identical.

It sounds horrible, and the photos of starvation victims in concentration camps or the Third World really are horrible, but in practice, experts say that death by starvation is about as peaceful as it gets. The real science at work is little more than calorie deprivation, which as anyone who has ever attempted a New Year's resolution diet can tell you simply involves taking in fewer calories, via food, than your body burns off going through the daily task of staying alive, powering the breathing, heartbeat, and other basic bodily functions that every one of us requires. Once this calorie deprivation reaches severe levels and duration it becomes malnutrition, which can cause organ damage and death.

But instead of feeling pain, patients who have come close to death by starvation report feeling a sense of euphoria, of being detached from their body, as their major systems shut down due to lack of food or water. The "pain" that most of us associate with hunger is only an issue for those who are trying to survive on less than their bodies need, but not cutting out calories entirely (e.g., dieters). After about twenty-four hours, the body adapts and the hunger pains disappear, helped along by the release of ketones and endorphins in the body that cause those feelings of euphoria.

And it's all because our bodies are designed for this. Back when we were hunting and gathering, steady food was not guaranteed. Sometimes our ancestors would come home with fresh meat, and sometimes they would be unlucky and have to go to bed hungry. That was simply the way it was. But hungry hunters are poor hunters, so the body adapted to neutralize those hunger pains and allow prehistoric humans to get the job done even between kills.

We are the beneficiaries of this evolution.

True, starvation is not painful. In fact, it's normal. It is typical for people to, in the last few days of life, forgo food and water as they near death. It's a natural and normal part of the end-of-life process that many experts feel helps to soften the blow of death itself.

"What my patients have told me over the last twenty-five years is that when they stop eating and drinking, there's nothing unpleasant about it—in fact it can be quite blissful and euphoric," Dr. Perry G. Fine, vice president of medical affairs at the National Hospice and Palliative Care Organization in Arlington, Virginia, told the *Los Angeles Times* in 2005, as part of a story of the then-evolving saga of Terri Schiavo, the forty-one-year-old who was then starving to death in a Florida hospital. "It's a very smooth, graceful and elegant way to go."

The reason for this is that the body goes into survival mode as soon as it realizes the food and water are being cut off. It starts digging into its fat and protein stores to get the energy it needs, which works for a while but soon starts to impact basic bodily functions. Protein and muscle loss from starvation can interrupt the heartbeat and lead to cardiac arrest, or a weakened immune system can leave a victim susceptible to pneumonia or other diseases. Whatever the case, eventually they will fall into a coma and die within about two weeks.

We know most of this thanks to a groundbreaking study conducted in 1993 at Duke University Medical Center, when a cancer patient decided to give up eating and pass away rather than continue her painful course of treatment. Dr. Robert Sullivan, her doctor, observed her decline over the course of the next forty days, documenting exactly what she was going through along the way.

And it didn't look bad. She reported no pain, rather experiencing that euphoria we have discussed, and she was lucid and talking for weeks. When the end finally came, she simply slipped into a coma as if it was a deep sleep and died.

The body has some very powerful tools at its disposal to minimize the pain and suffering of death, and its reaction to starvation is a good example of the lengths it will go to make things easier in the event of severe malnutrition.

Dysentery/Giardia

"You have died of dysentery."

Readers over a certain age likely well remember the classic computer game, *The Oregon Trail,* which challenged game players to complete the difficult and dangerous journey from Independence, Missouri, to Oregon's Willamette Valley, almost entirely via text-based gameplay.

Introduced in 1971, the game was a staple in elementary and middle school classrooms throughout most of the 1980s and '90s (and it may well still be popular), often the intense focus of attention during group "computer time," back when one PC was shared among dozens of kids. It was educational, teaching about the real life and death struggles that occurred on the Oregon Trail in the nineteenth century, but it was also fun and engaging—the prototypical 1980s computer game.

It was also pretty difficult to complete. Even playing it now, on one of the many online platforms for it, making it all the way to Oregon is far from a foregone conclusion, even for an adult game player who has been around the block when it comes to video games for the better part of thirty years.

After buying a wagon and mule team, stocking up on supplies, and heading out onto the plains, my *Oregon Trail* experience always seems to end up the same way. I make it for a few weeks, even reach a few of the resupply stations along the way, but sooner or later, inevitably, I see the same message flash across the screen.

"You have died of dysentery."

It's no different than it was in 1985, when I was playing the game on the Apple IIE in my elementary school. Apparently my *Oregon Trail* skills have not improved over the years.

But the real lesson here, the real question that the game has been asking of players all along, is: "What is dysentery"? I can't remember knowing very much about it as a fourth grader, and I certainly wasn't alone in that. In fact, the "you have died of dysentery" line has emerged as a full-on meme in this digital age, a catchphrase that old-school gamers use (a little too often) in casual conversation.

Kids in the '70s had no idea what dysentery (also known as shigellosis) was all about. That was the point of an educational game such as *The Oregon Trail*, to get a conversation started and raise new questions. It's not like anyone was really "dying of dysentery" in the regular course of Western life in those days. It was a foreign concept from an earlier time.

But dysentery was and is a very real condition that can and does still kill thousands of people around the world every year, particularly in the developing world.

At the most basic level, dysentery is a form of gastrointestinal distress that involves frequent diarrhea and some stomach pain. The condition can be caused by a wide variety of different things, ranging from viruses to bacteria, and even parasites, leading to an inflammation of the colon. These symptoms usually clear up on their own in about a week, allowing the patient to return to normal activity over time. But in some cases, left untreated, shigellosis can leave its victims severely dehydrated and malnourished, as the body is flushing out the colon so quickly that it is unable to draw any nutrients from the food a person is eating. Eventually, in this weakened state, the body simply runs out of energy and vital functions begin to shut down.

As you can probably imagine, it must be an unpleasant way to go.

The good news is that there are good reasons that "you have died of dysentery" is regarded as a disease of the past. For the most part, modern sanitation practices—such as water purification, bleach for surface cleaning, and antibiotics—have made dysentery a rare occurrence in North America, although it does still strike many thousands every year in the developing world. The rise and fall of diseases such as dysentery can be traced back to human settlement patterns throughout history, as we moved from small, rural communities to big, bustling, and often filthy and unclean cities. With poor sanitation came repeated bouts of dysentery. Fortunately, it didn't take too long for our ancestors to make this connection and correct the problem.

According to the CDC, "The 19th century shift in population from country to city that accompanied industrialization and immigration led to overcrowding in poor housing served by inadequate or nonexistent public water supplies and waste-disposal systems. These conditions resulted in repeated outbreaks of cholera, dysentery, TB, typhoid fever, influenza, yellow fever, and malaria. By 1900, however, the incidence of many of these diseases had begun to decline because of public health improvements, implementation of which continued into the 20th century. Local, state, and federal efforts to improve sanitation and hygiene reinforced the concept of collective 'public health' action (e.g., to prevent infection by providing clean drinking water). By 1900, 40 of the 45 states had established health departments. The first county health departments were established in 1908."

These programs included everything from proper sewage disposal to standardized water treatment programs and new efforts in food safety and food handling. Many cities in the first half of the twentieth century even went out into their communities in efforts to educate local residents on not only the importance of proper sanitation but also how to maintain a safe, clean home.

But this wasn't soon enough to save scores of people throughout history from the scourge of a dysentery-led death. Its victims include the famous "Lone Woman" who lived alone on San Nicolas Island off the coast of California for nearly two decades before succumbing to dysentery just two weeks after being transported to Santa Barbara, still a Spanish colonial outpost, in 1853. Even Jack London, the California-based author of classics such as *Call of the Wild* and *White Fang*, was said to have suffered from bouts of dysentery for the last few years of his hard-charging life, eventually succumbing at just forty years of age.

Although the disease is largely eradicated in North America, dysentery remains a major threat and aggressive killer in the developing world, where antibiotic strains are becoming increasingly common. There is no known vaccine yet, and in places where access to clean, safe medical care is hard to come by, water-borne diseases such as dysentery are unfortunately common.

* * *

Of course, *clean* and *sanitized* aren't words that can be used to describe the typical backcountry campsite or outdoor environment either, no matter where in the world you are. It's nature; it is, by definition, not sanitized.

That's why, for hikers and other backcountry users, the parasite that is most associated with intestinal distress in the outdoors goes by one name: giardia.

Technically, giardia, which is a microscopic parasite, goes by a few different names, including such fun-sounding ones as "Giardia intestinalis," but the general idea is the same. An unusually hardy little parasite, giardia gathers in water, food, or on surfaces that have been contaminated with feces, either from infected humans or animals, and once ingested, can last in the body for a week or more, leading to symptoms that seem to go on and on regardless of treatment. Most of the time, infected water supplies such as mountain streams and untreated water are the source of giardia infections in the backcountry.

Infection is simple. If you drink contaminated water, the parasite gets into your body and then you become a potential source of further contamination. According to the CDC, giardia is transmitted in what are called cysts or hard shells that protect the parasite and allow it to survive both on surfaces and in the body for a long time. They are "instantly infectious" and plentiful. The CDC says that an infected person can release as many as 10 billion giardia cysts every day through their stool, though the next victim can be infected by ingesting as few as ten cysts.

The fun part (if there is one) is that most infected human carriers of the giardia parasite don't even realize they're infected since symptoms typically don't show up for at least two or three weeks after ingesting the cysts. On the one hand, this delay can be seen as upside when traveling in the backcountry for a short time. If you're out for a week-long distance hike and accidentally ingest giardia on the first day, chances are good that you won't be laid up with symptoms until you get home. Or, if you're overseas, the nature of the infection might allow you to travel back to where you started before hitting you head on.

But once it happens, oh boy. Based on the CDC's numbers, giardia is the most frequently diagnosed intestinal parasitic disease in the United States and, like dysentery, giardia can create intense intestinal distress and chronic diarrhea. Cases can range from mild to acute and include everything from gas to greasy stools and abdominal cramping, nausea, dehydration, joint swelling, hives, and more. And those hard-shelled cysts make giardia a very tough bug to pass, with symptoms often lingering for two weeks or more.

Although drugs are available to treat giardia, many people will allow the infection to run its course rather than seeking true medical help, as diagnosis requires lab work on multiple stool samples and that process can take as long as the symptoms themselves last. Drinking enough water to maintain your body's natural defenses and simply riding it out is an effective plan of attack.

So prevention is key, particularly when traveling in the backcountry and living in the, as mentioned, "dirty" world of the outdoors. Giardia as a parasite knows no range or season and can be found worldwide, wherever the conditions it prefers are right. It's not something that can be avoided or simply ignored. It is everywhere and an ever-present threat.

Treat All Water: Nowhere is giardia more common that in bodies of water, from streams, to ponds, to open collection pools. If there is standing or untreated water around, chances are very good that giardia is in it. That's why we, as a species, treat our water to kill and remove the creepy crawlies that are lying in wait in it, waiting to make us sick. Fortunately, treating water, even in the backcountry, is not difficult. When bottled water, or water you bring in from a known safe source, is not available, the CDC simply recommends boiling all water for one minute at a rolling boil in order to kill the parasites, viruses, bacteria, and whatever else is in it. Alternatively, a water filter that has been rated by the National Safety Foundation can be used to filter out many cysts and other bugs, though further processing with chemicals is usually required to fully eradicate the bacteria and viruses that are small enough to fit through the filter.

There's a reason that water filters and purification systems are required equipment for all outdoor adventures.

Wash Your Hands: The rules from preschool still apply. Any time you use the bathroom, touch an animal, touch garbage, clean a wound, or work around food, you need to wash your hands with soap and water for a solid twenty seconds, or use the trick of humming "Happy Birthday" as you wash to make sure you do it long enough. This is enough time to remove any bugs that may be hitchhiking on your skin and could end up in your mouth, food, or elsewhere. In the backcountry, where running water is not an option, hand sanitizer can be useful, as is washing with a container of previously treated water that you then discard.

Keep It Clean: Indoors, the CDC has a long list of recommendations for preventing giardia contamination in the kitchen, bathroom, and elsewhere that reads like a list of commonsense household chores, including disinfecting all hard surfaces, properly cleaning cooking tools, wearing gloves when handling any potential contaminants, etc. Of course, absolutely none of this applies when your potential contaminant source is the stream flowing past your campsite and the only hard surface you have access to is the plate you use for every meal. In the backcountry, cleanliness is relative, but an understanding of where giardia contamination comes from (i.e., feces) and a practice of avoiding all contact with potential sources can go a long way toward preventing infection. Of particular note, it's worth keeping in mind that washing dishes and cookware, though important, should never be done in potentially infected water such as a stream. Washing with contaminated water can result in infection just as drinking contaminated water does.

Exposure/Hypothermia

The White Mountains of New Hampshire are notoriously rugged and rocky, with temperature swings that rival higher peaks such as the Colorado Rockies, making them among the roughest terrain on the Eastern seaboard.

The weather there can be extreme as well.

For more than sixty years, the weather station on the summit of the 6,288-foot-high Mount Washington, the tallest peak in the East, held the world record for fastest wind gust ever recorded with a 231 mile per hour breeze that was recorded on April 12, 1934. (It surrendered that title in 1996, when an unmanned weather station on Barrow Island, off the northwest coast of Australia, recorded gusts of 253 miles per hour during Typhoon Olivia.)

Still, the White Mountains are not to be messed with.

That makes the region somewhat unique in the east. Most of the Appalachian chain, of which the Whites are part of the northern highlands segment, are relatively low and manageable, certainly when compared to their high mountain cousins out west. As a general rule, lower altitudes mean less extreme, less dangerous conditions, with shorter approaches and less exposure above treeline, making the backcountry comparatively less intimidating and more approachable here than in other parts of the world.

Not so in the White Mountains. This part of the Appalachians was formed, along with all the rest, some 100 million years ago by the collision of the North American Plate with mainland North America. But the Northeast, unlike the southern segments of the chain, saw heavier glaciation over time, leaving sharper, more heavily exposed features and rocky expanses that are rarely found in other parts of the East. Good examples of this in action include the formation of glacier-shaped notches and passes in the region, including Tuckerman Ravine on Mount Washington and King Ravine on Mount Adams. That history has left behind a landscape that's noticeably sharper and more challenging than its neighbors. (It's no accident that the history of rock climbing in the Northeast traces its development directly back to the exploration of Mount Washington and other nearby rocky peaks.)

Add in the prevailing weather trends in the area, and you have the recipe for a dangerous, difficult place.

But the mountains of New Hampshire are also very close to major population centers such as Boston and New York City, making them a popular destination for hikers and climbers from all over the Northeast. You can drive to the visitors' center at the base of Mount Washington in less than four hours from Boston, barely seven hours from New York.

That proximity means that not only do large crowds often find their way to the New Hampshire mountains but that many times some of those adventurers come out unprepared for what they're going to find in the hills once they get there.

That wasn't the case when Kate Matrosova came to the White Mountains in February 2015 for a winter traverse of the snow-covered peaks, however. A Russian national living in New York, Matrosova was an experienced high-altitude adventurer with a string of difficult climbs all over the world to her credit. Her husband dropped her off at the base of Mount Madison, from where she planned to continue on across Mount Adams, Mount Jefferson, and Mount Washington before rendezvousing again at the base of Washington. The hike makes up about half of what is known locally as the "Presidential Traverse," from the historical figures the mountains are named after, and covers more than fifteen miles in total.

But she didn't make it.

Matrosova's body was found about a day after she started the hike, in an exposed area between the summits of Mount Madison and Mount Adams. According to official reports, the area had seen temperatures as low as 30 degrees below zero Fahrenheit and winds in excess of 100 miles per hour when Matrosova was attempting her traverse. She had activated her emergency beacon, so authorities knew where she was during the storm, but rescuers were unable to reach her before she died of exposure to the extreme temperatures.

Matrosova was thirty-two years old.

Attempting the Presidential Traverse, even part of it, in winter is by definition a difficult hike, but it is by no means unheard of. The hike is considered something of a Northeast classic, and every year thousands complete the two- to three-day adventure in all four seasons. Still, even for an adventurer as skilled as Matrosova, the conditions can be extreme. The average monthly temperature on Mount Washington in February is 6.1 degrees Fahrenheit, and the surrounding peaks offer similar conditions, as well as high winds and frequent winter storms.

"Regardless of the season, a Presidential Traverse is not a hike to take on lightly," wrote Philip Werner, on his blog, SectionHiker. com, about the route. "Besides being physically strenuous, bad weather, including snow, lightning, hail, and whiteout conditions are a constant threat and one of the main reasons for bailing out part way through. This hike is also almost entirely above treeline (resembling a moonscape), so good compass and map skills are a must."

The entire route, of which Matrosova completed only part, includes a full eleven miles above treeline and more than 10,000 feet of elevation gain, making for an extremely difficult hike even in perfect conditions. The trail up Mount Madison gains 3,500 feet of the total elevation gain for the full hike in less than the first four miles, and all ten of the presidential peaks on the full traverse are above 4,000 feet.

The rewards—hiking for days across a barren landscape in a sea of white—are substantial, and rare in the East, but the risks of the route in winter are well known to rescuers and hikers in the area.

"If you are going to hike in this type of weather you need to be in a more sheltered area, not up on an open exposed ridgeline," New Hampshire Fish and Game Lt. Jim Goss told Manchester TV station WMUR after the body was recovered. "There's just no room for error in a place like that."

* * *

Of all the risks in the backcountry, dying of "exposure" is probably the least understood.

Technically, the term refers to death as a result of exposure to the elements—whether it is extreme heat, extreme cold, or something else—over a long period of time. The human body is capable of adapting to many different challenging conditions and changes in the environment, but eventually the struggle to stay alive in poor conditions without adequate protection simply catches up to you and the body surrenders.

Most of the time, when we're hot our bodies are able to cool off by sweating. When we're cold, shivering helps to activate our tissues and (at some level) helps to keep us warm. Once those natural defenses have been exhausted, however—after spending so long in a hot, dry environment, that our body no longer has any moisture left to sweat out and cool itself with, for example—the environment is able to begin to do real damage to our systems.

This is where "exposure" as a cause of death comes in.

The classic example of this generally involves the cold. As in the example above, hikers, hunters, or other adventurers get lost in the backcountry in the dead of winter. Without easy access to shelter, they end up spending more time exposed to the elements—cold, snow, ice, wind, etc.—than expected and they start to experience injuries as a result. Maybe the ice leaves them with some frostbite on exposed areas. Maybe the lack of food leads to starvation. Or maybe the cold causes

For the most part, exposure is a matter of preparation, but it can kill much faster than most expect.

hypothermia. Either way, their bodies are pushed to the brink of death by exposure to the winter elements.

It's also worth noting here that "exposure" often refers to several different problems occurring at once. I may not die simply by sitting in an ice-cold room with my shirt off, but that situation is very likely to cause hypothermia, which can very easily kill me. Or I may not die simply as a result of it being a hot day. But those severe temperatures can dehydrate me quickly, leaving my body unable to properly adapt to the environment.

This conglomeration of causes can make deaths by exposure somewhat hard to track. Every year, hundreds of people—both in the backcountry and in hospitals—die as a result of heat-related injuries. In fact, according to the Centers for Disease Control, more than 7,000 people died this way in the United States from 1999 to 2009, an average of approximately 600 per year. There is wide variability here, though. The highest year for heat-related deaths in this stretch was 1999 with 1,050, while the lowest was 2004 with just 295.

From 1999 to 2010, a total of 7,415 deaths in the United States, an average of 618 per year, were associated with exposure to excessive natural heat. The highest yearly total of heat-related deaths (1,050) was in 1999 and the lowest (295) in 2004. Approximately 68 percent of heat-related deaths were among males.

But that's just from heat.

On the flipside, nearly 17,000 people died as a result of cold exposure–caused hypothermia from 1999 to 2011, for an annual average of just over 1,300. These hold pretty steady from year to year, with 2010 showing the most hypothermia-related deaths with 1,536, and 2006 with the least, at 1,058.

What this data shows us, then, is that the old mountaineers' axiom is true: a lot more people die of excessive cold than die of excessive warmth. Our bodies are simply better equipped to handle exposure to hot temperatures than they are cold temperatures, and we're better able to regulate our body temperatures in those climates as a result.

Think about it, when you start to get overheated and dehydrated in the backcountry, what do you do? You drink water, and you soon start to feel better. When deep cold sets in while traveling in a remote area, though, our options are far more limited. We can put on a heavy coat in order to trap our body's heat and keep it close to our body, helping to keep us warmer by preventing heat loss. But that only works when our body is healthy enough to generate and give off heat. Once we're too cold, that process slows down and our core temperature will start to drop. Although they can be useful for protection from the elements, no coat will generate that heat for us.

And then there is the simple fact that exposure to cold can get at us in so many different ways. With heat, dehydration is the primary and almost exclusive risk. But cold cannot only cause hypothermia but frostbite, snow blindness, and other injuries that are very real risks in the cold, and each will need to be addressed in its own way. (Cold can even cause dehydration, too, as intensely cold air contains less moisture than rich, warm air. As we breathe that dry air into our bodies, dragging down our core temperature, it further dehydrates us from the inside out, multiplying the damage that the cold can do.)

To use our coat example again, even if exposure victims are able to get their coats on and use them to help raise their body temperature, what if they don't have any gloves? Or they don't have a hat? They are still at severe risk of frostbite regardless of how warm their core is (to some extent), and exposure in the cold is a multilevel problem that often is not easy or quick to address.

All of that said, the conventional wisdom around exposure is that it is, at least comparably, one of the more pleasant ways to die in the outdoors. According to the stories from survivors who have nearly died of exposure, only to be rescued and resuscitated at the last moment, it is almost as simple as going to sleep. By definition, a body that is succumbing to exposure—either to the hot or cold—has given up and is no longer fighting for survival. It can no longer sweat or shiver or otherwise anymore, so it is slowing down in order to maintain basic life functions such as breathing and a heartbeat. Sound familiar? That is roughly what happens when we fall asleep every night. Our body slows down and enters a calm, relaxed state. Exposure is roughly the same thing, except in those cases the body is not relaxing in order to recharge for the next day but rather as a last-ditch survival mechanism.

It really is just like going to sleep.

* * *

"Hypothermia is very common, and a lot of times it's not recognized," says emergency medicine specialist Dr. Edward Otten. "It's very common in the city. You get a 40 degree day and rain, you're more likely to get hyperthermia than you are if it's 15 degrees, because people don't dress all the time in 40 or 50 degree weather for the weather. They go out in their T-shirt, and their shorts, and they get wet. You see this all the time."

The crazy thing, he says, is that more people die from hypothermia in the summer than in the winter, because in the winter people don't go out into the mountains or the wilderness without wearing proper clothing, and shelter, and plenty of food and everything else they might need. They're experienced. They're prepared. They know that going outside in the winter can be dangerous so they don't even attempt it without knowing what they're doing.

In the summer, though, you'll see tourists heading out in their T-shirts and flip flops, trying to climb Pike's Peak or descend into the Grand Canyon in one day. They have no idea what they're getting into, they aren't geared up for it, and they simply aren't prepared for the changing conditions that are common in the mountains year-round. All of a sudden, a hailstorm or a rain storm rolls in and they get soaked. Then they and their T-shirt get cold. Then they get hypothermia. Here in Colorado, for instance, it seems that not a month goes by in the summer or fall when some tourist from Texas or California gets stuck in the mountains, unprepared, and unaware of how quickly the weather can change in the high country. And they get in trouble. "They think they're at Disney World," Dr. Otten jokes, as if someone will come and rescue them if something happens.

But it's not that simple.

"I see hypothermia most often in people who are wet," Dr. Otten says. "People who get dunked in the lake or a river, doing a river crossing, falling in the water, and they can't dry out, and they can't get any dry clothes or warm clothes put on, or people out in rainstorms who get soaking wet and they don't have dry clothes or shelter, hypothermia, I think, is very common in those groups of people."

The real problem is that hypothermia often goes unnoticed, so much so that many people don't even recognize it in themselves, even in the advanced stages. As with heatstroke, it can be difficult to see in yourself, which is why it is so critical to have someone with you who can watch for it and treat you if you need it.

"I was canoeing one time with one of the smartest people I ever knew," Dr. Otten says, "and it started to drizzle. I put on my rain jacket and he didn't, he was just wearing a cotton T-shirt. We stopped at an island to camp and I said, 'Well, I'll set up the tent, and you go ahead and get the stove going, and we'll having something to eat.' I got the tent all set up and put the stuff in. I went over and he was just sitting there; he had burned up like fifteen matches trying to light the stove. He lost his hand-eye coordination, he was disoriented, he could barely stand up. He was hypothermic. He didn't recognize it."

That's why, just as with heat illnesses, you have to prevent hypothermia, rather than focus on treating it once you get there. Once you have hypothermia it can be very difficult to recover from, especially if you're out in the wilderness, facing the elements. And if you're by yourself, you'll end up dead. The reason for this is that cerebellum function is the first thing to go when someone gets hypothermia. Very quickly they can go from functioning normally to having difficulty walking, difficulty with hand-eye coordination, and even difficulty keeping track of what they're doing. This is why many people often do not recognize it in themselves, since the first thing you see is a change in mental status with lowering temperature, and that makes it harder for their brain to process.

Without a traveling companion who can recognize hypothermia in you and address it, you'll just keep getting more and more hypothermic. As disorientation creeps in, things get weird and victims behave in ways that injure themselves further. They'll take their clothes off. They won't dry off. They'll just wander around and not find shelter. Even before that stage, they'll have trouble doing simple tasks such as putting up a tent, or putting on clothes, or unzipping a sleeping bag, leaving them exposed to further injury.

"It's just like people who get dunked in the water in their sailboat, or their kayak, and instead of getting out of the water, even if they have to crawl on top it, they stay in the water because when you get out of the water the wind makes them feel cold," Dr. Otten says. "Well, that's how you die. You lose heat forty times faster in water than you do in air, so you always want to get as much of your body out of the water as possible. That's why a life jacket, any kind of thing that's floating around, getting up on it and getting out of the water will increase your chance for survival. Staying in the water, you're going to die. It may take you three to four hours, but you're probably going to drown."

CHAPTER 6
Hazardous Terrain

Rockslide

All the Johnson family wanted to do was go for a hike.

The weather was nice that October day, the kids had the day off from school, and they had family in town visiting for vacation. They wanted to show off their active, fun life in Buena Vista, Colorado.

So they took their guests—two cousins from Missouri—up to Agnes Vaille Falls in nearby Nathrop, a popular day hiking spot for families from all over the Arkansas Valley. It isn't generally considered a very challenging hike, or even a very long one, and it is typically very crowded. A clearing at the base of the falls makes for a stunning vantage point.

Except, on that day, tragedy struck at the base of those falls, as a rockslide—likely triggered by the early fall freeze-thaw process in the Colorado High Country—came roaring over the edge of the falls, burying the entire Johnson family, and their two houseguests, under boulders as big as cars. Five family members were killed instantly, including parents Dwayne and Dawna Johnson, their eighteen-year-old daughter Kiowa-Rain Johnson and family members Baigen Walker, ten, and Paris Walkup, twenty-two.

The sole survivor of the rockslide, thirteen-year-old Gracie Johnson, later told investigators that she was saved when her father, Dwayne, jumped on top of her at the last moment to protect her from the impact of the rocks. Rescuers later found her alive under the rock pile at the falls, suffering from a few broken bones but nothing major. Dwayne Johnson had traded his own life for hers, pushing her under a larger boulder that protected her from the bulk of the falling rock.

The debris field covered fifty yards, and rocks continued to fall even as rescuers worked to remove the bodies from the scene. It took more than twenty-four hours to stabilize the site to allow access.

"The slope itself started moving downhill," Chaffee County Undersheriff John Spezze told the *Denver Post* the day after the incident, explaining that the steep and rocky terrain was a danger to recovery crews because it was so unstable. "We had to get [the recovery team] out of there because the slope was sliding, and it was so unstable. It is very loose, rocky terrain. These engineers, they work in a mine and . . . they tell us this is a very dangerous area. There are rocks in there the engineers estimate are 100 tons. I've never seen something like this."

In the small river town of 3,000 people, the reaction was immediate. The Johnsons were well known around town, and universally beloved. The story even made the rounds in the national media, with Gracie appearing on the *Today Show* and other outlets following her recovery.

"We may never get over this," family friend Jennifer Eggleston told CNN after the incident. "They were so much a part of every single thing we ever did. You won't be able to find a single person in this town that they did not touch."

A heartbreaking, terrible story to be sure, but in the aftermath of the Johnson family tragedy, investigators were left with the mystery of why. Why had the ground given way so suddenly? How had the rocks been perched so precariously? And, most of all, why did this happen when and where it did?

Rockslides are technically a type of landslide that occur when a slope breaks free from whatever support is holding it in place—be it bedrock or gravel or other materials—and collapses as one mass, rather than in individual boulders, gaining steam as it tumbles downhill and releasing other rocks as it passes. Whereas landslides involve loose dirt, rockslides contain—no surprise here—rocks and boulders.

They are fairly common in the Rocky Mountains, where loose rocks and small slides close highways and back roads all over the state every summer. It doesn't take much to set them off. Mountains are by definition little more than giant piles of rocks—I am simplifying here—so loose rock can be found all over the surface of any hill or mountain. Add in some steep terrain, an open area to run through and a reason to let loose—be it a careless hiker, an earthquake, or simply some runoff from a heavy rain—and you have all the ingredients you need for a slide.

The problem becomes worse in the fall when, as temperatures start to drop, water that seeps within fractures in the rock freezes into ice and expands, pushing out rocks that are otherwise well supported, causing falls. It doesn't take much to get a good slide going once the stability of the entire wall has been compromised, as falling materials serve to further destabilize the slope bed, pulling additional rocks free and gaining in strength as it falls.

After all, as the saying goes, nothing starts a rock fall like falling rock. Or something like that.

Experts later determined that water had been to blame at the Agnes Vaille Falls also. The area had seen heavy fall rains in the days and weeks heading up to the rockslide, loosening the footing under the large boulders at the top of the falls and setting them up to fall. What's more, freezing temperatures the night before likely further loosened the rocks. So, when rock started to fall from a cliff shelf above the falls, the rest of the wall was primed to let loose.

"It could be that we have had so much moisture and rain, you could have gotten moisture in those fractures, and those could have lubricated those fractures and created the rockslides," Karen Berry of the Colorado Geological Survey told CNN. "That might have been a contributing factor."

Still, as with most rockslides and landslides, warning signs are rare in these cases.

"The place is visited by thousands of people every summer. Nobody has said anything looked out of place," Spezze said. "It's just, unfortunately, bad timing—and nature."

* * *

A rockslide is, quite simply, any incident in which rocks slide down a slope. It's essentially an avalanche of rocks, a wave of stone cascading downhill and coming to rest on valley floor or other level area down below.

Rockslides occur constantly. In rocky, hilly areas they are simply part of the landscape, the erosion process in action. That puts them in the same category as mudslides and landslides, both collapse events that are capable of sending tons of, depending on the type of slide, rocks, mud, or dirt down a slope at high speed.

All of that means there are as many causes for these types of events as there are factors in the world.

You might know the trail, but do you know what risk is looming overhead?

The 2014 Oso disaster, for example, sent approximately one square mile of mud down on top of the town of Oso, Washington, killing forty-three people, redirecting a local river and all but obliterating the town. In that case, a known unstable slope let loose as the result of more than a month of heavy rain, 200 percent above normal.

Two years later, an earthquake near Kumamoto, Japan, loosened several hillsides, triggering a number of landslides and caused widespread damage, including one that destroyed a local bridge. Similarly, an earthquake that struck Pakistan's Kashmir region in 2005 killed some 100,000, many being caught up in the landslides that the earthquake unleashed.

The Agnes Vaille Falls rockslide, on the other hand, happened on a sunny day in an area that hadn't seen anything in the way of weather or seismic activity. The rocks just fell down.

And that's not uncommon with rockslides. Unlike mudslides or landslides, before which the affected area is generally fairly stable and quiet, the only thing keeping a rocky slope from crumbling down is the weight of the rocks themselves. Gravity is holding the whole thing together like a giant Jenga set. It should come as no surprise, then, that even the slightest change in that delicate balance—a freeze-thaw cycle that loosens a few rocks near the bottom of the pile, animal activity high up on the slope, erosion, or even a hot, sunny day that heats the rocks and causes some of the gaps between them to expand—can cause the whole thing to let loose.

That very fact makes them all but impossible to predict or foresee. A given rocky slope is going to let loose and slide exactly when it, and gravity, decide it is time to. Little else can predict that. True, the freeze-thaw cycle does lead to an increase in rockslides in the fall, but when and where exactly they will happen is a mystery. The same can't be said for mudslides and landslides, which are more often triggered by specific events, but the lesson remains the same.

And for our purposes, that is OK. Knowing that slides like these can happen at any time means that backcountry travelers need to be constantly vigilant. Know what a typical rockslide slope looks like.

Keep an eye out for areas where you might get caught in the event of a slide. And watch the weather before your trip to identify any particular patterns—like that month of rain in Oso—the might suggest the possibly of a slide in the near future.

Avalanche

Alex Lowe and Dave Bridges were two of the preeminent mountaineers in the world when, in 1999, an avalanche brought their high-altitude careers suddenly and violently to a close. It happened on Shishapangma Mountain in Chinese Tibet, part of an American expedition that was seeking to be the first to ski off the summit of the 26,291-foot mountain.

At the time, such feats were the hot thing to do in mountaineering—in 2000, Slovenian ski instructor Davo Karnicar became the first person to ski nonstop down from the 29,035-foot summit of Mount Everest to Everest Base Camp at 17,500 feet, completing the feat in a little more than five hours without ever taking his skis off and setting a world record in the process. The feat completed a challenge that Japanese climber Yuichiro Miura started in 1970, when he skied about 6,600 feet down Everest, from the Lhotse face to the Yellow Band near the mountain's summit, resulting in the documentary film, *The Man Who Skied Down Everest*. Finally, in 2015, Kit DesLauriers became the first person to ski down all off the world's Seven Summits, the highest peaks on all seven continents, when she completed her own run down from the summit of Everest.

But Lowe and Bridges were no daredevils. At the time, Lowe himself was widely considered the most talented climber on the planet; one of his climbing partners even called him "lungs with legs" in reference to his superhuman endurance and strength at altitude. But he was also an expert skier who had sought out backcountry runs in many of the world's most remote places.

"It's been a passionate goal of mine," he told MountainZone.com before the 1999 expedition, "to ski off an 8,000 meter peak. I guess there's a lot of people sort of looking to do this and try to ski off

Everest. But for me, it's got to be an aesthetic and quality run. And Shisha Pangma has the best ski line of any of the 8,000 meter peaks. It's just an absolutely straight shot right down the Southwest Face. That's going to be a good one."

It all came together that year, and Lowe was slated, along with his climbing partner Conrad Anker, to become the first American to ski off of an 8,000-meter peak. Aspen-based photographer Bridges, an experienced mountaineer in his own right, was invited along to document the feat for NBC and The North Face.

But tragedy struck before the climb could really even get started.

On October 5, 1999, while Lowe, Bridges, and Anker were scouting for routes up the mountain, an ice ridge far up the mountain broke loose, sending a wave of snow and ice down to where they were climbing near base camp around 16,500 feet. The broad, steep slopes of Shishapangma allowed the avalanche to grow into a massive wave of destruction 500 feet wide, barreling down over the three men at nearly 80 mph.

Within seconds, all three were engulfed, with Lowe and Bridges tumbling over a ridge and Anker being thrown clear by a wind gust. When an avalanche is rushing downhill at full speed, it pushes a "bubble" of air in front of it, creating a false wind that, like a bomb explosion, is capable of delivering an explosive force in excess of the ice and snow itself. It was this force that threw Anker more than 100 feet clear, breaking several of his ribs and very likely saving his life.

The rest of the nine-person expedition—including expert skiers Andrew McLean, Mark Holbrook, Hans Saari, and Kristoffer Erickson—had been scouting a different part of the mountain and avoided the avalanche entirely.

Anker was injured but able to walk off of the debris field and lead what would become a nearly two-day search for his two missing climbing partners. They combed what remained of the avalanche field looking for a glove, a backpack, anything that would direct them to their friends. It went through the night and into the next day, with climbers from all over the mountain pitching in to help.

They wouldn't find anything.

"From my perspective there was just this big white cloud, and then it settled and there was nothing there," Anker later told *Outside* magazine about the incident. "And it was just so massive and so big. There wasn't that sense of closure."

In fact, it would be more than sixteen years before the bodies of Lowe and Bridges were found, when a pair of German climbers were on Shishapangma in April 2015, looking to develop a new route of the mountain. A month later, the bodies were recovered and funeral services were completed.

It was closure for the families, but far from a true explanation.

In fact, avalanches don't often come with much in the way of explanation. They are such a common part of travel in the mountains that they are an accepted risk of the sport, and mountaineers like Lowe are fully aware of the ever-present threat whenever they're on the high peaks. Avalanches cannot be prevented, but careful travel can minimize a party's exposure to them—either by traversing in relatively safer areas, or limiting time in avalanche terrain to early in the day when snowpack is colder and more stable.

But the slide on Shishapangma was something different. Lowe, Anker, Bridges, and the rest of the team were all very experienced mountaineers and they knew how to travel safely in avalanche country. By all accounts, they did everything right. But when a serac—ice ridge—breaks 6,000 feet over your head, creating a massive avalanche that's nearly as wide as two football fields, there really is almost nothing you can you. A force like that is going to overwhelm every precaution a climber takes on the mountain, barreling over less dangerous terrain and engulfing anyone that stands in its way.

The 1999 team knew the risks, knew what to do to minimize those risks, took all reasonable precautions, and yet still lost two members of their expedition to what was a typical incident on that mountain.

There really was nothing they could do.

* * *

At the most basic level, avalanches are collections of snow, ice, rock, and other debris that tumble down a mountainside as a group, often picking up steam as they go and expanding to cover an area of thousands of square feet. They can be triggered on a steep slope, fall hundreds of feet in mere seconds, before coming to rest where the slope mellows out and their potential energy runs out.

They are extremely dangerous in the backcountry because of their speed and destructive power, as well as their sheer size, making them difficult to avoid in the moment. Those caught in an avalanche can end up buried under several feet of extremely dense, heavy snowpack, making escape difficult, if not impossible, on their own. Death occurs as a result of suffocation when buried, or by injuries caused by the rush of ice and rock. Some victims are even dragged by an avalanche through trees or rock fields, where injuries occur.

Avalanche injury data can be difficult to obtain and isn't always accurate, in part because of the all-or-nothing nature of the slides themselves. Injuries can often go unreported because, as they were likely in an area where they shouldn't have been when they triggered the avalanche (in the case of self-triggered slides), the injured party doesn't want to call attention to it.

Fatality information is on the whole more reliable, because the victims in those cases aren't around to protest and the snow sports industry as a whole has spent a lot of time and money both studying avalanches and their causes and working on ways to minimize the risk to the population.

At the topline, according to the most recent ten years' worth of data compiled and studied by the Colorado Avalanche Information Center, a program under the Colorado Department of Natural Resources, twenty-seven people die every winter as a result of avalanches in the United States. This includes incidents in states as far flung as Alaska, Colorado, New Hampshire, Montana, and, yes, even Arizona (the desert state has suffered one avalanche fatality to date, in 1995), in a range of activities including hiking, climbing, mining, snowmobiling, and more, including highway work, which must be a particularly unpleasant way to go, while at work. All that said, the vast majority of avalanche fatalities in this country tend to happen where and when you'd expect: in the Western United States when skiers venture into the backcountry to earn their turns.

This fact plays out in the general numbers of avalanche fatalities, which have been trended upward for years. In fact, the winters of 2008 and 2010 were the deadliest since recordkeeping began in the 1950s with thity-six fatalities each, and nine of the last twenty winters have seen more than thirty avalanche fatalities in this country. The worldwide average is about 150 annually.

According to a forty-five-year study of slide deaths, conducted by Denver Health Medical Center's Division of Emergency Medicine and published in 1999 in *Wilderness Environmental Medicine*, a total of 440 victims were killed in 324 fatal avalanches in the second half of the twentieth century, and the data came to some interesting conclusions. The average avalanche victim at that time was 27.6 years old, a man (83.7 percent) and a climber (25.5 percent), backcountry skier (22.7 percent), out-of-bounds skier who has ducked under the boundary rope at an established ski resort (10 percent), or snowmobiler (6.8 percent). The study concluded that deaths among in-bounds skiers, highway workers, and motorists were declining, while incidents involving out-of-bounds skiers, snowmobilers, ski patrollers, and backcountry skiers were on the rise.

Why?

More and more people are heading out into the backcountry, often times placing themselves at risk without even realizing it.

According to the Snow Sports Industries America's (SIA) 2015 industry fact sheet, sales of what the group terms "backcountry accessories"—including avalanche beacons, probes, shovels, and climbing skins—increased 12 percent year over year by 2015, and Alpine/Alpine Touring boots, which are used by backcountry skiers to allow them to climb up a snow-covered slope and later ski back down in, made up 16 percent of the overall ski boot market that year, an all-time high. Overall, sales of backcountry-ready skis, boots, and accessories are up to

$54 million annually and the SIA estimates that as many as six million skiers and snowboarders are now heading out into the backcountry, in some form or another.

For an industry like skiing, which has been in decline for more than a decade, the increasing popularity of the backcountry is seen as a much-needed lifeline. At the 2017 SIA Snow Show in Denver, the industry's largest annual trade show, backcountry was front and center nearly everywhere, with even traditional resort skiing brands—such as Rossignol, Aplina, and Head—moving into backcountry gear as quickly as possible. According to the *Aspen Times,* legacy ski brand Salomon even featured its MTN Lab and MTN Explore lines of backcountry boots as the focus of its booth setup that year, just another indication of where the snow sports market is headed.

A decade ago—hell, even two years ago—backcountry skiing and snowboarding represented only a sliver of the overall winter sports market and was barely visible at events like the annual SIA. That has changed in a big way.

But there's a dark side to this trend.

Writing in *Outside* magazine in February 2017, former skiing editor Marc Peruzzi mourned the carefree and fun golden era of downhill skiing in the 1960s and '70s, before the sport became fragmented into segments based on specific types of skiing: extreme, freestyle, and now backcountry.

"Skiing participation has flatlined for 20 years," he wrote. "Snowboarding, sadly, is in decline. Backcountry skiing has the energy now, but its high cost of entry—dying in an avalanche—will meter participation as the larger sport awaits the next revolution."

That's what the market is doing, and what comes next is anyone's guess, but when it comes to avalanches and their behavior, we actually know quite a bit about what causes snow to slide, where it will let loose, and how to avoid being involved in the first place. According to the US Forest Service's National Avalanche Center, avalanches kill more people every year on National Forest land than any other natural hazard, and avoiding them is a simple matter of knowing what causes them and where, and then avoiding those areas whenever possible.

Avalanches can happen on slopes between twenty and forty degrees. Gravity pulls snow down steeper slopes before enough can build up to create an avalanche hazard, and on milder slopes there is rarely enough potential energy to cause snow buildup to slide. The sweet spot for avalanches is a slope angle of roughly degrees. Recent snowfall and heavy snow loads on top of looser, less defined snow layers can also create the conditions for a slide, and cracks in the snow and the sound of those layers collapsing under the weight of the top snow are two tell tale signs that a slope may be ready to slide. Triggers can include anything from additional new precipitation, wind gusts, a temperature change, or the presence of humans or animals.

The American Avalanche Association has determined that as much as 90 percent of all fatal avalanches are triggered by the victim or someone in their party.

As a general rule, when traveling through the backcountry in the winter, the NAC recommends a few key questions to ask.

- Is this slope steep enough to slide? (Per the NAC: "The best way to determine whether the terrain is steep enough is to measure it with a slope meter. Slopes less steep than about 30 degrees rarely avalanche, while slopes steeper than about 35 degrees can and often do avalanche. If a slope is steep enough to be exciting . . . it is probably 35 degrees or steeper!")
- Is the snowpack unstable?
- What has the recent weather been?
- Is this slope connected to something that might slide?

This is where it gets complicated, and where the Lowe team got in trouble in China. The area where they were traveling was not steep enough to slide and seemed relatively safe, but far over their heads, many thousands of feet up the mountainside but connected directly to their location, conditions were primed for an avalanche and as soon as the cornice collapsed, it set in motion a chain of events that killed the two climbers far down below.

* * *

It's all about knowing the terrain and understanding what you are getting into, explains Ethan Greene, executive director of the Colorado Avalanche Information Center (CAIC). A former ski patroller, Greene went on to earn his Masters while studying snow drift formation and his PhD on snow microstructures and metamorphism, and he brings that deep theoretical understanding to the very practical, day-to-day work of avalanche forecasting.

According to Greene, the surprising thing is that you don't really need to know very much to go out into the backcountry snows and return safely. It all depends on what you want to do and how much preparation you're willing to do.

"If you want to go climb a building, or go skiing in Colorado and be on steep slopes in the middle of winter, you're going to have to have

More than any other outdoor risk, travel in avalanche country calls for careful planning, research, and a healthy respect for the power of the mountains.

a fair amount of knowledge to do that," he says. "But if you want to go snowshoeing in Rocky Mountain National Park, on some trails, and enjoy the winter time in Colorado, or other places, you can do that safely without having a huge amount of knowledge."

Much of what goes into avalanche safety, at least on the practical level, is being able to recognize anything strange and out of place so you can avoid it. Current avalanche activity in the immediate area is the obvious indicator that there is potential for future avalanches, as are areas of cracking and sounds of collapsing layers within the snow pack (often referred to by forecasters as a "whoomping" sound) that can indicate areas of instability in the snow. Those are all going to be very short-term signs that avalanches have potential in a given area, and are what Greene refers to as "minute-by-minute" signs that a slide is possible. However, a wider, more long-term view can be helpful in determining not only which areas are likely to slide but also where avalanche activity is going forward.

"What you want to do is go to the weather reports and start to look at what's been happening over [the last several] hours and days. Most avalanches happen during or after a loading event, and those loading events are heavy precipitation, snowfall, or wind," he says. "Rain on snow would be another red light, a flashing warning sign that the avalanche risk is going to increase dramatically. [And] any large warming event where you're going to start to get melted snow pack and get water into the snow pack."

Get Informed: Knowledge is power in avalanche country, and there are various different ways to gain access to local information before venturing out into potentially dangerous conditions. It depends on where you are going, Greene says. In developed areas with safety groups, and rangers, and avalanche research centers such as the CAIC, you'll likely have access to deep, detailed information about conditions and risk factors specifically tailored to that area on that day. Greene suggests taking this information on the avalanche condition and going through it just as you would a weather forecast. You'll want to know what the downrange forecast is so you'll have a place to start and a good idea of what you might be getting into and what the conditions are going to be like. With that information in hand, safe travel through avalanche country is simply a matter of following the guidance of professional avalanche forecasters and taking their conditions reports seriously. Stay out of the areas where slides are likely forecast to happen or where conditions have been determined to be optimal for them, and travel carefully through areas of known avalanche activity.

This is backcountry safety 101.

But it's when visiting remote areas or places that don't have public avalanche information programs that you'll really need to have solid backcountry analysis skills. In those cases, you really won't have much information to start with beyond the regular weather forecast, so you'll need to stop and think more about what's been happing in the weather, what's been happening in the snow pack, and what the last week or so has been like in the area you're visiting. Forecasters often talk about obvious times of snow pack instability, so what you're looking for are conditions in the recent past that would suggest the snow is overweight and unstable, ready to slide.

"You're going to a place you've never been before and you really have no information," Greene says. "So you look around, see if there are any signs of recent avalanches. If so, what's the pattern in the char-acteristics, the terrain characteristics? Are these avalanches happening at high elevation, mid or low elevation? Are they all happening on the north or the south facing slopes? Are they breaking within the snow pack or are they breaking deeper down into the snow pack?"

All of this is a way to get an idea of what's been happening in the area and look for areas of rapid change. Are there big snowstorms mov-ing through? If so, that new snow on top of unstable snow layers may be enough to trigger an avalanche. Are rain showers in the forecast? That added water can further weaken the snow pack. Has there been a recent and rapid warm up that has started to melt the top layers of snow? This adds water to the snow pack as well, breaking down its structure deep within the snow. There are all signs that avalanche potential is on the rise quickly.

Know What You're Looking At: It's a fact, proven in high school physics classes all over the world, that some terrain is capable of producing avalanches and some terrain is not. Maybe it is too steep, maybe it is too flat, but forecasters know that slopes between thirty and forty-five degrees, and sometimes down to even twenty-five degrees, are where most avalanches occur. That range can be difficult to spot in the backcountry, so a slope meter is a good investment that will enable you to quickly and easily sight slope angles on the fly to determine which are safe versus which are potentially dangerous.

"You need a steep enough slope that, when the snow breaks away from the hillside, it's going to roll down the hill," Greene says. "So anything below about twenty-five degrees is just going to sink into the hillside rather than roll down it. Then you also need enough snow to build up so that you have these different layers of snow, because that's where the fractures tend to run across, is between these layers. As you get up over fifty, sixty degrees, you tend to get a lot of shedding of the snow during big snow falls. You just don't end up with this kind of layer cake structure and you just get constant loose snow slipping avalanches. It's the same thing that you would see in the sand dunes."

Get Out of the Way: The simple fact is, depending on the size of the avalanche, survival depends largely on how quickly and how effectively you can get out of its way without getting caught up in it.

Slab avalanches, which generally start as a result of fractures in the snow, are the big ones that typically kill people, Greene says, and if you're seeing huge avalanches like that rolling down the hill then the only thing you can really do is avoid them. This means not only getting out from underneath the floats where they are running but far, far away. Large slab avalanches are capable of running over flat areas and continuing far beyond their original slopes, so you really need to give them a wide berth where possible.

"A lot of it depends on how sensitive things are, and what the conditions are like," he says. "If you're seeing avalanches, then you want to give them a fairly wide berth. But it may be that all you need to do is stick to the ridgeline where you can stay on a low angle slope and avoid some of the steeper terrain. It really depends."

Glacier Travel

It was cold but clear in late November 2015, when husband-and-wife climbers Alison and Thomas Fountain left their home in McMinnville, Oregon, about forty miles southwest of Portland, and started the two-hour drive east to Marion Falls, near the base of Mount Jefferson, in the Willamette National Forest. As part of the chain of volcanoes that dot this part of the Pacific Northwest, the 10,500-foot Mount Jefferson is the second-highest peak in Oregon, after Mount Hood, and is a popular weekend destination for hikers and climbers from the coastal areas.

It is also, like many of the other high peaks in the area, heavily glaciated and rocky, with areas near the top of the cone and on its slopes showing evidence of glacial erosion that have been going on since the Ice Age. Today, five named glaciers remain on Mount Jefferson, including the Milk Creek, Jefferson Park, Russell, Waldo, and Whitewater glaciers. Whitewater is the largest of the group, covering an area of nearly two miles and extending from near the summit of the peak down to about 7,500 feet on the east side of the mountain. Waldo is Mount Jefferson's other most prominent glacier, named for John Breckenridge Waldo, a prominent Oregon politician and environmentalist in the nineteenth century, covering a large area on the high southeast slope of the mountain.

None of this is remotely unusual. Oregon lies in the so-called "Ring of Fire," the geological region that roughly outlines the Pacific Ocean and is marked by increased seismic and volcanic activity. The area, which extends from the west coast of the United States to Alaska, eastern Russia, Japan, Indonesia, and New Zealand, is home to more than 75 percent of the world's volcanoes and has seen nearly 90 percent of all the world's earthquakes over the years. This seismic activity is especially apparent in the Pacific Northwest, where volcanic activity on the eastern edge of the Ring of Fire over the course of millennia has dotted the landscape with the rocky cones of dormant (and active) volcanoes. From Washington's Mount Rainer and Mount Saint Helens to Mount Hood and Mount Jefferson in Oregon, all of the high peaks in the region share this history. Mount Jefferson last erupted roughly 15,000 years ago.

Glacial activity is part of the equation in this part of the world as well, and during the last Ice Age ice flows carved out much of Mount Jefferson, and the other Northwestern peaks—except for Mount Saint Helens, of course, which got its latest facelift as a result of a major eruption in 1980—leaving them roughly as we see them today. The glaciers that remain on these mountains are a mere sliver of the ice and snow that used to cover this region in antiquity.

But they are still adequate for climbing and hiking fun, and that is exactly what the Fountains where looking for when they parked their car at the Marion County trailhead that November day and hiked up to the Jefferson Park Glacier climbing area at roughly 8,800 feet. Both were experienced climbers who had bagged peaks all over the Pacific Northwest, including previous visits to Mount Jefferson, and came adequately equipped to climb.

But tragedy struck in the afternoon, when Thomas fell into a crevasse and became stuck within the glacier. Crevasses are deep cracks or fissures that form in glacial ice, often as a result of movement in the ice over the rigid bedrock below. They are often nearly vertical, with slick, deep blue ice walls that are all but impossible to climb, and can extend down as much as 150 feet into the ice and stretch for hundreds of yards across the ice sheet. To make matters worse, snowfall will sometimes build up on top of these openings, creating snow bridges that obscure the hazard but are not strong enough to support the weight of a human on top of them, effectively turning the crevasse into a hidden trap door that can collapse under a hiker or climber at any time. And, given that crevasses can open and close repeatedly as a glacier ages, they make for an ever-changing landscape of hidden risks for anyone walking on the ice above.

For climbers, the risk is simple. One minute they're making their way along the face of the glacier, and the next they are plunging deep into the ice, out of sight and with almost no way to climb out on their own. Depending on the depth and orientation of the glacier, and whatever injuries the victim suffers on the way down, aid from above with ropes and support is often the only hope of rescue from a deep crevasse.

That is exactly what happened to Thomas Fountain that day as he and his wife were attempting to reach the summit. He took a wrong step, slid an estimated 500 feet down the side of the mountain, and slipped down into the crevasse that eventually took his life. Alison was unharmed in the incident and was able to text for help after the fall, but poor weather conditions meant that she had to spend the ensuing night alone, in the cold, and exposed on the side of Mount Jefferson.

A nurse by training, she climbed down into the crevasse itself to spend one last night with her husband, checking his vital signs in the darkness, several bones in his arms and hands broken after the fall, and speaking with him to keep him alert. He eventually died as a result of his head injuries.

Rescuers finally made it to their location, over what was described as particularly difficult terrain, early the next morning, evacuating them off of the mountain by helicopter. Thomas became the first person to die on Mount Jefferson since 2001.

A terrible accident, the incident served to remind many in the Pacific Northwest climbing community of the dangers that lurk on even the most popular and well-traveled of their local mountains. Even the most experienced, best equipped climbers—and the Fountains were both that day in 2015—can encounter situations that they cannot foresee and cannot prevent in the moment, and glacier travel is rife with hidden dangers.

* * *

Glaciers are, in the eyes of those who study and document, very similar to living, breathing things. Although they are formed from ice, snow, and water, they are constantly evolving and changing, growing larger in the winter months, shrinking down in the summers, and slowly changing their location over the course of time. They are rivers of ice, ever moving toward the sea.

Of course, none of this is directly visible to the human eye. For example, in the summer of 2012, observers from the University of Washington recorded the fastest-ever speed for a glacier, tracking the forward progress of the Jakobshavn Glacier, Greenland's largest, at a blistering 10.5 miles per year. That doesn't seem like much, but when you think about it in feet—roughly 151 feet per day—the reality of the situation becomes clear.

"We are now seeing summer speeds more than four times what they were in the 1990s, on a glacier which at that time was believed to be one of the fastest, if not the fastest, glacier in Greenland," lead author Ian Joughin, a glaciologist at University of Washington Polar Science Center, told the university's press office when the results of the study were reported in 2014.

But Jakobshavn, which also happens to be the glacier that is believed to have created the iceberg that sunk the Titanic, is an anomaly, the fastest-moving glacier in the world. Worldwide, glacier speed depends on a long list of variables including thickness, ambient temperatures, slope, snowfall levels, and more, resulting in glaciers that move as little as zero feet per year as well as others that slip along by as much as half a mile. Rising temperatures worldwide have been changing glacier behaviors in some parts of the world, leading to dramatic pullbacks in places such as Montana's Glacier National Park and even Jakobshavn, which is retreating from the Greenland interior by about half a mile per year, but climate change and glaciers are complicated and the results aren't uniform. In some parts of the world, deep in Alaska for instance, glaciers are actually growing in size, even as others nearby are shrinking.

Glacier ecology is complicated.

All that said, even with the changes that are going on in global climate right now, chances are very good that glaciers will be with us for some time, at least as long as anyone reading this book is alive. This is a very good thing for the human race, as well as anyone interested in visiting the unique and beautiful frozen worlds of these slow-moving giants. But glacier travel does present its own challenges, as illustrated by the story about the Fountains from earlier in this chapter. For, as special as glaciers are, they are very different than the Earth of stone and soil that most of us are familiar with and as a result present a number of unique risk factors.

Granted, this is not a risk factor that most, or many, people face in the outdoors. Only a small portion of the population ventures out in the winter at all (compared to, say, day hikers in the summer), and even among those that do, glaciers are not a common destination for many. This is literally a fraction of a fraction.

As a result, fatality and injury statistics on glacier travel are almost impossible to find, and even those numbers that do exist are very small. Those who do spend time on the surface of glaciers, either in North America or elsewhere in the world, tend to be very careful and experienced; this is not a landscape that many people venture into unprepared. But that is not to play down the very real risks that do exist in glacier travel, and those risks, as well as the common ways that experienced winter climbers and hikers address them, are the reason that this chapter is in this book.

Just because few people die on glaciers doesn't mean there aren't some very real risks there.

Crevasses: The deep fissures in the face of a glacier are literally torn open by the force of ice moving over bedrock, with part of the glacier continuing forward and another part staying put (at least for the time being). A crevasse is literally a tear in the surface of the glacier, and as such they can form effectively anywhere and close up or reopen at unexpected times. Think of a glacier as a slow-moving stream of sand moving down a mild slope. Some of it will move easily on the top of the stack, while the sand nearer the bottom will get hung up on the surface it is moving across and will move slower. Although difficult to picture with sand, the slower-moving sections of a glacier can become hung up and tear apart from the faster-moving part on top, leading to the creation of crevasses. (This is also how avalanches function, with the lower portions of the snowpack often staying put when the snow on top of a weak layer slides.) When snow falls on top of a glacier it can form snow bridges over the tops of crevasses, hiding them from view. Mapping the ever-changing array of crevasses on a given glacier is effectively impossible, so climbers rely on ropes, connecting each member of a party together so that those on the surface can pull up anyone who falls in, as well as ice axes and probes to test the ground before moving forward.

Glacier Storms: In places like Iceland where glaciers are plentiful and near many human settlements, what are known as "glacier storms" is a concern. These low-level snowstorms form when strong winds, another common feature in Iceland, blow across glaciated landscapes, whipping up the top layers of snow and creating whiteout conditions, even on blue sky days. The risk with these "fake" storms is that they can rise up very quickly and last for hours, leaving hikers potentially lost in the swirling snow with no idea which way to go and no way to avoid falling into a crevasse. Even rescuers can't find hikers who get caught on glaciers in the midst of these storms before the victim usually freezes to death. Careful orienting whenever traveling in glacier country is critical.

Calving: One of the most stunning phenomenon in nature, glaciers are constantly "calving," or birthing new icebergs as large chunks of ice break off from the edge of a glacier where it reaches open water, letting loose with a deafening, primordial crack that sounds like a gunshot. These can be as small as basketballs or as large as US states—in January 2017, a massive fifty-mile-long rift along the edge of a glacier sheet in Antarctica resulted in the calving off of a piece of ice larger than New York's Long Island, while the largest known iceberg in human history calved from the Ross Ice Shelf in Antarctica in March 2000, resulting in a floating piece of ice that measured 183 miles long by 23 miles wide—and can be both immediately and long-term dangerous. For anyone walking on a glacier or viewing it from the water, either in a kayak or larger boat, these iceberg calvings are a very immediate danger and a very good reason to always keep your distance from the edge of an active glacier. As for the long-term implications of this natural phenomenon, the name "Titanic" should say it all.

"So, for us, we're usually dealing with glaciers that we know really well, and we aren't often on unknown terrain," says Robert Jantzen, a mountaineering guide with International Mountain Guides, based near Washington's Mount Rainier, who we met earlier in the book. "And here on Rainier we're usually dealing with crevasses that are five, ten, fifteen, twenty feet across, not much bigger. Up in Alaska, you can deal with 100-foot-across crevasses."

The reason this scale is important to guides like Jantzen is that climbers always need to be spaced out along the ropes in such a way that, if you're crossing a snow bridge over one of these big cracks, you don't have two people on the snow bridge at any one time. That's typically not a challenge when dealing with the "small" crevasses on a mountain like Rainier, but when those gaps widen to 100 feet across

Glacial ice is slow moving and massive, but it can also trap unsuspecting hikers and climbers and leave them lost in a frozen, inescapable landscape.

and more, as mentioned, that's when careful route planning comes into play. One of the primary things that guides focus on when crossing a crevasse field, Jantzen says, is making sure this rope travel technique, which is critical to keeping climbers safe in the event of a fall, is working properly and keeping people safe, rather than becoming an extra liability. "You rope a bunch of people together and then you stick them all on the same snow bridge, you've actually created more of a liability and less safety," he says.

"As we're traveling, we're paying really close attention to what's above us," he explains. "Is there a slope, or if the glacier's moving uphill and we're going right up the glacier, is there a point on it where we enter avalanche terrain? Or a place where an avalanche could occur above us, and take us down?"

On glaciers, he says, avalanches are an ever-present hazard, because even a small slide can knock a team member off into a crevasse, and then bury them in the crevasse, which would make them very hard to rescue. So climbers are always watching the avalanche conditions closely, checking for the risk factors, and traveling in such a way that they are not exposed to overhead hazards.

Navigation on the glacier face is essentially like any other trail, with map, compass, GPS, and a general sense of direction. But Jantzen says he's also looking for what are called "compression zones," which are areas on the glacier where the ice is moving slower than the surrounding area for some reason.

"In these compression zones the ice all builds up together and forms a big solid block, instead of being all cracked up in big crevasses," he says. "Those compression zones can give you a pretty good highway. You're looking for micro-terrain features, any indications of a crevasse. Make sure to try and keep your travel more in compression zones."

Of course, this being a glacier, the landscapes that you're crossing and the hazards that you are looking for are constantly changing. Over the course of the season, Jantzen says, it changed very significantly, building up under new ice and snow in the winter and accelerating its move down the mountain in the summer heat. As this process plays out, the same spot on a glacier can go from a supported zone of compression and a really safe place to an unsupported and risky area in the course of just a few days or weeks.

"Our camp, on Ingraham Flats on Rainier, is a good example to the zone of compression," he explains. "When we put it there in May it was in a really safe area. As the glacier below it moved and collapsed, due to the warming trend of summer, we had to keep moving our camp up into a smaller and smaller zone of compression, because it became unsupported and actually opened up into crevasses, where we originally placed the camp."

It sounds intimidating, but Jantzen says in reality glaciers can be fun, dynamic environments. When you get a hot week and the glacier warms up a bit, you'll start to see crevasses opening up in new areas, creating gaps of seven feet or more over the course of a week pretty easily in the summer. Safe travel in this type of environment, of course, takes a little more awareness than it does over solid ground, but glacier exploration is a unique, special treat that anyone who is comfortable in the backcountry should experience at least once in their life, and it's something where a little knowledge goes a long way. For instance, IMG leads groups up Mount Rainier all time in which no one on the climb has any mountaineering experience. In those cases, they stick to a couple of known safe routes and the guide make all of the decisions for them—setting up the rope, choosing the routes, safeguarding them in terrain they don't yet understand—but they are usually able to get to the summit safely even without knowing everything that's going on. Even more experienced climbers who make such trips, they may not be 100 percent comfortable with crevasse rescues and other advanced techniques, but by knowing the general do's and don'ts and using good common sense, they are able to keep themselves out of trouble even without the help of guides.

"I think the biggest thing with having common sense is knowing when you're out of your league and having your exit strategy," Jantzen says. "I learned to climb by biting off more than I could chew for a while, and that was really fun and I learned a lot, but I had a long time there, as I was first starting to be a climber, where I didn't make many summits. Each time I'd progress a bit further and eventually I recognized that I had to keep to my limits and my comfort level, to be responsible for what I was doing, and then I'd back off. That's something really important to keep in mind in the mountains: know your limits and have a plan to back off when you need to."

Snow Blindness/Changing Weather Conditions

The San Gabriel Mountains in Southern California run roughly east to west on the north side of the Los Angeles metro area. Situated between the Mojave Desert and the San Joaquin Valley north of Santa Barbara, the San Gabriels mainly consist of low peaks and rolling, grass covered hills, some of which can be quite steep. The foothills of the Santa Monica Mountains, immediately to the south of the San Gabriel chain, is better known to movie fans and tourists worldwide as the Hollywood Hills.

Neither of these areas is particularly high in terms of elevation. Mount San Antonio, which is commonly called Mount Baldy, is the highest peak in the chain as well as Los Angeles County, its often snow-covered peak looming over the city, but even it barely cracks 10,000 feet. Compared to the high California peaks of the Sierra Nevada or the Pacific Northwest, these mountains seem entry-level, and their proximity to a major metro area and walk-up access makes them very appealing peaks for a wide range of hikers.

But that doesn't mean they are easy, or safe. Far from it, in fact.

The weather in these mountains has a well-deserved reputation for unpredictability, with sunny skies giving way to blinding snowstorms, and back again, all in the course of a few hours. This fact is something like a mountain version of the "mircoclimates" that Californians are so proud of. Defined as "the essentially uniform local climate of a usually small site or habitat," microclimates are common along the Pacific coast and are simply atmospheric conditions that change rapidly from one area to the next. Sit at a beachfront café in Santa Barbara and it's 75 degrees and sunny. But get in your car and drive over the San Gabriels into Los Olivos, and once you get there it might be 105 and overcast. In the meantime, the mountains themselves are fogged in and barely above freezing.

Those are all microclimates.

The phenomenon, which is not isolated to California, is the result of air masses from the ocean rapidly cooling the air over land, with sometimes surprising effects. Combined with the dry, desert air covering California to the east, the variability of weather in the state is one of its hallmarks. (And can be surprising to anyone who considers LA the land of endless sunshine year-round. In addition to the Santa Ana winds, which pull hot, dry air in from the east every fall, southern California even has its own monsoon season in late June, drenching the area daily and causing the occasional mudslide along the coast.)

All of this means changeable weather in LA, and downright dangerous weather up in the hills surrounding the city. On Mount Baldy, for example, temperatures have been known to swing dozens of degrees in both directions, not only as you climb and descend the mountain but as you pass through different temperature zones on its slopes. Snow can roll in on the lower slopes after a hiker reaches the summit, for instance, forcing them to trudge through unexpected weather on the way down, or vice versa.

In this way, it is not too different from Mount Washington in New Hampshire, another mountain near a coastline that is famous for its wicked weather. On April 12, 1934, for instance, the record for measured wind speed (noncyclone) was set at its summit when the Mount Washington Observatory recorded gusts of 231, and its climate in general can put up highs in the fifties and lows in the negative fifties. Mountain weather can always be erratic, but in these coastal areas it is even more so.

But Mount Baldy is a popular hike, and the summit routes are often crowded with day hikers in nice weather. It's also a beautiful summit, completely tree-free—hence the somewhat obvious name— that offers unobstructed views from the desert to the ocean, including the entire sprawling LA metro area, something unique and precious in such a densely populated area. When the sun is shining, it can be a great way to spend a few hours away from the beach, which is likely exactly what Michelle Yu was thinking when she set out to hike Baldy on December 4, 2010.

It was December, true, and winter hikes of the mountain generally call for ice axes and crampons, and Yu was an experienced mountaineer who was properly equipped for the season. A local who had climbed Baldy dozens of times, Yu also had climbing experience on Denali, Mount Rainier, Mount Shasta, and other high peaks, and was believed to simply be heading out to Mount Baldy as a training climb for her next adventure. (She was found with more than 40 pounds of rocks in her backpack, training for her upcoming climb in the Andes.)

But she didn't make it back.

As described by David Whiting in the *Orange County Register* after the incident, variable weather conditions on the mountain can challenge any climber, no matter how experienced or prepared they are.

"Ron Campbell, *Register* writer and accidents and incidents investigator for the Sierra Club's local safety committee, didn't take much equipment that day and turned around at the ski hut, a place where climbers often gear up for the mountain's slippery slopes," Whiting wrote in a 2013 column. "Campbell signed the log book at 8:20 a.m. and had supper with his family that night. Michelle Yu signed the log about 8:30 a.m. Her body was recovered five days later."

The reason?

We may never know exactly. Search and rescue teams found her body at the bottom of a steep, ice-covered slope more than 2,100 feet below the summit of the mountain about a week after she was reported missing. It is believed that she lost her way as weather conditions on the mountain deteriorated, leading her to lose her footing or make a wrong turn that led to her death. Whatever the specific circumstances that led to her death, the simple fact that an experienced climber like Yu, who had brought the correct gear for a winter climb and knew the area well, could still fall victim to the whims of mountain weather should serve

Snow glare can be worse than the glare that comes off the water.

as a warning for all. Preparation can only get you so far when it comes to surviving in the backcountry. Sometimes a little common sense, and knowing when to turn back in the face of poor conditions, is all it takes.

"Checking the weather report before you go is important," says hiking guidebook author Randi Minetor, "and keeping an eye on what's really happening around you. Right now I'm working on a book called *Death on Mount Washington* where it's all about weather. People set out on a seventy degree day and they start down the trail, and all of a sudden it's thirty and snowing in August. They never took into consideration that might happen. In this day of twenty-four-hour newscasts and weather in the palm of your hand, there's no excuse for not knowing that something may change."

On any trip into the backcountry, she says, you need to be prepared with the clothing that you're going to need for any type of weather: rain, snow, heat, cold, etc. And you need to be prepared to hunker down in the event that conditions change rapidly and you aren't able to get out in time. This generally means carrying extra food, some sort of basic shelter, as well as extra water and a way to light a fire.

It's also critical to know when to turn back, to recognize when conditions get too bad to continue forward and the best course of action is a hasty retreat.

"That's a big thing on Mount Washington," Minetor says. "People will figure they got this far and they want to go for the summit. It's a trail, it's not like it's climbing, it's an established trail. But they just encounter a level of weather up there that they are just not prepared for at all."

Mount Washington in particular is an interesting case because the mountain itself is so accessible. It is less than four hours from Boston, and there is a road all the way up to the top that is open to drivers from May to October. (Anyone who has spent any time at all in the Northeast has surely seen the "THIS CAR CLIMBED MT. WASHINGTON" bumper stickers.) Surely a mountain like that isn't as tough as everyone says it is, right? Many people have driven up to the summit, taken in the view, so hiking up there seems like it probably is not any different.

Wrong. Mount Washington, as mentioned elsewhere in this book, is home to some of the most extreme weather on the planet and those August snowstorms are all but a regular occurrence up there.

"I actually have a friend who [climbed Mount Washington in the winter] a couple of weeks ago," Minetor says. "It's bitter cold. It's crazy cold. It's windy. The wind is unbelievable at the top of the mountain. There's a woman who died up there just a couple of years ago because she decided to do the President's Range, all five peaks in one go. She didn't make it to the second one. She got caught in the snowstorm. It's one thing to encounter weather you don't expect, but there's no excuse in February not knowing it's going to snow. You need to be prepared for that."

In these situations, she says, carrying extra clothing is critical. For one thing, extra layers can help keep you warm. But staying dry is the big thing. Once you get wet—whether it's in winter or the height of summer—you get chilled and can't warm up. Left too long, this can develop into hypothermia, and then you're in real trouble.

"Just being familiar [with the weather patterns in the area you're visiting] is really important," Minetor says. "And if you're not familiar, being extra cautious about what you're going to need so that you come home alive."

Getting Lost

It never should have happened.

Sixty-six-year-old Geraldine "Gerry" Largay had been out on the trail for the better part of four months by then. She had taken classes on hiking discipline and tracking. Was well supplied and supported by her husband and well known among the other hikers on the trail. She was tracking her progress in a trail diary, having completed more than 1,000 miles of the 2,168-mile Appalachian Trail.

But still, she got lost. Hopelessly, imperceptibly lost, after wandering off the trail to use the bathroom near the Bigelow Preserve in Western Maine.

To the hikers she—trail name: "Inchworm"—encountered that day in 2013, it was as if she simply disappeared. Now you see her, now you don't. The only clue left behind was a selfie she took of herself that morning as she prepared to leave the shelter where she had spent the previous night.

"In somm trouble," she texted to her husband, George, who was waiting at the Route 27 intersection twenty-two miles away for a resupply stop that day. "Got off trail to go to br. Now lost. Can u call AMC to c if a trail maintainer can help me. Somewhere north of woods road. XOX."

Rural Maine isn't known for good cell service and the text never went through. She tried ten times in an hour with no luck.

The next day she tried again: "Lost since yesterday. Off trail 3 or 4 miles. Call police for what to do pls. XOX."

Again, nothing.

By this time, Gerry's husband had grown concerned about her whereabouts and notified local rangers. An official search was launched, scouring the area between her last known location, the AT shelter where she had spent the night before her disappearance, and the Route 27 meeting point.

For days they searched, with teams of volunteers, aircraft, and dogs. The search expanded to include state police, national park rangers, and fire departments from all over the country, digging into the ridges and valleys, going on every tip they could find.

They found nothing.

Eventually, the trail grew cold and the search was called off. Largay was given up for dead.

For two years, Largay's disappearance remained a mystery, just one more missing piece in the ever-expanding story of the Appalachian Trail. Every year, hundreds of hikers like Gerry set out to thru-hike the whole 2,168 miles, and countless thousands more venture out for hours, days, and weekends in the wilderness. People go missing. Accidents happen. It is not entirely unheard of for hikers to simply wander off, leave the trail, and never be heard from again.

Largay was just one more of those. A dreamer who, maybe, when faced with the reality of hiking 2,000-plus miles, decided that it just wasn't worth the pain and suffering, wasn't worth sleeping on the ground and hiking in the rain, wearing the same clothes day after day, and just left. It had happened before.

But that wasn't the case this time.

According to the ranger who found her body, a full two years after she wandered off the trail to use the bathroom, it wasn't until he was nearly on top of the remains of her tent that he realized what he was seeing. A tent, partially collapsed, was almost completely camouflaged by the surrounding underbrush, and only Gerry's green backpack was immediately identifiable. Rangers later found maps, a jacket, a flashlight, and a space blanket scattered around the site, along with proof that the victim had tried to scrape together a means of survival after she got lost.

There were burn marks on nearby trees that looked man-made, proof that she had tried to start a fire for warmth or to be seen. And her bedding was built up, with "small trees, pine needles and possibly some dirt in an attempt to keep her tent out of any water."

Located near the border of Navy-owned and public properties, the site was in very dense woods a good distance from the AT.

With the mystery of her whereabouts solved, the question in the case shifted to: How long had Gerry Largay spent out away from the trail after she got lost?

Clearly, she had been out on her own for some time, long enough to make camp, string up some space blankets for shade, work on making a fire, and attempt to get out. This had not been a simple overnight experience for her.

Her trail diary held the final clue.

Covered with a thin layer of growing moss and with Gerry's handwritten inscription on the front cover—"George Please Read XOXO"—the book contained regular entries that continued through most of August, nearly a month after she had gone missing. According to her notes, she had spent a few days wandering the area after making a wrong turn across a stream, looking for hills or ridges or any other landmarks that she could use to figure out her position and get back to the trail.

Later study would show that she survived alone in the woods for a full twenty-six days after getting lost.

As if that were not heartbreaking enough, she had several missed opportunities over the course of those twenty-six days. Based on maps made of the discovery site, tracker dogs had come within 100 yards of her on at least two separate occasions. Had she pitched her tent in a nearby clearing, search aircraft might have spotted her. And had she been able to start a fire, the smoke may have directed rangers in her direction.

In the end, the tragedy was simply a case of too many things going wrong at the same time.

Through her ordeal, though, Largay remained fully aware of her situation, writing in her journal some two weeks after getting lost: "When you find my body, please call my husband George and my daughter Kerry," she wrote. "It will be the greatest kindness for them to know that I am dead and where you found me—no matter how many years from now. Please find it in your heart to mail the contents of this bag to one of them."

* * *

Whenever someone gets lost in the backcountry, and particularly when they die as a result, it's all too easy to say "it never should have happened." I should know. I started this chapter with those exact words.

But the truth is, it happens all too often, and no case is like another.

From people who find their own way out, go unreported, or simply disappear without anyone noticing, it is all but impossible to accurately estimate how many people get lost in the woods in a given year. The conventional wisdom among search and rescue professionals is that roughly 2,000 people get lost on hikes in the United States every year, although the vast majority of these eventually find their way to safety, either on their own or with the help of rescuers. Anecdotally, these numbers are on the rise, with the ninety search and rescue teams associated with the Mountain Rescue Association, which runs rescue teams in twenty states, reporting as many as 3,000 rescue missions each year, up sharply in the last decade.

But, as with everything, the true number depends on too many variables to count. Forest rangers with the New York State Department of Environmental Conservation say that they search for about 200 lost or stranded people every year—which would put the whole country on pace for as many as 10,000 lost people annually—to the local officers with Larimer County Search and Rescue, which conducts about seventy rescue operations on Colorado's Front Range every year.

But, despite all this variability, one thing that everyone in search and rescue can agree on when it comes to lost and stranded hikers is that time matters.

Paul Dudchenko, the author of *Why People Get Lost* told the *Little-Things* blog that all humans are born with an internal compass, or sense of direction, that generally helps keep us oriented as we go about our day-to-day lives. The trouble, he says, comes when we find ourselves in an environment that we're unfamiliar with and can't immediately identify.

"It usually is very good because we walk around familiar landmarks by which we can orient ourselves," he said. "But if we are someplace where there is no ability to correct it, our compass starts to drift."

That's why, Dudchenko says, that the first seventy-two hours after getting lost are critical. Up until that point, the body's internal compass is still able to determine direction based on where it started, hopefully finding the way back to the trail or campsite. Wait too long, though, and it gets more and more difficult to make out which way is which in the landmark-free environment of the backcountry, making it increasingly difficult for a victim to find their way out. Add to that the stress and challenge of spending several nights exposed in the wilderness, sometimes without adequate food or water, and the situation can quickly become critical.

Gerry Largey's lengthy stay in the woods after she got lost is the exception in these cases, not the rule.

That's why, Larimer County Search and Rescue's Don Davis told *The Coloradoan* that weathering those first seventy-two hours comes down to three things: a positive mental attitude, proper equipment, and knowledge of how to take care of yourself in the wilderness. Of these, he says that having a positive mental attitude accounts for 80 percent of the overall success.

Be Prepared: The US Forest Service advises that the best tool anyone can use to help prevent getting lost in the outdoors is advanced planning. "You must expect the unexpected and plan accordingly," the agency writes on its website. "Even if you are going out for just a few hours, pack enough essentials that you can stay hydrated, fueled and prepared for any type of weather." This includes more than enough food and water for whatever activity you have planned, a compass or GPS, up-to-date maps of the area, appropriate clothing and gear for the terrain you'll be exploring, blankets, flashlights, waterproof matches, and anything else you'll need to survive a night alone in the wilderness.

Keep Others Informed: All that said, the first rule of safe travel in the backcountry, no matter where you are going or what you are doing, is telling someone what you have planned and how long you'll be gone. A friend, a family member, a neighbor, anyone who will notice if you don't return on schedule and can notify authorities to search for you. Make sure they know exactly where you're going, what you're driving, where you plan to park, when you'll return, and which trails you'll be using, so that rescuers will have a starting point to plan their response. The Forest Service also recommends checking in with the local ranger district or forest office ahead of your departure to keep them informed of your plans and to find out about any special warnings, fire updates, flooding, trail conditions, and more.

Keep It Simple: When you sense that you've lost your way, immediately stop moving and take stock of your situation. Can you retrace your steps and find your way back to where you started? Do you see any recognizable landmarks? Can you judge how long you've been walking since you last knew where you were? At this point, according to the Forest Service, panic is your greatest enemy so it is critical to remain calm, keep your wits about you, and plan you next move carefully. Use your compass to orient yourself, stay on a trail if you already are and don't make a move until you're sure about where you're going and what you're trying to accomplish. Unless you're very confident about where you are and what you should do, it's always best just to stay put.

Hunker Down: Rather than wandering around aimlessly, exhausting yourself, or simply getting further away and more disoriented, often (very, very often) the best tactic when lost in the woods is simply to sit still and weather the wait while until rescuers find you. This was Largey's response and, although it did not work out for her, is widely accepted as the most effective by nearly all search and rescue workers. A lost hiker who is staying in one place will generally last much longer, allowing rescuers more time and a larger window to find the victim and help them. This starts with shelter: find or create something that will protect you from the elements and give you a safe, dry place to sit and wait. Then, work on building a fire. This will not only keep you warm, and eventually give you a way to cook any food you find, but will also serve as a powerful signal to rescuers. Not only are fires visible from great distances after dark but the smoke and smell of something as small as a campfire can be detected for miles, drawing attention to your location. That done, find a water source, whether it's a clean stream or a condensation trap system. Only then, and remember that the human body can last a week or more without food, when you have all of that taken care of, should you start thinking about and looking for food.

All that done, the only thing left to do is wait, prepared to signal for help if rescuers get close.

"The slogan on our website is 'We get lost so you don't have to,' so I've spent a lot of my life being lost in the woods," laughs Randi Minetor, the author of more than forty guidebooks to hiking and camping across the United States. "It's so easy to do even when trails are marked clearly. You take that one step in the wrong direction on a side trail and

It doesn't matter how well prepared you are, if you don't know where you are—or how to get out—you're in trouble.

the next thing you know you're completely surrounded by unfamiliar things and you don't know where you are."

She should know. Minetor and her husband Nic, who takes the photographs that are featured in her books, spend months out of the year exploring the parks and trails, often in areas that they have never visited before. Getting lost, and getting found again, are just part of the job description for a guidebook author.

That's why she carries not one but two GPS units—one that's creating a course for her to follow and another that's stocked with maps, data points, and other information for her to reference in the field. And she also carries a total of twelve extra batteries at all times, effectively eliminating the risk of a dead GPS unit in the woods. This is her standard hiking kit at all times, even when she's going out for less than an hour, because, as she says, you just never know. You probably won't need all of it, but the one time that you do you'll be glad it's there. Besides, none of this is very heavy.

"That's my theory about it is, if there's technology, use it," Minetor says. "I know that people go out on trails and say, 'I want to commune with nature and I want to leave all my technology behind and I want to have a real wilderness experience.' I, unfortunately, keep reading about people who do this and don't come home."

That's why she's such a strong proponent of using technology in the backcountry. We have access to GPS now, we have access to directional tools that don't require a cell connection to work and we have access to beacons and distress signal devices that can summon help in the event that something goes wrong. There is simply no reason for people to become lost in the woods anymore. Don't be afraid of using technology.

"Ideally, you should be able to use a compass," she admits. "But I know that not everybody goes through Boy Scouts and Girl Scouts and learns to do that anymore, so a GPS device is a really good thing to carry with you because you can press a button and backtrack and get back to the main trail, in no time at all, once you recognize that you're lost. It's a simple precaution and isn't it wonderful we live in the future where we have these things that are available to us."

Personally, I did go through Boy Scouts and was trained in the proper use of map and compass (circa the 1980s), so tend to come at this problem as more of a completist than Minetor, though she does admit that no trip into the backcountry is complete without a good compass and a map of the area you're visiting—in particular, Minetor suggests the backcountry maps produced by National Geographic, which are available for most of the popular recreation areas in North America and offer a level of trail-by-trail, ridge-by-ridge detail that can be hard to find in physical maps these days. They're also printed on a sort of lightweight plastic material that is impervious to water and essentially impossible to destroy. Basic map and compass skills are not difficult to learn and, at the very least, having a compass that can show you which way is north versus south can be very useful in determining the way toward the nearest road, trailhead, or town when all else fails. Used in partnership with a good, up-to-date maps (because an old map that shows, for example, logging roads that are no longer there or lacks information about more modern trail systems), a basic compass can deliver a lot of information in the backcountry that will help anyone, even those who are not map and compass experts, at least determine their rough location.

Of course, all of this boils down to one word, which would also qualify as the unofficial motto of this book: preparation. Recovering and finding your way back safely when lost in the woods isn't an in-the-moment solution. It relies almost entirely or proper preparations being made before the trip starts, before you hit the trail, and before you get lost. And, in this case, preparation includes everything from buying a map of the area you're visiting, learning how to use the compass that's been in the bottom of your pack since high school, buying a GPS device and learning how to use it, studying your planned route, and making sure you pack bring everything you need for it all to work when you need it (read: spare batteries).

Minetor has seen this in action for herself many times.

"We were at the Grand Canyon last year at Christmas time and we saw people setting off down the Bright Angel Trail in their flip flops in December, carrying no water, no food," she says. "Just, you know, blindly going down the trail. [Note: Bright Angel Trail starts on the south rim and descends roughly 4,000 over eight miles down to the edge of the Colorado River at an average grade of 10 percent.] They obviously hadn't done any research, had no idea what they were getting into, did not take into consideration that it's not really a trail you should do in one day. Because what they didn't know was that, once they were down they would have to come back up, and that's a long day on Bright Angel. These are people who have not done the least bit of research to figure out what they're going to encounter and what they're getting into. But that step is critical, and research is one of the things we stress a lot when we go out on trails. It keeps you from getting lost because you'll know what to look for and where you're going."

Acknowledgments

As I STATED AT THE start of this book, I am no expert on wilderness survival. I'm not a doctor, I'm not a high-altitude mountaineer, and I'm not someone who has ever spent weeks or months living off the land.

But that's why I decided to write this book in the first place.

It's an open secret that writers tend to take on projects that interest them personally, in order to justify spending hours and hours researching a topic that they might not be able to do otherwise. And this book is no exception.

The fact is, the great thing about writing a book like this is spending time with the real experts in this field, learning more about what they know, what they do, and picking their brains for information. A book is not a writing project but a research project, and for this one I have dozens of people to thank for their help and support. In addition to all the subject matter experts I met with who were so generous with me to share their time and expertise, there are so many people beyond the course list and bibliography who guided me along the way.

First of all, big thanks go to Jay Cassell, Ken Samelson, Leah Zarra, Nicole Frail, and everyone at Skyhorse Publishing for taking a chance on me and publishing my work. The same goes for Andy Ross and all of my editors (you know who you are).

And it's not every day that a writer gets to call out some of their former colleagues, especially when they show up in the bibliography.

But this time I referenced a lot of work from people I consider friends: Hawes Spencer, the founder and editor of the late-great alt weekly *The Hook* in Charlottesville, Virginia; Will Harlan, the editor of *Blue Ridge Outdoors* who published some of my first work; Frederick "Rico" Reimers, the one-time editor of *Paddler* magazine that published my actual first story ever; and Jenny Depper from AOL, and Yahoo/Associated Content before that. Thanks to you all.

This book is for Kristin.

Interviews

Dwyer, Joseph, PhD. Professor of Physics specializing in cosmic rays and gamma ray astronomy, University of New Hampshire, Durham, New Hampshire; November 2016

Forbes, Rachel. Executive Director, The Grizzly Bear Foundation; Vancouver, British Columbia; February 2017

Greene, Ethan. Executive Director, Colorado Avalanche Information Center; Boulder, Colorado; January 2017

Hackett, Dr. Peter. Executive Director, Institute for Altitude Medicine; Telluride, Colorado; February 2017

Jantzen, Robert. Mountaineering Guide, International Mountain Guides; Ashford, Washington; February 2017

Maguire, Kathy. Curator of Amphibians and Bugs, Reptile Gardens; Rapid City, South Dakota; January 2017

McIntosh, Mike. Founder and Director, the Bear With Us Sanctuary and Rehabilitation Centre for Bears; Ontario, Canada; March 2017

Minetor, Randi. Author, *Death in Glacier National Park* and fifty other titles; Rochester, New York; March 2017

Mussen, Eric, PhD. Professor of Entomology (ret.) at the University of California, Davis; Davis, California; January 2017

Otten, Dr. Edward. Professor of Emergency Medicine, Director, Toxicology; Associate Director, Cincinnati Drug and Poison Information Center; University of Cincinnati Medical Center; Cincinnati, Ohio; March 2017

Platnick, Norman. Curator Emeritus of the Division of Invertebrate Zoology at the American Museum of Natural History; New York, New York; March 2017

Seeley, Tom, Professional guide with Arizona Rock & Canyon Adventures; Phoenix, Arizona and Executive Director of the American Canyoneering Association; February 2017

Starr, Oliver. Wolf activist and educator; San Francisco, California; December 2016

Steinberg, Michele. Manager of Wildland Fire Operations, National Fire Protection Association; Quincy, Massachusetts; March 2017

Yost, Jeff. Terrestrial Biologist, Colorado Parks and Wildlife; Steamboat Springs, Colorado; March 2017

Yovovich, Veronica, PhD. Wildlife Conflict Specialist, Mountain Lion Foundation; Sacramento, California; January 2017

Bibliography

ABC News. "Survivor of Mountain Lion Attack Gives Thanks." January 21, 2004. http://abcnews.go.com/GMA/story?id=128077&page=1

ABS Alaskan. "Sunlight Hours by Month in Alaska." 2016. http://www.absak.com/library/average-annual-insolation-alaska

Alaska Department of Fish and Game. "Brown/Grizzly Bear Hunting in Alaska." ADFG.alaska.gov, 2017. http://www.adfg.alaska.gov/index.cfm%3Fadfg=brownbearhunting.main

Alexander, Harriet. "Swarm of 800,000 Bees Kill Man in Arizona." *The Telegraph*, October 9, 2014. http://www.telegraph.co.uk/news/worldnews/northamerica/usa/11151083/Swarm-of-800000-bees-kill-man-in-Arizona.html

Allyn, Matt. "How to Prevent a Bear Attack." *Men's Journal*, 2014. http://www.mensjournal.com/travel/mountain-wilderness/how-to-prevent-a-bear-attack-20140923

Andrews, Travis. "'I Thought This Was the End': Montana Man Tells of 2 Ferocious Battles with Same Grizzly Bear." *Washington Post*, October 3, 2016. https://www.washingtonpost.com/news/morning-mix/wp/2016/10/03/drenched-in-blood-montana-man-tells-tale-of-surviving-two-run-ins-with-same-grizzly-bear/

Appelbaum, Yoni. "Blizzards and the Birth of the Modern Mayor." *The Atlantic*, January 26, 2015. https://www.theatlantic.com/politics/archive/2015/01/blizzards-and-the-birth-of-the-modern-mayor/384833/

Associated Press. "17-Year-Old Boy Killed By Lightning During Northern Arizona Hike." Weather.com, July 22, 2016. https://weather.com/news/news/northern-arizona-lightning-death-wade-young

Associated Press. "Buzz Aldrin Says Altitude Sickness Forced His South Pole Evacuation." *Los Angeles Times*, December 3, 2016. http://www.latimes.com/world/la-fg-buzz-aldrin-20161203-story.html

Associated Press. "Central Texas Man Stung to Death by Bees." *Albuquerque Journal*, August 26, 2016. https://www.abqjournal.com/834272/central-texas-man-stung-to-death-by-bees.html

Backpacker Editors. "American Climber Alex Lowe Presumed Dead." *Backpacker*, October 6, 1999. http://www.backpacker.com/survival/american-climber-alex-lowe-presumed-dead/

Backstrom, Lauren. "NFPA's Ray Bizal Attends Yarnell Hill Fire Memorial Service and Honors 19 Firefighters." NFPA Blog, July 15, 2013. https://community.nfpa.org/community/fire-break/blog/2013/07/15/nfpas-ray-bizal-attends-yarnell-hill-fire-memorial-service-and-honors-19-firefighters

Bailey, Ronald. "North America's Most Dangerous Mammal: How Best to Deal with the Menace of Bambi." *Reason*, November 21, 2001. http://reason.com/archives/2001/11/21/north-americas-most-dangerous

Barish, Robert, MD, and Thomas Arnold, MD. "Bee, Wasp, Hornet, and Ant Stings." Merck Manual (Consumer), 2016. http://www.merckmanuals.com/home/injuries-and-poisoning/bites-and-stings/bee%2c-wasp%2c-hornet%2c-and-ant-stings

Barks, Cindy. "Yarnell Fire Cost: Over $4 Million." *Prescott Daily Courier*, June 18, 2016. http://www.dcourier.com/news/2016/jun/18/yarnell-fire-cost-over-4m/

Baron, David. *The Beast in the Garden: A Modern Parable of Man and Nature*. New York: W.W. Norton, 2003.

Baron, David. "The Cougar Behind Your Trash Can." *New York Times*, July 28, 2011. http://www.nytimes.com/2011/07/29/opinion/the-cougar-behind-your-trash-can.html

Bekoff, Marc, Ph.D. *The Animals' Agenda: Freedom, Compassion, and Coexistence in the Human Age*. Boston: Beacon Press, 2017.

Bennett, Robert, and Richard Vetter. "An Approach to Spider Bites. Erroneous Attribution of Dermonecrotic Lesions to Brown Recluse or Hobo Spider Bites in Canada." *Can Fam Physician*, August 2004. https://www.ncbi.nlm.nih.gov/pmc/articles/PMC2214648/

Blevins, Jason. "Relatives of Four Killed by Carbon Monoxide in Aspen-area Home to Keep Fighting After Dismissals." *Denver Post*, November 12, 2011. http://www.denverpost.com/2011/11/12/relatives-of-four-killed-by-carbon-monoxide-in-aspen-area-home-to-keep-fighting-after-dismissals/

Blumhardt, Miles. "Q&A with Don Davis." *Coloradoan*, May 4, 2003. http://www.wisesurvival.com/QandAwithDonDavis.shtml

Boroff, David. "Arizona hiker, 17, Just Graduated High School Before Lightning Fatally Struck Him on State's Highest Peak." *New York Daily News*, July 22, 2016.
http://www.nydailynews.com/news/national/arizona-hiker-17-struck-killed-lightning-article-1.2721620

Bourjaily, Phil. "Special Report: On Coyote Attacks and the Death of Canadian Folk Singer Taylor Mitchell." *Field & Stream*, November 2009. http://www.fieldandstream.com/blogs/hunting/2009/11/special-report-coyote-attacks-and-death-canadian-folk-singer-taylor-mitchell

Brenner, Lisa. "Autopsy Shows Michele Yu Fell To Her Death On Mt. Baldy." *LAist*, December 11, 2010. http://laist.com/2010/12/11/autopsy_shows_michele_yu_fell_to_he.php

Brook, Pete. "Keeping a Wolf at Home to Save the Species." *Wired*, May 2013. https://www.wired.com/2013/05/camille-seaman-arctic-wolf/

Buddle, Chris. "Spiders Do Not Bite." *Arthropod Ecology*, February 15, 2012. https://arthropodecology.com/2012/02/15/spiders-do-not-bite/

Burfoot, Amby. "The Last Run." *Runner's World*, January 19, 2007. http://www.runnersworld.com/runners-stories/the-dangers-of-running-in-the-heat

Burnham, Mary. "Virginia's Ramseys Draft Wilderness: Rugged and Remote." *Backpacker*, May 31, 1997. http://www.backpacker.com/trips/virginia/virginia-s-ramseys-draft-wilderness-rugged-and-remote/

Campbell, Jon. "How Coyotes Conquered New York." *Village Voice*, October 12, 2016. http://www.villagevoice.com/news/how-coyotes-conquered-new-york-9207914

Canterbury, Dave. *Bushcraft 101: A Field Guide to the Art of Wilderness Survival*. Avon, MA: Adams Media, 2014.

Carey, Julie. "Case of 1996 Slayings of Shenandoah Hikers Not Cold to FBI." NBC 4, June 1, 2016. http://www.nbcwashington.com/news/local/1996-Slayings-Shenandoah-Hikers-Julie-Williams-Lollie-Winans-Not-Cold-FBI-381600361.html#ixzz4Yy5D7f4Q

Carroll, Rick. "Judge Drops Criminal Cases in Aspen Carbon Monoxide Fatalities." *Aspen Times*, November 4, 2011. http://www.aspentimes.com/news/judge-drops-criminal-cases-in-aspen-carbon-monoxide-fatalities/

CBS News. "Teen Survives First Confirmed Wolf Attack in Minn." August 27, 2013. http://www.cbsnews.com/news/teen-survives-first-confirmed-wolf-attack-in-minn/

Colorado Avalanche Information Center. "Statistics and Reporting." CAIC, 2017. http://avalanche.state.co.us/accidents/statistics-and-reporting/

Condon, Scott. "Surging Backcountry Popularity Captures Ski Industry's Attention." *Aspen Times*, February 2, 2015. http://www.aspen-times.com/news/surging-backcountry-popularity-captures-ski-industrys-attention/

Currie, Carol McAlice, and Zach Urness. "Love and Loss on Mount Jefferson." *Statesman Journal*, January 17, 2016. http://www.states-manjournal.com/story/news/2016/01/17/love-and-loss-mount-jefferson/78367928/

Daily Mail. "Thai Woman Sets New World Record . . . for Holding Scorpion in Her Mouth." December 22, 2008. http://www.daily-mail.co.uk/news/article-1100222/Thai-woman-sets-new-world-record—holding-scorpion-mouth.html

Dell'Amore, Christine. "Bear Mauling in Wyoming: Why Do They Attack?" *National Geographic*, September 19, 2014. http://news. nationalgeographic.com/news/2014/09/1409018-grizzly-bears- attack-wyoming-animals-science-nation/

Denver Channel Staff. "Survivor of Rock Slide that Killed Buena Vista Family: 'I'm Doing Really Well'" *Denver Post*, December 5, 2013. http://www.denverpost.com/2013/12/05/survivor-of-rock-slide- that-killed-buena-vista-family-im-doing-really-well/

Depper, Jenny. "Photo Found After Flooding Reveals Final Image of 7 Hikers." *AOL.com*, September 18, 2015. http://www.aol.com/arti- cle/2015/09/18/photo-found-after-flooding-reveals-final-image- of-7-hikers/21238150/

Dickman, Kyle. "19: The True Story of the Yarnell Hill Fire." *Outside*, September 17, 2013. https://www.outsideonline.com/1926426/19- true-story-yarnell-hill-fire

DiGiulian, Sasha. "How to Overcome Fear in the Face of Extreme Risk." *Outside*, December 27, 2016. https://www.outsideonline .com/2145146/how-overcome-fear-face-extreme-risk

Dudchenko, Paul. *Why People Get Lost: The Psychology and Neuroscience of Spatial Cognition.* New York: Oxford University Press, 2010.

Dvorak, Petula. "Virginia Mother Who Died After Wasp Sting Lived a Life Worth Remembering." *Washington Post*, August 4, 2014. https:// www.washingtonpost.com/local/virginia-mother-who-died-after- wasp-sting-lived-a-life-worth-remembering/2014/08/04/d16c9b- de-1bff-11e4-ab7b-696c295ddfd1_story.html

Edney, Anna. "Newly Found Virus Linked to Kansas Death After Tick Bite." *Bloomberg*, February 20, 2015. https://www.bloomberg.com/ news/articles/2015-02-20/newly-found-virus-linked-to-kansas- man-s-death-after-tick-bite

Emerson, Clint. *100 Deadly Skills: Survival Edition: The SEAL Oper- ative's Guide to Surviving in the Wild and Being Prepared for Any Disaster.* New York: Touchstone Publishing, 2016.

Etchison, Amanda. "Arizona Temp Records Toppled by Deadly Heat Wave." *Arizona Republic*, June 19, 2016. http://www.azcentral.

com/story/news/local/phoenix-weather/2016/06/19/tempera-tures-top-daily-record-phoenix-yuma/86118102/

Federal Bureau of Investigation. "Crime in the United States: 2014." https://ucr.fbi.gov/crime-in-the-u.s/2014/crime-in-the-u.s.-2014/offenses-known-to-law-enforcement/murder

Flores, Adrian, Tadesse Haileyesus, and Arlene Greenspan, PhD. "National Estimates of Outdoor Recreational Injuries Treated in Emergency Departments, United States, 2004–2005." *Wilderness & Environmental Medicine*, 2008. http://www.bioone.org/doi/pdf/10.1580/07-WEME-OR-152.1

Gardner, Jennifer. "The Rising Cost of Wildfires." Center for Insurance Policy and Research, April 2014. http://www.naic.org/cipr_newsletter_archive/vol11_wildfires.pdf

Garrison, Laura Turner. "Where Are They Now? Diseases That Killed You in Oregon Trail." *Mental Floss*, May 28, 2014. http://mental-floss.com/article/28968/where-are-they-now-diseases-killed-you-oregon-trail

George, Jerry. "Wolf Attack a Tragic, Cautionary Tale." *San Francisco Chronicle*, January 14, 2006. http://www.sfgate.com/homeand-garden/article/Wolf-attack-a-tragic-cautionary-tale-2543491.php

Godfrey, Ed. "Felder Family Has Been Involved with Rattlesnake Event Each of its 67 Years." *The Oklahoman*, April 30, 2006. http://newsok.com/article/1830437

Goodier, Rob. "Why Does Everyone Climb Everest in May?" *Popular Mechanics*, May 21, 2012. http://www.popularmechanics.com/adventure/outdoors/a7725/why-does-everyone-climb-everest-in-may-9035510/

Greiner, Thomas H. "Carbon Monoxide Concentrations: Table (AEN-172)." Department of Agricultural and Biosystems Engineering, Iowa State University, August, 1997. https://www.abe.iastate.edu/extension-and-outreach/carbon-monoxide-concentrations-table-aen-172/

Gunderman, Richard. "CDC: Bees are the Deadliest Non-Human Animals in America." *Government Executive*, August 21, 2015.

http://www.govexec.com/management/2015/08/bees-are-deadliest-non-human-animals-america-cdc/119328/

Gurubacharya, Binaj. "Risks in Climbing Everest in Focus as 3 Die, 2 Go missing." Associated Press, May 23, 2016. http://bigstory.ap.org/article/30c48ae14fff44bbaf02f06602405c52/indian-climber-3rd-die-mount-everest-recent-days

Hahn, Dave. "The No Fall Zone." *Outside*, December 21, 2006. https://www.outsideonline.com/1909236/no-fall-zone

Hardy Diagnostics. "The Most Deadly Animals on the Planet." 2016. http://www.hardydiagnostics.com/wp-content/uploads/2016/05/The-Most-Deadly-Animals.pdf

Harlan, Will. "Ancient Appalachia: The Southeast's Old-Growth Forests." *Blue Ridge Outdoors*, July 1, 2005. http://www.blueridge-outdoors.com/magazine/july-2005/ancient-appalachia-the-southeasts-old-growth-forests/

Hauser, Christine. "In a Montana Bear Attack, Lessons on Hope, Survival and First Aid." *New York Times*, October 7, 2016. http://www.nytimes.com/2016/10/07/health/in-a-montana-bear-attack-lessons-on-hope-survival-and-first-aid.html

Heck, Kaylee. "Texas Farmer Killed After Tractor Disturbs Bee Hive." ABC News, July 1, 2015. http://abcnews.go.com/US/texas-farmer-killed-tractor-disturbs-bee-hive/story?id=32154938

Henderson, Doug, and Dennis Paulson. "Snakes of North America." Slater Museum of Natural History, University of Puget Sound, Tacoma, Washington, October 1995. http://www.pitt.edu/~mcs2/herp/SoNA.html

Herrel, Katie. "Ask A Bear: How Many Bear Attacks, Really?" *Backpacker*, December 1, 2009. http://www.backpacker.com/news-and-events/news/trail-news/ask-a-bear-how-many-bear-attacks-really-2/#sthash.TxDJBKMO.dpuf

Herrel, Katie. "One Hiker Dies, Two Rescued on Mount Rainier." *Backpacker*, June 11, 2008. http://www.backpacker.com/news-and-events/news/trail-news/one-hiker-dies-two-rescued-on-mount-rainier/

Hickey, Hannah, and Bárbara Ferreira. "Greenland's Fastest Glacier Sets New Speed Record." *UW Today*, February 3, 2014. http://www.washington.edu/news/2014/02/03/greenlands-fastest-glacier-sets-new-speed-record/

Hill, Craig. "Rescuers Spot Climber Believed Dead on Mount Rainier, 2 Others Airlifted to Madigan." *The Olympian*, March 28, 2016. http://www.theolympian.com/outdoors/article68633192.html

Hill, Greg. "How to Stay Safe in the Backcountry." *Outside*, January 20, 2017. https://www.outsideonline.com/2146696/how-stay-safe-backcountry-greg-hill

Hunt, Elle. "Sydney Man Dies After Redback Spider Bite, Although Not Yet Clear Bite to Blame." *The Guardian*, April 11, 2016. https://www.theguardian.com/environment/2016/apr/12/sydney-man-dies-after-redback-spider-bite

Illinois Department of Public Health, Division of Environmental Health. "Mosquitoes and Disease." March 29, 2017. http://www.idph.state.il.us/envhealth/pcmosquitoes.htm

Ingraham, Christopher. "Chart: The Animals That Are Most Likely to Kill You This Summer." *Washington Post*, June 16, 2015. https://www.washingtonpost.com/news/wonk/wp/2015/06/16/chart-the-animals-that-are-most-likely-to-kill-you-this-summer/?utm_term=.aa092a8e7fb5

International Association of Antarctica Tour Operators. "Statement from White Desert about South Pole Medical Evacuation." December 1, 2016.

Jensenius, John S. Jr. "A Detailed Analysis of Lightning Deaths in the United States from 2006 through 2015." NOAA, January 2016. http://www.lightningsafety.noaa.gov/fatalities/analysis06-15.pdf

Johnson, Dr. Stephen A. "Frequently Asked Questions About Venomous Snakes." University of Florida Department of Wildlife Ecology and Conservation, 2007. http://ufwildlife.ifas.ufl.edu/venomous_snake_faqs.shtml

Joling, Dan. "DNA Samples Confirm Wolves Killed Southwest Alaska Teacher." *Alaska Dispatch News*, December 6, 2011. https://www.

adn.com/alaska-news/article/dna-samples-confirm-wolves-killed-southwest-alaska-teacher/2011/12/06/

Kan, Kenneth. "Wildfire in Arizona: Remembering the Fallen Firefighters and Their Courage" Property Insurance Coverage Law blog, July 2, 2013. http://www.propertyinsurancecoveragelaw.com/2013/07/articles/insurance/wildfire-in-arizona-remembering-the-fallen-firefighters-and-their-courage/

Kaplan, Karen, and Rosie Mestel. "Ceasing Food and Fluid Can Be Painless." *Los Angeles Times*, March 23, 2005. http://articles.latimes.com/2005/mar/23/science/sci-schiavodeath23

Kathmandu Post. "Briton dies from altitude sickness." December 27, 2016. http://kathmandupost.ekantipur.com/news/2016-12-27/briton-dies-from-altitude-sickness.html

Kilgannon, Corey. "Barber by Day, Wily Coyote Whisperer by Night." *New York Times*, January 27, 2017. https://www.nytimes.com/2017/01/27/nyregion/coyotes-barber.html

Kirby, Jen. "Why Coyotes Are Flourishing in New York City." *New York* magazine, May 20, 2015. http://nymag.com/daily/intelligencer/2015/05/coyotes-new-york-city.html

Koerner, Claudia. "Four Dead, Others Missing as Frostbite, Sickness Strike Climbers on Mount Everest." *Buzzfeed.com*, May 22, 2016. https://www.buzzfeed.com/claudiakoerner/two-dead-and-others-missing-as-frostbite-sickness-strikes-do?utm_term=.bc2Mz-rDZdV#.pwXP95r7dX

Kosoy, Olga, Amy Lambert, Dana Hawkinson, Daniel Pastula, Cynthia Goldsmith, Charles Hunt, and Eric Staples. "Novel Thogotovirus Associated with Febrile Illness and Death, United States, 2014." *Emerging Infectious Diseases Journal*, May 2015. https://wwwnc.cdc.gov/eid/article/21/5/15-0150_article

KTVQ. "A Grizzly Bear Decides to see the Tourists in Montana." CNN, June 27, 2015. http://www.cnn.com/videos/us/2015/06/27/grizzly-bear-encounter-ktvq.ktvq

Kushner, David. "Is Your GPS Scrambling Your Brian?" *Outside*, November 15, 2016.

https://www.outsideonline.com/2135771/your-gps-scrambling-your-brain

Lamplugh, Rick. "This Is The Number of People Killed By 'Fearsome' Wolves." *The Dodo*, October 20, 2015. https://www.thedodo.com/how-many-people-killed-by-wolves-1413351180.html

Langley, Ricky L. "Animal Bites and Stings Reported by United States Poison Control Centers, 2001–2005." *Wilderness & Environmental Medicine*, March 2008. https://www.ncbi.nlm.nih.gov/pubmed/18333665

Letsky-Anderson, Christine. "Appalachian Trail – Skyland to Big Meadows." *Virginia Trail Guide*, June 6, 2010. https://virginia-trailguide.com/2010/06/06/appalachian-trail-skyland-to-big-meadows/

Lewis, Crystal. "Why Was Buzz Aldrin at the South Pole? The 86-Year-Old Still Has a Lot to Explore." *Romper*, December 1, 2016. https://www.romper.com/p/why-was-buzz-aldrin-at-the-south-pole-the-86-year-old-still-has-a-lot-to-explore-23918

Lieberman, Josh. "Wolf Attacks Teen In Minnesota: How Rare Are Wolf Attacks On Humans?" *International Science Times*, August 28, 2013. http://www.isciencetimes.com/articles/5954/20130828/wolf-attack-how-rare-minnesota-noah-graham.htm

LiveScience. "Fear of Spiders Can Develop Before Birth." February 8, 2010. http://www.livescience.com/9808-fear-spiders-develop-birth.html

Lobdell, William. "Cougar's Victim Won't be 'Prisoner of the Drama.'" *Los Angeles Times*, May 15, 2008. http://articles.latimes.com/2008/may/15/local/me-lion15

Lofholm, Nancy. "Hiker Slowly Starves as He Treks Colorado's Back-country." *Denver Post*, August 1, 2009. http://www.denverpost.com/2009/08/01/hiker-slowly-starves-as-he-treks-colorados-backcountry/

Main, Douglas. "The Surprising Cause of Most 'Spider Bites.'" *Live Science*, July 5, 2013. http://www.livescience.com/37974-he-surprising-cause-of-most-spider-bites.html

Marciniak, Kristin. *Surviving in the Wilderness.* Minneapolis: Lerner Publishing, 2014.

Maynard, Matt. "How to Survive a Swim in the Antarctic." *Outside,* December 28, 2016. https://www.outsideonline.com/2146171/ how-survive-swim-antarctic

Mayo Clinic Staff. "Carbon Monoxide Poisoning: Symptoms and Causes." Mayo Clinic, 2017. http://www.mayoclinic.org/diseases-conditions/carbon-monoxide/basics/symptoms/con-20025444

McLachlan, Marilynn. "12 Extreme Facts about Mount Everest." *New Zealand Herald*, April 23, 2014. http://www.nzherald.co.nz/world/ news/article.cfm?c_id=2&objectid=11242928

McIntosh, Mike. "Less Growling, More Snorting: Expert Explains Frightened Bear Behavior." Canadian Broadcasting Company, March 9, 2017. http://www.cbc.ca/news/canada/calgary/fright-ened-bear-behaviour-1.4017740

Medred, Craig. "Moose with Calves Charges Pack of Mountain Bikers at Anchorage's Kincaid Park." *Alaska Dispatch News*, September 28, 2016. https://www.adn.com/wildlife/article/ moose-calves-charges-pack-mountain-bikers-anchorages-kincaid-park/2014/05/28/

Medred, Craig. "Wolves Killed Alaska Teacher in 2010, State Says." *Alaska Dispatch News*, December 6, 2011. https://www.adn. com/outdoors/article/wolves-killed-alaska-teacher-2010-state-says/2011/12/07/

Miles, Kathryn. "'When You Find my Body, Please Call my Husband,' Missing Hiker Wrote." *Boston Globe*, May 25, 2016. https://www. bostonglobe.com/metro/2016/05/25/hiker-who-died-after-disap-pearing-from-appalachian-trail-survived-for-weeks/KAcHuKS-dYVHNTNu0qQobvK/story.html

Miller, Michael. "'Covered With Bees, and a Swarm Pursuing': Man Dies After Being Stung More Than 1,000 Times in Arizona Park." *Washington Post*, May 27, 2016. https://www.washingtonpost.com/ news/morning-mix/wp/2016/05/27/covered-with-bees-and-a-swarm-pursuing-man-dies-after-being-stung-more-than-1000-times-in-ariz-park/

Mills, Kylen. "Oklahoma Man Dies from Rattlesnake Bite." OKCFox, September 13, 2016. http://okcfox.com/news/local/oklahoma-man-dies-from-rattlesnake-bite

Minetor, Randi. *Death in Glacier National Park: Stories of Accidents and Foolhardiness in the Crown of the Continent.* Guilford, CT: Lyons Press, 2016.

Minetor, Randi. *Death in Zion National Park: Stories of Accidents and Foolhardiness in Utah's Grand Circle.* Guilford, CT: Lyons Press, 2017.

Mitchell, Kirk. "Mountain Lion Attacks Boy on Boulder Trail." *Denver Post*, April 15, 2006. http://www.denverpost.com/2006/04/15/mountain-lion-attacks-boy-on-boulder-trail/

Molinet, Jason. "NYC Financial Analyst, Married to JP Morgan Exec, Dies of Exposure During Solo Hike in New Hampshire Mountains." *New York Daily News*, February 17, 2015. http://www.nydailynews.com/news/national/nyc-hiker-found-dead-n-h-mountains-article-1.2118000

Montana Fish, Wildlife & Parks. "Grizzly Bear Population Monitoring: Northern Continental Divide Ecosystem." 2017. http://fwp.mt.gov/fishAndWildlife/management/grizzlyBear/monitoring.html

Mountain Lion Foundation. "Counting Lions: How Many Lions are in the United States?" 2016. http://mountainlion.org/us/-us-population.asp

Mount Washington Observatory "Normal, Means and Extremes: Weather Conditions on Mount Washington." 2017. https://www.mountwashington.org/experience-the-weather/mount-washington-weather-archives/normals-means-and-extremes.aspx

Moxley, Tonia. "Tennessee Cougar Sightings Pose Questions for Virginia." *Roanoke Times*, January 1, 2017. http://www.roanoke.com/news/virginia/tennessee-cougar-sightings-pose-questions-for-virginia/article_aff1a4ec-ab02-555d-9b18-a0379510b59a.html

Murray, Christopher. "Global, Regional, and National Age-Sex Specific All-Cause and Cause-Specific Mortality for 240 Causes of Death, 1990–2013: a systematic analysis for the Global Burden of

Disease Study 2013." *Lancet*, January 10, 2015. https://www.ncbi. nlm.nih.gov/pmc/articles/PMC4340604/

National Interagency Fire Center. "Wildland Fire Statistics: 2017." January 2017. https://www.nifc.gov/fireInfo/fireInfo_statistics. html

National Park Service. "Fatalities at Mt. Rainier National Park." 2016. http://www.mountrainierclimbing.us/sar/fatalities.php

National Weather Service. "Lightning Deaths: 2017." 2017. http://www.lightningsafety.noaa.gov/fatalities.shtml

National Weather Service. "Wind Chill Safety." Weather.gov, 2017. http://www.weather.gov/bou/windchill

Netter, Sarah. "Faulty Heating Connection Leads to Carbon Monoxide Death of Family." ABC News, December 3, 2008. http://abcnews.go.com/US/story?id=6376209&page=1

New York State Department of Environmental Conservation. "Search and Rescue: Lost in the Woods." 2017. http://www.dec.ny.gov/regulations/57053.html

New York Times Staff. "12 Hikers Are Swept Away By Flash Flood in a Canyon." *New York Times*, August 14, 1997. http://www.nytimes.com/1997/08/14/us/12-hikers-are-swept-away-by-flash-flood-in-a-canyon.html

Nordin, Barbara. "After Rice: New Questions in Park Murders." *The Hook*, March 18, 2004. http://www.readthehook.com/94820/cover-after-rice-new-questions-park-murders

Offerman, Steven, MD, Patrick Daubert, MD, and Richard Clark, MD. "The Treatment of Black Widow Spider Envenomation with Antivenin *Latrodectus Mactans*: A Case Series." National Institutes of Health, Summer 2011. https://www.ncbi.nlm.nih.gov/pmc/articles/PMC3200105/

O'Malley, Julia. "Woman Killed by Wolves Left Behind Vivid Blog of Alaska Life." *Anchorage Daily News*, March 15, 2010. http://www.mcclatchydc.com/news/nation-world/national/article24576631.html

Paajanen, Terri. *A Complete Guide to Surviving in the Wilderness: Everything You Need to Know to Stay Alive and Get Rescued.* Ocala, FL: Atlantic Publishing Group, 2014.

Pacific Energy Center. "Guide to California Climate Zones and Bioclimatic Design." 2006. http://www.pge.com/includes/docs/pdfs/about/edusafety/training/pec/toolbox/arch/climate/california_climate_zones_01-16.pdf

Packer, Randall. "How Long Can the Average Person Survive Without Water?" *Scientific American.* https://www.scientificamerican.com/article/how-long-can-the-average/

Page, Atkins, Shockley, and Yaron. "Avalanche Deaths in the United States: a 45-Year Analysis." *Wilderness Environmental Medicine*, Autumn 1999. https://www.ncbi.nlm.nih.gov/pubmed/10560307

Paltzer, Seth. "The Other Foe: The U.S. Army's Fight against Malaria in the Pacific Theater, 1942-45." Army Historical Foundation, April 30, 2016. https://armyhistory.org/the-other-foe-the-u-s-armys-fight-against-malaria-in-the-pacific-theater-1942-45/

Peruzzi, Marc. "Opinion: 'Skiing' Was the Magazine the Sport Deserved." *Outside*, February 13, 2017. https://www.outsideonline.com/2156826/ode-skiing-magazine-1948-2017

Peterson, Lee Allen, and Roger Tory Peterson. *A Field Guide to Edible Wild Plants: Eastern and Central North America (Peterson Field Guides).* New York: Houghton Mifflin Harcourt, 1999.

Potterfield, Peter. "Is There Anything This Guy Can't Climb?" *MountainZone.com*, 1999. http://www.mountainzone.com/climbing/99/interviews/lowe/

Pree, Richard. "Snakes and the Eight Stages of Agitation." ABC Northern Tasmania, May 21, 2010. http://www.abc.net.au/local/stories/2010/05/21/2906297.htm

Reimers, Frederick. "What's in Bear Spray?" *Outside*, September 23, 2016. http://www.outsideonline.com/2115456/packing-heat

Richardson, Lance. "New York Needs Coyotes." *Slate.com*, July 31, 2015. http://www.slate.com/articles/health_and_science/science/2015/07/

coyotes_in_new_york_and_chicago_urban_ecology_of_rats_geese_
deer_feral_cats.html

Rivas, Anthony. "New Tick-Borne Disease Identified In Kansas Man, Kills Him In 11 Days." *Medical Daily*, February 22, 2015. http://www.medicaldaily.com/new-tick-borne-disease-identified-kansas-man-kills-him-11-days-323146

Roach, James M, and Robert B. Schoene. "High-Altitude Pulmonary Edema." Medical Aspects of Harsh Environments, 2002.

Rochat, Scott. "Experts Say 'Zero Chance' that Black Widow Killed Seale." *Longmont Times-Call*, July 22, 1011. http://www.timescall.com/ci_18533006

Rosenbloom, Perry. "Preventing & Surviving a Moose Attack." Glacier National Park Travel Guide, January 3, 2015. http://www.glacier-national-park-travel-guide.com/moose-attack.html

Rosenfeld, Scott, and Peter Stark. "The 10 Worst Ways to Die in the Wild." *Outside*, June 25, 2013. https://www.outsideonline.com/1928291/10-worst-ways-die-wild

Russell, Suzanne. "Rutgers Student Killed in Bear Attack." *USA Today*, September 22, 2014. http://www.usatoday.com/story/news/nation/2014/09/22/bear-attack-rutgers-student-killed/16078383/

San Francisco Globe. "Man Dies from Tick Bite, but it Had Nothing to do with Lyme Disease." *San Francisco Globe*, January 18, 2017. http://sfglobe.com/2015/04/27/he-died-from-a-tick-bite-but-it-had-nothing-to-do-with-lyme-disease/

Schaffer, Grayson. "Alex Lowe's Body Found on Shishapangma." *Outside*, April 30, 2016. https://www.outsideonline.com/2075001/alex-lowes-body-found-shishapangma

Schaffer, Grayson. "Special Report: The Keyhole Seven." *Outside*, May 24, 2016. https://www.outsideonline.com/2072666/special-report-keyhole-seven

Schandelmeier, John. "Wave the Flag (or Your Parka) When Dealing with Ornery Moose." *Alaska Dispatch News*, December 21, 2016. https://www.adn.com/outdoors-adventure/2016/12/21/wave-the-flag-or-your-parka-when-dealing-with-ornery-moose/

Sexton, Connie Cone. "A Brief History of Arizona's Deadly Flash Floods." *Arizona Republic*, September 15, 2015. http://www.azcentral.com/story/news/local/arizona/2015/09/15/brief-history-arizonas-deadly-flash-floods/72335682/

Siler, Wes. "How to Stop Surviving and Start Living Well Outdoors." *Outside*, April 26, 2016. https://www.outsideonline.com/2072801/how-stop-surviving-and-start-living-well-outdoors

Siler, Wes. "What Todd Orr's Mauling Teaches Us About Bear Attacks." *Outside*, October 11, 2016. https://www.outsideonline.com/2124656/what-todd-orrs-mauling-teaches-us-about-bear-attacks

Shoichet, Catherine, Kyung Lah, and Jack Hannah. "Colorado Rock Slide Kills 5 Members of One Family; Teen Survives." CNN, October 2, 2013. http://www.cnn.com/2013/09/30/us/colorado-hikers-rockslide/

Snowsports Industry Association. "SIA Snow Sports Key Trends." 2017 http://www.snowsports.org/research-surveys/downhill-consumer-intelligence-project/key-trends/

Spector, Dina. "What to Do If You Are Attacked By a Pack of Wolves." *Business Insider*, June 28, 2012. http://www.businessinsider.com/what-to-do-if-you-are-attacked-by-a-pack-of-wolves-2012-6

Spencer, Hawes. "Runner Down: The Life and Death of Kelly Watt." *Hook*, August 11, 2005. http://www.readthehook.com/97528/cover-runner-down-life-and-death-kelly-watt

Stark, Peter. "Frozen Alive." *Outside*, March 7, 2016. https://www.outsideonline.com/2152131/freezing-death

Stark, Peter. *Last Breath: The Limits of Adventure*. New York: Ballantine Books, 2002.

Starr, Oliver. "Animal Behavior: Would a Lone Adult Wolf Be Able to Take Down an Unarmed, Athletic Adult Human? (Starr's Attack Story)" *Quora.com*, April 7, 2016. https://www.quora.com/Animal-Behavior-Would-a-lone-adult-wolf-be-able-to-take-down-an-unarmed-athletic-adult-human

State of Arizona. "Yarnell Hill Fire: Serious Accident Investigation Report." September 23, 2013. http://www.iawfonline.org/Yarnell_Hill_Fire_report.pdf

Steele, Lauren. "This Man Survived a Worst-Case Bear Attack—Here's How." *Men's Journal*, 2017. http://www.mensjournal.com/adventure/articles/this-man-survived-a-worst-case-bear-attack-heres-how-w443088

Stencel, Christine. "Report Sets Dietary Intake Levels for Water, Salt, and Potassium To Maintain Health and Reduce Chronic Disease Risk." National Academies of Sciences, Engineering and Medicine, February 11, 2004. http://www8.nationalacademies.org/onpinews/newsitem.aspx?recordid=10925&_ga=1.189400107.1889174396.1485367407

Stewart, Creek. *Survival Hacks: Over 200 Ways to Use Everyday Items for Wilderness Survival.* Avon, MA: Adams Media, 2016.

Stewart, Sarah. "Well known Oklahoma Rattlesnake Hunter Dies from Snake Bite." KFOR, September 16, 2016. http://kfor.com/2016/09/16/well-known-oklahoma-rattlesnake-hunter-dies-from-snake-bite/

Thomas, Michael. *Wild Survival: Learn How To Escape Attack Of A Dangerous Wild Animal When No One Around.* Seattle, WA: CreateSpace, 2016.

Thompson, Andrea. "Large Iceberg Looks Poised to Break Off of Antarctica." *Scientific American*, January 6, 2017. https://www.scientificamerican.com/article/large-iceberg-looks-poised-to-break-off-from-antarctica/

Tomlinson, Stuart. "Keizer Man is First to Die Climbing Mount Jefferson Since 2001." *The Oregonian*, November 30, 2015. http://www.oregonlive.com/pacific-northwest-news/index.ssf/2015/11/keizer_man_is_first_to_die_cli.html

Tribune Staff. "Utah Floods That Killed 19 Show Dangers of Popular Desert Canyons." *Chicago Tribune*, September 17, 2015. http://www.chicagotribune.com/news/nationworld/ct-utah-floods-20150915-story.html

U.S. Centers for Disease Control and Prevention. "Achievements in Public Health, 1900–1999: Control of Infectious Diseases." *Morbidity and Mortality Weekly Report*, July 30, 1999. https://www.cdc.gov/mmwr/preview/mmwrhtml/mm4829a1.htm

U.S. Centers for Disease Control and Prevention. "Anopheles Mosquitoes." CDC.gov, October 21, 2015. https://www.cdc.gov/malaria/about/biology/mosquitoes/

U.S. Centers for Disease Control and Prevention. "Avoiding Mosquito Bites: Zika, Dengue, Chikungunya." CDC.gov, December 7, 2016. https://www.cdc.gov/features/stopmosquitoes/

U.S. Centers for Disease Control and Prevention. "Elimination of Malaria in the United States (1947–1951). CDC.gov, November 9, 2012. https://www.cdc.gov/malaria/about/history/elimination_us.html

U.S. Centers for Disease Control and Prevention. "New CDC Study First To Present National Outdoor Recreational Injury Estimates." CDC.gov, June 10, 2008. https://www.cdc.gov/media/press-rel/2008/r080610.htm

U.S. Centers for Disease Control and Prevention. "Number of Heat-Related Deaths by Sex - National Vital Statistics System, United States, 1999–2010." CDC.gov, September 14, 2012. https://www.cdc.gov/mmwr/preview/mmwrhtml/mm6136a6.htm

U.S. Centers for Disease Control and Prevention. "Tickborne Diseases of the United States." CDC.gov, February 8, 2016. https://www.cdc.gov/ticks/diseases/index.html

U.S. Centers for Disease Control and Prevention. "Venomous Snakes: Symptoms and First Aid." CDC.gov, 2017. https://www.cdc.gov/niosh/topics/snakes/symptoms.html

U.S. Consumer Products Safety Commission. "National Electronic Injury Surveillance System—Data Highlights, 2015." CPSC.gov, 2016. https://www.cpsc.gov/s3fs-public/2015%20Neiss%20data%20highlights.pdf

U.S. Fish and Wildlife Service. "North Dakota Field Office: Gray Wolf." 2016. https://www.fws.gov/northdakotafieldoffice/endspecies/species/gray_wolf.htm

U.S. Forest Service. "If You Get Lost." 2017. https://www.fs.fed.us/visit/know-before-you-go/if-you-get-lost

U.S. Forest Service. "Mountain Lion Facts." 2017. https://www.fs.fed.us/visit/know-before-you-go/mountain-lions

Walsh, Michael. "Colorado Hiker Encounters Mountain Lion, Records Instead of Running as he Stares Death in Face." *New York Daily News*, September 26, 2013. http://www.nydailynews.com/news/national/colo-hiker-encounters-mountain-lion-records-stares-death-face-article-1.1468430

Wanshel, Elyse. "How to Survive The First 72 Hours When Lost In The Woods." *Little Things*, 2017. https://www.littlethings.com/how-to-survive-in-the-woods/

Watts, Amanda. "Man Dies After Being Stung by Bees More Than 1,000 Times." CNN, May 27, 2016. http://www.cnn.com/2016/05/27/us/bee-sting-death/

Weather.com. "Record-Breaking Heat Scorches the Southwest; Tucson Sees Hottest Day in 20+ Years." Weather Channel, June 21, 2016. https://weather.com/forecast/regional/news/dangerous-record-heat-southwest-plains

Webber, Carolyn. "Experts Urge Awareness After Bees Kill Arizona Hiker." *Backpacker*, June 3, 2016. http://www.backpacker.com/news-and-events/experts-urge-awareness-after-bees-kill-arizona-hiker/

Weller, Robert. "Carbon Monoxide Deaths in Aspen Lead to Indictments." *Huffington Post*, July 28, 2010. http://www.huffingtonpost.com/robert-weller/carbon-monoxide-deaths-in_b_661171.html

Westfall, Scottie. "Coyotes Make it to Colombia." *Retrieverman.com*, March 31, 2012. https://retrieverman.net/2012/03/31/coyotes-make-it-to-colombia/

Whelen, Luke. "How to Survive a Shark Attack, Plus Skills for 9 Other Emergencies." *Outside*, January 2017. http://www.outsideonline.com/2129276/how-survive-shark-attack-plus-skills-9-other-emergencies

WISTV. "West Columbia Man Dies After Being Bitten by Rattlesnake." WISTV, June 13, 2016. http://www.wistv.com/story/32209469/west-columbia-man-dies-after-being-bitten-by-rattlesnake

World Food Programme. "Zero Hunger Program Overview." 2017. http://www1.wfp.org/zero-hunger

World Health Organization. "Global Health Observatory Data: Number of Malaria Deaths 2000–2015." WHO, 2016. http://www.who.int/gho/malaria/epidemic/deaths/en/

Xu, Daniel. "TN Officials Confirm First Sighting of Mountain Lion in 100 Years." *Outdoor Hub*, December 9, 2015. http://www.outdoorhub.com/news/2015/12/09/tn-officials-confirm-first-sighting-mountain-lion-100-years/

Yardley, William, Matt Pearce, and Nigel Duarasept. "Seven Hikers' Descent into Doom at Zion National Park." *Los Angeles Times*, September 20, 2015. http://graphics.latimes.com/zion-flash-flood/

Yeoman, Barry. "Murder on the Mountain." *Out*, November 1, 1996. http://barryyeoman.com/1996/11/murder-on-the-mountain/

Yuhas, Alan. "Hiker Who Went Missing on Appalachian Trail Survived 26 Days Before Dying." *The Guardian*, May 25, 2016. https://www.theguardian.com/us-news/2016/may/26/hiker-who-went-missing-on-appalachian-trail-survived-26-days-before-dying

Ziegler, Zachary. "Missing Hiker Found Dead; 4th Victim of Record Heat Wave." Arizona Public Media, June 21, 2016. https://news.azpm.org/s/39935-tucson-hits-high-of-115/

Zietman, Nina. "The Gruesome Truth Behind Those Murders On America's Famous Appalachian Hiking Trail." *Mpora*, October 30, 2015. https://mpora.com/outsiders/the-gruesome-truth-behind-those-murders-on-americas-famous-appalachian-hiking-trail

Zuckerman, Laura. "Researcher Killed by Bear in Wyoming Wilderness." Reuters, September 15, 2014. http://www.reuters.com/article/us-usa-bear-wyoming-idUSKBN0HA2G420140915

Index

A

Acclimatization, 162
Acute mountain sickness (AMS),
    159–161, 163
Aldrin, Buzz, 158–159
All, John, 150
Allergy
  bee sting, 102
  scorpion, 106
Altitude sickness, 157–166
Anderson, Kaden, 111–112
Animals, large
  bears as, 7–20
  cats as, 20–29
  coyotes as, 50–59
  moose as, 29–39
  wolves as, 39–50
Anker, Conrad, 214–215
Ants, 96
Attack
  bear, 7–14
  cat, 20–29
  coyote, 50–59
  human, 59–67
  moose, 29–39
  wolf, 39–50
Avalanche, 213–224

B

Backing away, 29, 49
Baron, David, 22, 25
Bear bells, 19
Bears, 7–20
Bear spray, 17, 20
Bed netting, 88
Beecham, John, 13
Bees, 92–102
Berner, Candice, 39–41
Berry, Karen, 210
Bestler, Alex, 92–93
Big cats, 20–29
Bird, Chip, 52
Bites
  snake, 68–73
  spider, 73–83
Bizal, Ray, 135–136
Black Forest Fire, 138
Black widow spider, 76–77,
    80–81
Blizzard, 142–148. *See also* Frostbite
Booth, Reed, 93
Bourbon virus, 89
Brazilian wandering spider, 75, 80
Bridges, Dave, 213–215
Brown recluse spider, 80

Bryson, Bill, 62
Buddle, Chris, 78–79

C

Calving, 229–233
Campbell, Ron, 235
Canyons, slot, 110–123
Carbon monoxide poisoning, 166–173
Carnegie, Kenton, 43
Cats, big, 20–29
Churchill, Winston Branko, 189–190
Cold. *See* Blizzard; Frostbite;
    Hypothermia
Cougar. *See* Cats, big
Coyotes, 29, 50–59
Crevasses, 228–229

D

Davis, Don, 242
DDT, 83–84, 87
Death Zone, 149–152
Dehydration, 173–186
Drowning, 110–123
Dudchenko, Paul, 241–242
Dwyer, Joe, 130–132
Dysentery, 193–199

E

Eggleston, Jennifer, 209
Ehrlichiosis, 90–91
Emergency room visits, 1
Exposure, 199–207

F

Felder, Tony, Sr., 69–70
Fighting back, 25
Fine, Perry G., 192
Fire, 133–142
First aid, 4
Flash floods, 110–123
Flooding, 110–123
Food, 16. *See also* Starvation
Forbes, Rachel, 14–17

Forest fire, 133–142
Fountain, Alison, 224
Fountain, Thomas, 224–226
Fox, Camilla, 57–58
Frostbite, 149–157. *See also* Blizzard

G

Gehrt, Stanley, 56
George, Jerry, 44
Getting lost, 238–247
Giardia, 193–199
Gibby, Alex, 181
Glacier storms, 229
Glacier travel, 224–233
Granite Mountain Hotshots, 134–136
Great Fire of 1910, 137
Greene, Ethan, 220–224
Greenspan, Arlene, 1

H

Hackett, Peter, 163–166
Handwashing, 198
Harkins, Sarah, 97
Heartland virus, 91
Heatstroke, 180–186
Heeschen, George, 181
High altitude cerebral edema
    (HACE), 160–162, 165
High altitude pulmonary edema
    (HAPE), 160–162, 165
Hillary, Edmund, 149
Hjelle, Anne, 22–23
Hornets, 96–97
House, scorpions in, 107
Humans, as attackers, 59–67
Hunger. *See* Starvation
Hypothermia, 199–207

J

Jantzen, Robert, 146–148, 155–157,
    230–233
Johnson, Dawna, 208
Johnson, Dwayne, 208

Johnson, Gracie, 208–209
Johnson, Kiowa-Rain, 208
Joughin, Ian, 227

K

Keen, Kelly, 53

L

Lamplugh, Rick, 42–43
Landslide, 208–213
Largay, George, 238
Largay, Gerry, 238–241
Latrodectus, 77
Laveran, Charles Louis Alphonse, 86
Lee, Adam, 61
Lightning, 123–133
London, Jack, 195
Lowe, Alex, 213–215
Lyme disease, 91

M

Maguire, Kathy, 88–89, 108–109
Malaria, 82–84, 87
Matrosova, Kate, 200–202
McCandless, Christopher, 187–189
McDonough, Brendan, 135
McIntosh, Mike, 18–20
Minetor, Randi, 65–67, 236–237,
    244–247
Mitchell, Taylor, 51, 53
Moose, 29–39
Mosquitoes, 82–89
Mosquito repellent, 88
Mountain lion. *See* Cats, big
Mountains. *See* Altitude sickness;
    Avalanche; Blizzard; Flash
    floods; Getting lost
Mount Everest, 149–152
Mussen, Eric, 98–101

N

Netting, bed, 88
Norgay, Tenzing, 149

O

Oakland "Firestorm of 1991," 138
O'Brien, Mike, 52
Orr, Todd, 7–14
Otten, Edward, 183–186, 205–207
Outdoor Industry Association, 1–2

P

Panthers. *See* Cats, big
Peruzzi, Marc, 218–219
Pike, Gareth, 103–104
Platnick, Norman, 79–82
Pollock, George Freeman, Jr., 59
Predators
    bears as, 7–20
    cats as, 20–29
    coyotes as, 50–59
    wolves as, 39–50
Pumas. *See* Cats, big

Q

Quatela, Anthony, III, 175

R

Redback spider, 75
Reynolds, Mark, 23
Rice, Darrell David, 61
Rockslides, 208–213
Ross, Ronald, 86–87

S

San Souci, Darryl, 126
Scorpions, 102–109
Seeley, Tom, 120–123
Shouting, 19, 25, 49
Sleeves, for mosquitoes, 88
Slot canyons, 110–123
Smith, Brady, 126
Snakes, 68–73
Snow. *See* Avalanche; Blizzard;
    Glacier storms
Snow blindness, 142–143, 233–238

Spezze, John, 209
Spiders, 73–83
Staring down, 49
Starr, Oliver, 45–50
Starvation, 186–192
Steinberg, Michele, 139–142
Stinging insects, 92–102
Subervi, Larry, 175
Sullivan, Robert, 192
Sydney funnel-web spider, 75

T

Terrain , hazardous
  avalanche as, 213–224
  glaciers as, 224–233
  rockslides as, 208–213
Thow, Mick, 73
Ticks, 89–92

W

Waldo Canyon Fire, 138
Walker, Baigen, 208

Walkup, Paris, 208
Wasps, 92–102
Water treatment, 197
Watt, Kelly, 180–182
Whittaker, Pete, 145
Wildfire, 133–142
Williams, Julie, 60–61
Wilson, Dave, 68
Winans, Lollie, 60–61
Wolves, 39–50

Y

Yarnell Hill Fire, 133–136
Yost, Jeff, 36–39
Young, Wade, 124–126
Yovovich, Veronica, 27–29
Yu, Michelle, 235

Z

Zika virus, 84–85
Zuniga, Rogerio, 94